Betty Crocker

ANNUAL RECIPES

2007

This edition published in arrangement with Wiley Publishing, Inc.

General Mills

Director, Book and Online Publishing: Kim Walter

Manager, Cookbook Publishing: Lois Tlusty

Recipe Development and Testing: Betty Crocker Kitchens

Photography and Food Styling: General Mills Photo Studio

Editor: Kimberly Tweed

Book Designer: Tracey J. Hambleton

ISBN-10   1–59486–536–1
ISBN-13   978–1–59486–536–7

Printed in the United States of America

2   4   6   8   10   9   7   5   3   1   hardcover

Cover: Image Double Chocolate–Cherry Torte (page 269)

For more great ideas, visit www.bettycrocker.com

C O N T E N T S

Garlic and Lemon Roasted Turkey Breast (page 146)

Introduction

Welcome to the 2007 edition of *Betty Crocker Annual Recipes*. In this, our sixth edition, we've compiled your favorite recipes from the past year of *Betty Crocker* magazine and placed them in one convenient collection. There are more than 240 delicious and easy-to-make recipes, all sure to delight your friends and family at your next gathering.

New favorites, such as creamy Mexican Chicken and Sour Cream Lasagna and Margarita Shrimp Stir-Fry, complement traditional dishes with a twist, like Pesto-Stuffed Steaks and Country-Style Ribs and Sauerkraut.

You'll be amazed by the selections in our "Beverages and Appetizers" chapter! Your next summer party is sure to be the hit of the neighborhood when you present colorful trays of Firecracker Punch and Cosmos Slush. Caribbean Layered Dip and Sesame Toast Vegetable Bites will have guests smiling before you even fire up the grill.

And of course, there are desserts! Two chapters offer the best cupcakes, cookies, cakes and pies for every occasion. Wow them at the next bake sale by baking up bundles of Rainbow Sprinklers, Chocolate Chip Dream Bars or Confetti Caramel Bars. And don't forget about holiday baking—with Frosty Pumpkin Squares, Impossibly Easy French Apple Pie, Raspberry-Topped Eggnog Cheesecake or Cranberry Mousse, it will be tough to choose just one!

Aside from the pages of delicious recipes, you'll find all the latest information and tips to help around the kitchen. The sidebar on "Perfect Pies" will help you create a fabulous and flaky crust every time you bake. And "10 Top Tips for Cooking in a Slow Cooker" will give you everything you need to make the convenience of your slow cooker shine in the fabulous meals you set and forget and serve! Plus, almost every recipe has a specialized tip to help make all your meals quicker, faster or more delicious.

In a hurry? On a diet? Look for the "Quick" label to find all the recipes that can be prepared in 30 minutes or less. Recipes with "Low Fat" labels show you which dishes have 6 grams of fat or less per serving (3 grams or less in the sides and desserts), making it simple to stick to your diet and still eat everything you love.

Choosing what to make for big events and holidays might be a tough decision, so we've provided "Inspired Entertaining" menus, created to offer meal suggestions from start to finish. From New Year's Eve with friends to a backyard picnic for the neighborhood kids or just a special night with your family, you will find just the right combination of salads, soups, entrées and desserts to make your table shine. The "Seasonal Selections" section lists recipes arranged by time of year, helping you select the dish with the perfect ingredients to match the weather. And full-color photos of each dish let you see the amazing meals you'll make.

We hope you'll start enjoying this new edition of *Betty Crocker Annual Recipes* right away. Thank you for joining us for another year!

Betty Crocker

Inspired Entertaining

MENU SUGGESTIONS FOR EVERY OCCASION

Holidays, celebrations and special days are the perfect time to create a fantastic meal for your friends and family. Below you will find 12 inspired menus to help you select the perfect dish to make your guests feel special. From a romantic Valentine's dinner for just the two of you to a Fourth of July barbecue for the whole neighborhood, you'll find a great way to combine these delicious Betty Crocker recipes.

Countdown to the New Year

Cranberry-Topped Three-Cheese Spread (page 27)

Zesty Corn Dip (page 41)

Citrus-Marinated Shrimp Canapés (page 46)

Smoked Salmon Tarts (page 47)

Grilled Buffalo Chicken Sticks (page 49)

Assorted Spirits and Champagne

Super Bowl Sunday

Ham-Twisted Pretzels with Beer Dip (page 42)

Spicy Maple Chicken Drummies (page 49)

Pineapple Fruit and Rice Salad (page 56)

Grilled Open-Face Pork Sandwiches (page 96)

Assorted Beer and Beverages

A Lovely Evening for Two

Layered Ranch Salad (page 61)

Shrimp Alfredo Primavera (page 114)

White Chocolate Bread Pudding (page 252)

Wine or Champagne

Easter Day Celebration

Garlic-Rosemary French Rolls (page 2)

Italian Seafood Stew with Garlic-Herb Croutons (page 81)

Crown Roast of Pork (page 152)

Parmesan Broccoli (page 202)

Make-Ahead Sour Cream 'n Chive Mashed Potatoes (page 216)

Browned Butter Pound Cake with Caramel-Cashew Filling (page 278)

Assorted Beverages

Coffee and Tea

Girls' Movie Night

Cosmos Slush (page 22)

Bloody Mary Cocktail Spread (page 32)

Grilled Vegetable Salsa (page 40)

Grilled Margherita Pizza (page 85)

Seasonal Selections

Looking for something special to celebrate the start of summer? The perfect meal to warm your family on a cold winter night? Try something from one of these helpful lists, grouped by season, to select just the right dish for every occasion!

Spring

Summer

Fall

Winter

Anytime

Breads
and Breakfasts

A Delicious Way to Wake Up

Garlic-Rosemary French Rolls (page 2)

Ham and Swiss Brunch Bake (page 14)

Quick

Garlic-Rosemary French Rolls

Prep time: 10 min Start to finish: 20 min
(Photo on page 1)

1 package (12.4 ounces) frozen crusty French dinner rolls (10 rolls)

3 tablespoons olive or vegetable oil

1 teaspoon finely crushed dried rosemary leaves

½ teaspoon garlic powder

1 tablespoon shredded Asiago or Parmesan cheese, if desired

1. Heat oven to 425°F. Place rolls on ungreased cookie sheet. Bake 4 minutes.

2. Meanwhile, in small bowl or measuring cup, mix oil, rosemary and garlic powder. Remove rolls from oven. With serrated knife, carefully cut X shape in each roll, cutting about halfway through. Generously brush oil mixture over and into each roll. Sprinkle with cheese.

3. Bake 2 to 3 minutes longer or until golden brown. Serve warm.

10 rolls
1 Roll: Calories 140 (Calories from Fat 50); Total Fat 6g (Saturated Fat 0.5g); Cholesterol 0mg; Sodium 200mg; Total Carbohydrate 18g (Dietary Fiber 0g; Sugars 2g); Protein 4g
% Daily Value: Vitamin A 0%; Vitamin C 0%; Calcium 0%; Iron 6%
Exchanges: 1 Starch, 1 Fat
Carbohydrate Choices: 1

KITCHEN TIPS

● If you are really in a hurry, just omit the cutting step and brush the tops of the rolls with the olive oil mixture.

Low-Fat

Bread Machine Fresh Herb Bread

Prep time: 10 min Start to finish: 3 hr 40 min

1 cup plus 2 tablespoons water

2 tablespoons butter or margarine, softened

3 cups Gold Medal® Better for Bread® bread flour

2 teaspoons chopped fresh sage leaves

1 tablespoon chopped fresh basil leaves

1 tablespoon chopped fresh oregano leaves

2 teaspoons chopped fresh thyme leaves

¼ cup chopped fresh parsley

3 tablespoons instant nonfat dry milk

2 tablespoons sugar

1 teaspoon salt

1½ teaspoons bread machine yeast

1. Measure carefully, placing all ingredients in bread machine pan in the order recommended by the manufacturer.

2. Select Basic/White cycle. Use Medium or Light crust color. Remove baked bread from pan and cool on wire rack.

1 loaf (12 slices)
1 Slice: Calories 150 (Calories from Fat 20); Total Fat 2.5g (Saturated Fat 1g); Cholesterol 5mg; Sodium 220mg; Total Carbohydrate 29g (Dietary Fiber 1g; Sugars 3g); Protein 4g
% Daily Value: Vitamin A 4%; Vitamin C 0%; Calcium 2%; Iron 10%
Exchanges: 2 Starch
Carbohydrate Choices: 2

KITCHEN TIPS

- Bread machines with a bread pan capacity of 9 cups or larger work best for this recipe.
- No fresh herbs available? Use ½ teaspoon each of dried sage and thyme leaves and 1 teaspoon each of dried basil and oregano leaves.

Bread Machine Fresh Herb Bread

Orange-Honey Dinner Rolls

Prep time: 5 min Start to finish: 15 min

2 teaspoons honey
$1/2$ teaspoon grated orange peel
2 frozen crusty French dinner rolls (from 12.4-ounce package)

1. Heat oven to 425°F. In small bowl, mix honey and orange peel.

2. Bake rolls as directed on package. Immediately after removing rolls from oven, brush tops with honey mixture. Serve immediately.

2 servings
1 Serving: Calories 130 (Calories from Fat 15); Total Fat 1.5g (Saturated Fat 0g); Cholesterol 0mg; Sodium 200mg; Total Carbohydrate 24g (Dietary Fiber 0g; Sugars 8g); Protein 4g
% Daily Value: Vitamin A 0%; Vitamin C 0%; Calcium 0%; Iron 6%
Exchanges: $1/2$ Starch
Carbohydrate Choices: $1/2$

KITCHEN TIPS

- Having guests over for dinner? This recipe can easily be doubled or tripled.
- Serve these tasty dinner rolls with a breakfast casserole for Sunday brunch.

Southern Buttermilk Cornbread

Prep time: 10 min Start to finish: 40 min

$1/2$ cups yellow, white or blue cornmeal
$1/2$ cup Gold Medal all-purpose flour
$1/2$ cups buttermilk
$1/4$ cup vegetable oil
2 teaspoons baking powder
1 teaspoon sugar
1 teaspoon salt
$1/2$ teaspoon baking soda
2 eggs or $1/2$ cup fat-free egg product or 4 egg whites

1. Heat oven to 450°F. Grease bottom and sides of 9-inch round pan or 8-inch square pan with shortening or spray with cooking spray. In large bowl, mix all ingredients with spoon until blended. Beat vigorously 30 seconds. Pour batter into pan.

2. Bake 25 to 30 minutes or until golden brown. Serve warm.

12 servings
1 Serving: Calories 150 (Calories from Fat 50); Total Fat 6g (Saturated Fat 1g); Cholesterol 35mg; Sodium 370mg; Total Carbohydrate 19g (Dietary Fiber 0g; Sugars 2g); Protein 4g
% Daily Value: Vitamin A 0%; Vitamin C 0%; Calcium 8%; Iron 6%
Exchanges: $1/2$ Starch, 1 Fat
Carbohydrate Choices: 1

KITCHEN TIPS

- You can use this bread to make Bacon-Cornbread Stuffing (page 221); it makes $9/2$ cups of cubed cornbread.

Orange-Honey Dinner Rolls

Southern Buttermilk Cornbread

Quick

Grilled Herbed Stuffed Bread

Prep time: 15 min Start to finish: 15 min

1 ounce reduced-fat cream cheese (Neufchâtel), softened

$\frac{1}{8}$ teaspoon Italian seasoning
Dash of garlic salt

2 crusty dinner rolls (4 inches long), cut crosswise in half

1. Heat gas or charcoal grill for indirect heat as directed in owner's manual. Cut two 12 × 8-inch pieces of heavy-duty foil.

2. In small bowl, mix cream cheese, Italian seasoning and garlic salt. Spread on cut sides of rolls. Place each roll on center of foil piece. Fold foil over roll so edges meet. Seal edges, making tight $\frac{1}{2}$-inch fold; fold again. Allow space on sides for circulation and expansion.

3. Place packets over unheated area on grill. Cover and grill over medium heat 7 to 10 minutes or until rolls are heated through.

2 servings
1 Serving: Calories 220 (Calories from Fat 70); Total Fat 5g (Saturated Fat 2g); Cholesterol 10mg; Sodium 290mg; Total Carbohydrate 33g (Dietary Fiber 2g; Sugars 4g); Protein 7g
% Daily Value: Vitamin A 4%; Vitamin C 0%; Calcium 8%; Iron 10%
Exchanges: 2 Starch, 1$\frac{1}{2}$ Fat
Carbohydrate Choices: 2

KITCHEN TIPS

- Grill these rolls along with your entrée, starting 10 minutes before your entrée is done.
- Mix the cream cheese mixture up to 4 hours in advance and refrigerate. Spread it on the rolls when you are ready to grill.

Grilled Herbed Stuffed Bread

Quick
Double-Corn Muffins
Prep time: 10 min Start to finish: 30 min

$^2/_3$ cup milk

3 tablespoons vegetable oil

1 egg

$^3/_4$ cup Gold Medal all-purpose flour

$^3/_4$ cup cornmeal

2 tablespoons sugar

1 teaspoon baking powder

$^1/_2$ teaspoon salt

1 can (7 ounces) Green Giant® Niblets® whole kernel corn, drained, or 1 cup Green Giant Niblets frozen (thawed) whole kernel corn

1. Heat oven to 400°F. Grease bottoms only of 8 regular-size muffin cups with shortening or line with paper baking cups.

2. In medium bowl, beat milk, oil and egg with spoon. Stir in remaining ingredients except corn just until flour is moistened. Fold in corn. Divide batter evenly among muffin cups (about three-fourths full).

3. Bake 18 to 20 minutes or until golden brown. Immediately remove from pan to wire rack. Serve warm or cool.

8 muffins
1 Muffin: Calories 180 (Calories from Fat 60); Total Fat 7g (Saturated Fat 1g); Cholesterol 30mg; Sodium 260mg; Total Carbohydrate 26g (Dietary Fiber 1g; Sugars 5g); Protein 4g
% Daily Value: Vitamin A 2%; Vitamin C 0%; Calcium 6%; Iron 8%
Exchanges: $1^1/_2$ Starch, 1 Fat
Carbohydrate Choices: 2

KITCHEN TIPS

- For tender, light muffins, stir the batter just until the flour is moistened.
- Any leftover muffins are great the next day. Just be sure to store tightly covered.

Double-Corn Muffins

Betty Crocker
IN SEASON

A IS FOR APPLES

Apples are one of the most requested, most beloved, most popular fruits. They are perfect to take along for a snack, to transform into delicious desserts and to enhance recipes with color and natural sweetness.

Apple ABCs

Because there are thousands of varieties of apples, each with its own unique color, texture and taste, there are lots of ways to prepare them. Here are guidelines for choosing apples, depending on how you want to use them.

Applesauce apples don't need the same firmness as other cooking apples. If you want to reduce or omit the sugar when making applesauce, choose apples that are naturally sweetest. If you want to add sugar, here's a tip: When sugar is added at the beginning of cooking, it will help apples retain their shape and result in a chunkier applesauce. If you like smoother applesauce, cook the apples first, then stir in the sweetener.

TRY: Cameo, Crispin, Golden Delicious, Ida Red, Jonagold, Newtown Pippin, Northern Spy, Paula Red, Pink Lady, Rome

Baking apples are similar to pie apples; they should retain their shape when baked. If you're baking a whole apple, reduce shrinkage by peeling a 1-inch strip of skin around the center of the apple.

TRY: Cameo, Crispin, Golden Delicious, Granny Smith, Honeycrisp, Ida Red, Jonagold, Northern Spy, Pink Lady, Rome

Eating apples are those best for eating out of hand, using in salads and making caramel apples. Remember, these are simply suggestions because everyone has different tastes for tartness, firmness and sweetness.

TRY: Braeburn, Cortland, Fuji, Gala, Golden Delicious, Granny Smith, Honeycrisp, Jonagold, Jonathan, McIntosh, Paula Red, Red Delicious, Regent

Pie apples, as well as those for crisps, turnovers and dumplings, need to be firm enough to hold their shape when cooked. Many pie apples and baking apples can be interchanged.

TRY: Crispin, Golden Delicious, Granny Smith, Ida Red, Jonagold, Newtown Pippin, Paula Red, Rome

Use in Impossibly Easy French Apple Pie on page 261.

CHOOSE: Select apples that are shiny in appearance, not dull. They should be firm and free of bruises.

STORE: Although apples may look nice in a fruit bowl, they don't maintain freshness at room temperature because they will continue to ripen. Refrigerating apples keeps them full of flavor and crunch.

PREPARE: Apples that are cut up or sliced will turn brown fairly quickly once exposed to air. When adding to salads and other unbaked recipes, cut just before serving or, to prevent browning, toss in a mixture of one part citrus juice to three parts water. No citrus? Lemon-lime soda pop will also do the trick. Two large, 3 medium or 4 small apples will equal about a pound. This will yield about $2\frac{1}{2}$ cups chopped or sliced apples.

Nutrition highlights

Apples contain phytonutrients called flavonoids. These substances may protect the cells in your body from damage and lower the risk for several diseases. Along with onions and tea, apples are considered one of the richest sources of flavonoids.

What that might mean for your health

Flavonoids are linked to a lower risk of:
- Heart disease
- Asthma
- Cancer, especially lung cancer
- Diabetes

Eat the peel

Both the flesh and the peel of an apple contain flavonoids, but the peel has more— two to three times more.

Ideas for fitting apples into your day

- Include as an ingredient in lettuce salads
- Add to peanut butter or cheddar cheese sandwiches
- Garnish squash, carrot and pumpkin soups with a favorite variety
- Slice into wedges and dip into vanilla low-fat yogurt
- Add to quick bread and muffin batter
- Partner with peeled kiwifruit, oranges and raisins in a fruit salad
- Sauté and include in rice dishes or as part of a wine sauce poured over chicken

Raspberry-Banana Yogurt Salad

Prep time: 10 min Start to finish: 2 hr 10 min

³⁄₄ cup boiling water

¹⁄₂ package (4-serving size) sugar-free raspberry-flavored gelatin (1¹⁄₂ teaspoons)

1 container (6 ounces) Yoplait® Original 99% Fat Free red raspberry yogurt

¹⁄₂ cup fresh or frozen (thawed and well-drained) raspberries

1 small banana, sliced

1. In small bowl, pour boiling water over gelatin; stir until gelatin is dissolved. Stir in yogurt; gently stir in raspberries and banana. Pour into two 6-ounce custard cups.

2. Refrigerate about 2 hours or until set.

2 servings
1 Serving: Calories 100 (Calories from Fat 10); Total Fat 1g (Saturated Fat 0.5g); Cholesterol 0mg; Sodium 100mg; Total Carbohydrate 20g (Dietary Fiber 2g; Sugars 17g); Protein 5g
% Daily Value: Vitamin A 0%; Vitamin C 15%; Calcium 15%; Iron 0%
Exchanges: ¹⁄₂ Fruit, ¹⁄₂ Other Carbohydrate, ¹⁄₂ Skim Milk
Carbohydrate Choices: 1

KITCHEN TIPS

- If you have extra, garnish with fresh raspberries and banana slices.

Raspberry-Bannana Yogurt Salad

Quick & Low Fat
Creamy Mango Smoothies
Prep time: 10 min Start to finish: 10 min

2   mangoes, peeled, chopped (2 cups)

2   cups mango sorbet

2   containers (6 ounces each) Yoplait Original French vanilla yogurt

1½ cups milk

1. Place all ingredients in blender. Cover and blend on high speed until smooth.

6 servings (1 cup each)
1 Serving: Calories 220 (Calories from Fat 20); Total Fat 2g (Saturated Fat 1g); Cholesterol 5mg; Sodium 75mg; Total Carbohydrate 46g (Dietary Fiber 2g; Sugars 38g); Protein 5g
% Daily Value: Vitamin A 10%; Vitamin C 30%; Calcium 15%; Iron 0%
Exchanges: 1 Fruit, 1½ Other Carbohydrate, ½ Low-Fat Milk
Carbohydrate Choices: 3

KITCHEN TIPS

● For best flavor, choose ripe mangoes. The skins should be yellow with blushes of red.

Creamy Mango Smoothies

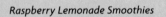

Raspberry Lemonade Smoothies

Peachy Chai Smoothies

Peachy Chai Smoothies

Prep time: 10 min Start to finish: 10 min

- 2 fresh peaches, peeled, sliced
- 2 containers (6 ounces each) Yoplait Custard Style® vanilla low-fat yogurt
- 1/3 cup chai tea latte mix (from 10-ounce package)
- 1/2 cup milk
  Ground nutmeg, if desired

1. Place all ingredients except nutmeg in blender or food processor.

2. Cover and blend on high speed about 1 minute or until smooth and creamy. Sprinkle individual servings with a dash of nutmeg.

3 servings (1 cup each)
1 Serving: Calories 230 (Calories from Fat 30); Total Fat 3.5g (Saturated Fat 1g); Cholesterol 10mg; Sodium 190mg; Total Carbohydrate 43g (Dietary Fiber 2g; Sugars 37g); Protein 9g
% Daily Value: Vitamin A 6%; Vitamin C 8%; Calcium 25%; Iron 0%
Exchanges: 1 1/2 Starch, 1 Fruit, 1 1/2 Skim Milk
Carbohydrate Choices: 3

KITCHEN TIPS

- For the sweetest smoothies with lots of peach flavor, use peaches that are very ripe.

Raspberry Lemonade Smoothies

Prep time: 10 min Start to finish: 10 min

- 2 ripe bananas, thickly sliced
- 1 1/2 cups fresh raspberries
- 2 containers (6 ounces each) Yoplait Original 99% Fat Free red raspberry yogurt
- 1 cup refrigerated raspberry lemonade (from 64-ounce container)

1. Place all ingredients in blender or food processor.

2. Cover and blend on high speed about 1 minute or until smooth and creamy.

4 servings (1 cup each)
1 Serving: Calories 180 (Calories from Fat 15); Total Fat 1.5g (Saturated Fat 0.5g); Cholesterol 0mg; Sodium 50mg; Total Carbohydrate 42g (Dietary Fiber 5g; Sugars 31g); Protein 5g
% Daily Value: Vitamin A 2%; Vitamin C 35%; Calcium 15%; Iron 4%
Exchanges: 1 Fruit, 1 1/2 Other Carbohydrate, 1/2 Skim Milk
Carbohydrate Choices: 2 1/2

KITCHEN TIPS

- Don't have fresh raspberries? Use frozen raspberries that are slightly thawed instead.

Ham and Swiss Brunch Bake

Prep time: 25 min Start to finish: 2 hr

1 loaf (1 pound) French bread, cut into ¹/₂-inch slices

2 tablespoons Dijon mustard

8 ounces thinly sliced cooked ham

8 ounces thinly sliced Swiss cheese

4 eggs

2 cups milk

¹/₄ cup grated Parmesan cheese

¹/₄ cup Progresso® plain bread crumbs

2 tablespoons chopped fresh parsley

3 tablespoons butter or margarine, melted

1. In ungreased 13 × 9-inch (3-quart) glass baking dish, arrange half of the bread slices, overlapping as needed. Brush bread in dish with mustard. Top evenly with ham and Swiss cheese, overlapping as needed. Top with remaining bread slices, arranging them over first layer of bread slices to make sandwiches.

2. In medium bowl, beat eggs and milk with wire whisk until well blended. Carefully pour over sandwiches. Cover and refrigerate at least 1 hour but no longer than 12 hours.

3. Meanwhile, in small bowl, mix Parmesan cheese, bread crumbs, parsley and butter.

4. Heat oven to 375°F. Sprinkle crumb topping over casserole. Bake uncovered 30 to 35 minutes or until sandwiches are puffed and golden brown.

10 servings
1 Serving: Calories 350 (Calories from Fat 150); Total Fat 17g (Saturated Fat 8g); Cholesterol 135mg; Sodium 810mg; Total Carbohydrate 29g (Dietary Fiber 1g; Sugars 4g); Protein 21g
% Daily Value: Vitamin A 10%; Vitamin C 0%; Calcium 35%; Iron 15%
Exchanges: 2 Starch, 2 Medium-Fat Meat, 1 Fat
Carbohydrate Choices: 2

KITCHEN TIPS

- Prepare this dish the night before. Cover and refrigerate the sandwiches separately from the topping.
- Add the topping just before baking. Serve with colorful spiced apple rings.

Ham and Swiss Brunch Bake

Ham and Hash Brown Casserole

Prep time: 15 min Start to finish: 1 hr 10 min

1 bag (1 pound 4 ounces) refrigerated hash brown potatoes

1½ cups diced cooked ham

2 cups shredded Colby or mild Cheddar cheese (8 ounces)

1 cup chive-and-onion sour cream potato topper

1½ cups milk

½ teaspoon peppered seasoned salt

1. Heat oven to 350°F. Spray 8-inch square (2-quart) glass baking dish with cooking spray.

2. In large bowl, mix potatoes, ham and 1½ cups of the cheese. Spread in baking dish. In same bowl, mix sour cream, milk and seasoned salt with wire whisk until well blended. Spoon over potato mixture; stir to mix. Cover baking dish with foil.

3. Bake 45 minutes. Sprinkle with remaining ½ cup cheese. Bake uncovered about 10 minutes longer or until bubbly and thoroughly heated.

6 servings (1¼ cups each)
1 Serving: Calories 450 (Calories from Fat 210); Total Fat 23g (Saturated Fat 14g); Cholesterol 70mg; Sodium 1030mg; Total Carbohydrate 39g (Dietary Fiber 3g; Sugars 7g); Protein 23g
% Daily Value: Vitamin A 15%; Vitamin C 10%; Calcium 40%; Iron 8%
Exchanges: 2 Starch, ½ Other Carbohydrate, 2½ Lean Meat, 3 Fat
Carbohydrate Choices: 2½

KITCHEN TIPS

● While the casserole bakes, microwave Green Giant frozen broccoli or another favorite green vegetable to serve as a side dish.

Ham and Hash Brown Casserole

Quick & Low-Fat
Seafood Frittata

Prep time: 10 min Start to finish: 20 min

1 teaspoon olive or vegetable oil

4 ounces fresh asparagus, cut into 2-inch pieces (1 cup)

¾ cup thinly sliced fresh mushrooms

½ cup chopped imitation crabmeat

¾ cup cheese-and-chive egg product

¼ cup shredded mozzarella cheese (1 ounce)

1. Brush oil over bottom and up sides of 10-inch nonstick skillet; heat over medium-low heat. Cook asparagus and mushrooms in skillet 3 to 4 minutes, stirring occasionally, until asparagus is crisp-tender. Reduce heat to medium-low. Stir in crabmeat. Cook until heated through.

2. Spread mixture evenly in skillet. Pour egg product evenly over mixture; do not stir. Cook 6 to 8 minutes or until egg is almost set. Sprinkle with cheese.

3. Set oven control to broil. Cover skillet handle with foil. Broil frittata with top 4 to 6 inches from heat 1 to 2 minutes or until cheese is melted and eggs are set. Cut in half; serve immediately.

2 servings
1 Serving: Calories 170 (Calories from Fat 60); Total Fat 7g (Saturated Fat 3g); Cholesterol 20mg; Sodium 690mg; Total Carbohydrate 8g (Dietary Fiber 1g; Sugars 1g); Protein 20g
% Daily Value: Vitamin A 25%; Vitamin C 10%; Calcium 15%; Iron 15%
Exchanges: 1 Vegetable, 2½ Very Lean Meat, 1 Fat
Carbohydrate Choices: ½

KITCHEN TIPS

● Nectarine slices are a quick, fresh in-season accompaniment.

Seafood Frittata

Blueberry Pancakes

Prep time: 2 min Start to finish: 3 min per batch

- 1 cup Bisquick Heart Smart™ mix
- 2/3 cup fat-free (skim) milk
- 2 tablespoons fat-free cholesterol-free egg product
- 3/4 cup blueberries

1. Stir ingredients except blueberries until blended. Gently stir in blueberries.

2. Pour by slightly less than 1/4 cupfuls onto hot greased griddle.

3. Cook until bubbles break on surface. Turn and cook until golden.

8 pancakes
1 Serving (4 pancakes): 300 Calories (Calories from Fat 40); Total Fat 4g (Saturated Fat 0g, Trans Fat 0g), Cholesterol 0mg; Sodium 720mg % Daily Value: Vitamin A 4%; Vitamin C 10%; Calcium 15%; Iron 15% Exchanges: 1/2 Fruit, 1/2 Milk, 3 Bread

Blueberry Pancakes

Beverages
and Appetizers

Serve Up Something Special

Smoked Salmon Tarts (page 47)

Sparkling Raspberry Lemonade (page 24)

Colada Cooler Punch

Prep time: 10 min Start to finish: 10 min

2 cans (12 ounces each) frozen piña colada mix concentrate, thawed

2 cans (12 ounces each) frozen white grape juice concentrate, thawed

6 cups cold water

12 cups (about 3 liters) lemon-lime soda pop
Lemon and lime slices

24 servings (1 cup each)
1 Serving: Calories 120 (Calories from Fat 0); Total Fat 0g (Saturated Fat 0g); Cholesterol 0mg; Sodium 15mg; Total Carbohydrate 30g (Dietary Fiber 0g; Sugars 30g); Protein 0g
% Daily Value: Vitamin A 0%; Vitamin C 40%; Calcium 0%; Iron 0%
Exchanges: 2 Other Carbohydrate
Carbohydrate Choices: 2

KITCHEN TIPS

● Make grape ice cubes by putting 1 or 2 grapes in each section of an ice-cube tray. Cover with water and freeze.

1. In large glass or plastic container, mix piña colada and juice concentrates. Stir in water.

2. Just before serving, pour into punch bowl. Add soda pop and lemon and lime slices. Serve over ice.

Colada Cooler Punch

Not-So-"Hard" Lemonade

Prep time: 15 min Start to finish: 2 hr 15 min

3 orange slices, each cut in half

3 lemon slices, each cut in half

3 small strawberries, cut lengthwise in half

6 green grapes

5 bottles (11.2 ounces each) lemon malt beverage, chilled

$1/3$ cup grenadine syrup

1. Remove any seeds from orange and lemon slices.

2. In ungreased 15 × 10 × 1-inch pan, place orange slices, lemon slices, strawberry halves and grapes in single layer. Freeze at least 2 hours until fruit is frozen.

3. When ready to serve, pour malt beverage into each of 6 tall glasses. Drizzle 1 teaspoon grenadine syrup into each glass. Place orange slice, lemon slice, strawberry half and 1 grape into each glass.

6 servings (²/₃ cup each)
1 Serving: Calories 120 (Calories from Fat 0); Total Fat 0g (Saturated Fat 0g); Cholesterol 0mg; Sodium 35mg; Total Carbohydrate 29g (Dietary Fiber 2g; Sugars 11g); Protein 1g
% Daily Value: Vitamin A 0%; Vitamin C 30%; Calcium 2%; Iron 0%
Exchanges: 2 Other Carbohydrate
Carbohydrate Choices: 2

KITCHEN TIPS

- For a beautiful layered cocktail, don't mix the grenadine syrup and malt beverages.
- Frozen chunks of fresh fruit make colorful and tasty "ice cubes" for any summertime beverage.

Not-So-"Hard" Lemonade

Cosmos Slush

Prep time: 10 min Start to finish: 8 hr 10 min

- 6 ounces frozen (thawed) limeade concentrate (from 12-ounce can)
- 3 tablespoons powdered sugar
- 2 cups citrus-flavored vodka or orange juice
- 1 cup orange-flavored liqueur or orange juice
- 4 cups 100% cranberry juice blend

1. Place limeade concentrate and powdered sugar in blender. Cover and blend on high speed until well mixed. Add vodka and orange liqueur. Cover and blend until well mixed.

2. In 13 × 9-inch glass baking dish, stir limeade mixture and cranberry juice until well mixed.

3. Cover and freeze at least 8 hours until slushy. Stir before serving.

14 servings (¹/₂ cup each)
1 Serving: Calories 90 (Calories from Fat 0); Total Fat 0g (Saturated Fat 0g); Cholesterol 0mg; Sodium 0mg; Total Carbohydrate 23g (Dietary Fiber 0g; Sugars 21g); Protein 0g
% Daily Value: Vitamin A 2%; Vitamin C 30%; Calcium 0%; Iron 0%
Exchanges: 1¹/₂ Other Carbohydrate
Carbohydrate Choices: 1¹/₂

KITCHEN TIPS

- For the most flavor and color, make this slush with 100% cranberry juice, not cranberry juice cocktail.
- Serve this version of the trendy Cosmopolitan martini in martini glasses. Put 2 or 3 fresh cranberries in the bottom of each glass.

Firecracker Punch

Prep time: 15 min Start to finish: 45 min

- ²/₃ cup red cinnamon candies
- 4 cups water
- 1 can (6 ounces) frozen lemonade concentrate, thawed
- ¹/₃ cup frozen (thawed) orange juice concentrate (from 6-ounce can)
- 1 bottle (1 liter) ginger ale
- 6 orange slices, cut in half

1. In 1-quart saucepan, cook cinnamon candies and 1 cup of the water over medium-high heat, stirring frequently, until candies are melted; remove from heat. Cool completely, about 30 minutes.

2. In large punch bowl, stir candy mixture, remaining 3 cups water, and the lemonade and orange juice concentrates until well mixed. Refrigerate until ready to serve.

3. Just before serving, gently stir in ginger ale. Garnish with orange slices.

12 servings (³/₄ cup each)
1 Serving: Calories 150 (Calories from Fat 0); Total Fat 0g (Saturated Fat 0g); Cholesterol 0mg; Sodium 15mg; Total Carbohydrate 37g (Dietary Fiber 2g; Sugars 34g); Protein 0g
% Daily Value: Vitamin A 4%; Vitamin C 80%; Calcium 4%; Iron 0%
Exchanges: 2¹/₂ Other Carbohydrate
Carbohydrate Choices: 2¹/₂

KITCHEN TIPS

- To decorate this punch for your Fourth of July bash, add frozen star-shaped ice cubes.

Cosmos Slush

Firecracker Punch

Quick & Low Fat

Pineapple Limeade

Prep time: 10 min Start to finish: 10 min

1 cup sugar
6 cups pineapple juice, chilled
1 cup lime juice
2 liters sparkling water, chilled
Lime slices, if desired

1. In large glass or plastic pitcher, mix sugar and juices. Pour half of mixture into another large pitcher.

2. Just before serving, stir 1 liter sparkling water into each pitcher. Serve over ice. Garnish with lime slices.

16 servings (about 1 cup each)
1 Serving: Calories 110 (Calories from Fat 0); Total Fat 0g (Saturated Fat 0g); Cholesterol 0mg; Sodium 0mg; Total Carbohydrate 26g (Dietary Fiber 0g; Sugars 25g); Protein 0g
% Daily Value: Vitamin A 0%; Vitamin C 25%; Calcium 2%; Iron 0%
Exchanges: 2 Other Carbohydrate
Carbohydrate Choices: 2

KITCHEN TIPS

● Use fresh or bottled lime juice.

Pineapple Limeade

Low Fat

Sparkling Raspberry Lemonade

Prep time: 10 min Start to finish: 3 hr 10 min
(Photo on page 19)

2 packages (10 ounces each) frozen raspberries in syrup, thawed
2 cans (12 ounces each) frozen pink lemonade concentrate, thawed
2 cans (11½ ounces each) frozen raspberry juice cocktail concentrate, thawed
12 cups water
4 cans (12 ounces each) lemon-lime soda pop
1 lemon, thinly sliced

1. Into 2 ice-cube trays, carefully spoon raspberries with syrup. Add enough water to just cover raspberries. Freeze about 3 hours or until firm.

2. In very large glass or plastic container, mix lemonade concentrate, raspberry juice concentrate and water. (Or mix 1 can of each concentrate and 6 cups water into each of 2 large pitchers.) Refrigerate until serving.

3. Just before serving, stir soda pop into lemonade mixture. Place ice cubes in glasses; pour lemonade mixture over ice. Garnish with lemon slices.

24 servings (about 1 cup each)
1 Serving: Calories 150 (Calories from Fat 0); Total Fat 0g (Saturated Fat 0g); Cholesterol 0mg; Sodium 15mg; Total Carbohydrate 37g (Dietary Fiber 1g; Sugars 34g); Protein 0g
% Daily Value: Vitamin A 0%; Vitamin C 25%; Calcium 0%; Iron 4%
Exchanges: 2½ Other Carbohydrate
Carbohydrate Choices: 2½

KITCHEN TIPS

● Mix the lemonade, raspberry juice and water up to 2 days ahead of time.

Lemon Tea Slush

Prep time: 20 min Start to finish: 24 hr 40 min

5   cups water

2   tea bags green tea

1   cup sugar

1   can (12 ounces) frozen lemonade
    concentrate, thawed

1   cup vodka

1   bottle (1 liter) sparkling water, chilled
    Lemon slices, if desired

1. In 2-cup microwavable measuring cup, microwave
   1 cup of the water on High until boiling. Add tea bags
   to boiling water; let steep 10 minutes. Remove tea
   bags; cool tea.

2. Meanwhile, in 2-quart saucepan, heat remaining
   4 cups water to boiling. Stir in sugar until dissolved.
   Remove from heat; cool 20 minutes.

3. In 3-quart plastic container, mix tea, sugar water,
   lemonade concentrate and vodka. Cover and freeze
   at least 24 hours.

4. To serve, place $2/3$ cup slush in each glass and fill
   with $1/3$ cup sparkling water; stir. Garnish with lemon
   slices.

Lemon Tea Slush

12 servings (1 cup each)
1 Serving: Calories 120 (Calories from Fat 0); Total Fat 0g (Saturated
Fat 0g); Cholesterol 0mg; Sodium 0mg; Total Carbohydrate 30g
(Dietary Fiber 0g; Sugars 28g); Protein 0g
% Daily Value: Vitamin A 0%; Vitamin C 8%; Calcium 0%; Iron 0%
Exchanges: 2 Other Carbohydrate
Carbohydrate Choices: 2

KITCHEN TIPS

- Store the slush in a covered container in the freezer for
  up to 1 month.
- Vodka keeps this beverage from freezing solid, so it
  keeps its slushy consistency.

Caribbean Layered Dip

Prep time: 20 min Start to finish: 20 min

1 package (8 ounces) cream cheese, softened

½ cup sour cream

1 tablespoon Old El Paso® taco seasoning mix (from 1.25-ounce envelope)

1 can (15 ounces) black beans, drained, well rinsed

½ cup chopped red bell pepper

½ cup chopped mango

2 tablespoons chopped fresh cilantro

1 to 2 teaspoons finely chopped jalapeño chilies

Lime-flavored or plain tortilla chips

24 servings (2 tablespoons dip and 3 chips each)
1 Serving: Calories 90 (Calories from Fat 50); Total Fat 6g (Saturated Fat 3g); Cholesterol 15mg; Sodium 150mg; Total Carbohydrate 9g (Dietary Fiber 1g; Sugars 1g); Protein 3g
% Daily Value: Vitamin A 8%; Vitamin C 10%; Calcium 2%; Iron 4%
Exchanges: ½ Starch, 1 Fat
Carbohydrate Choices: ½

KITCHEN TIPS

● Trim fat to 4 grams and calories to 80 per serving by using low-fat or fat-free sour cream and reduced-fat cream cheese.

1. In small bowl, mix cream cheese, sour cream and taco seasoning mix with spoon or electric mixer on medium speed until well mixed. Spread on 10-inch round serving plate.

2. Top cream cheese mixture with remaining ingredients except tortilla chips. Serve immediately or refrigerate until serving. Serve with tortilla chips.

Caribbean Layered Dip

Quick

Cranberry-Topped Three-Cheese Spread

Prep time: 15 min Start to finish: 2 hr 15 min

2 packages (8 ounces each) cream cheese, softened

1 cup freshly grated Parmesan cheese

$\frac{1}{2}$ cup Swiss almond cold-pack cheese food (from 8-ounce container)

$\frac{1}{4}$ teaspoon white pepper

$\frac{1}{4}$ teaspoon garlic powder

$\frac{1}{8}$ teaspoon salt

$\frac{1}{3}$ cup whole berry cranberry sauce

Sliced almonds, if desired

Assorted crackers

1. In medium bowl, beat all ingredients except cranberry sauce, almonds and crackers with electric mixer on medium-low speed until smooth.

2. Line 2-cup mold with plastic wrap. Spoon cheese mixture into mold. Cover and refrigerate until firm, at least 2 hours but no longer than 2 days.

3. When ready to serve, turn mold upside down onto serving plate and remove plastic wrap. Spoon cranberry sauce over mold; sprinkle with almonds. Serve with crackers.

32 servings (2 tablespoons spread and 2 crackers each)
1 Serving: Calories 100 (Calories from Fat 70); Total Fat 7g (Saturated Fat 4.5g); Cholesterol 20mg; Sodium 170mg; Total Carbohydrate 4g (Dietary Fiber 0g; Sugars 2g); Protein 3g
% Daily Value: Vitamin A 6%; Vitamin C 0%; Calcium 8%; Iron 2%
Exchanges: $\frac{1}{2}$ Medium-Fat Meat, 1 Fat
Carbohydrate Choices: 0

KITCHEN TIPS

● Shape cheese mixture into a 6-inch star or ball if you don't have a 2-cup mold.

Cranberry-Topped Three-Cheese Spread

Mozzarella and Basil with Marinara Sauce

Prep time: 15 min Start to finish: 15 min

- 8 ounces fresh mozzarella cheese, cubed
- 2 tablespoons chopped fresh basil leaves
- 2 cups chunky marinara sauce
  French baguette slices

1. Heat oven to 350°F. Place cheese cubes in shallow 2-quart casserole. Sprinkle with basil. Spoon marinara sauce around cheese.

2. Bake uncovered 8 to 10 minutes or until cheese is hot and bubbly. Serve with baguette slices.

10 slices (¼ cup sauce and 3 baguette slices each)
1 Serving: Calories 370 (Calories from Fat 90); Total Fat 10g (Saturated Fat 4g); Cholesterol 10mg; Sodium 930mg; Total Carbohydrate 58g (Dietary Fiber 3g; Sugars 4g); Protein 15g
% Daily Value: Vitamin A 10%; Vitamin C 6%; Calcium 25%; Iron 20%
Exchanges: 4 Starch, ½ Medium-Fat Meat, 1 Fat
Carbohydrate Choices: 4

KITCHEN TIPS

- Look for the marinara sauce near the refrigerated pasta or with the jars of pasta sauce.

Warm Cheddar and Olive Dip

Prep time: 10 min Start to finish: 10 min

- 1 container (8 ounces) sharp Cheddar cold-pack cheese food
- 1 package (8 ounces) cream cheese, cut into cubes
- ½ cup milk
- ¼ teaspoon garlic powder
- ¼ teaspoon pepper
- ½ cup salad sliced Spanish olives
- 1 loaf (10 ounces) French baguette bread, cut into 40 slices

1. In large microwavable bowl, place cold-pack cheese food, cream cheese and milk. Microwave uncovered on High 1 minute; stir. Continue microwaving 1 minute at a time, stirring after each minute, until smooth. Stir in remaining ingredients except bread.

2. Spoon dip into 1- to 2-quart slow cooker to keep warm; do not cover. Serve with bread. Dip will hold on Low heat setting up to 2 hours.

20 servings (2 tablespoons dip and 2 slices bread each)
1 Serving: Calories 130 (Calories from Fat 70); Total Fat 8g (Saturated Fat 4.5g); Cholesterol 20mg; Sodium 290mg; Total Carbohydrate 9g (Dietary Fiber 0g; Sugars 2g); Protein 5g
% Daily Value: Vitamin A 6%; Vitamin C 0%; Calcium 8%; Iron 4%
Exchanges: ½ Starch, ½ High-Fat Meat, 1 Fat
Carbohydrate Choices: ½

KITCHEN TIPS

- If dip becomes too thick, stir in milk, 1 tablespoon at a time.

Mozzarella and Basil with Marinara Sauce

Warm Cheddar and Olive Dip

Cream Cheese–Onion Spread

Prep time: 30 min Start to finish: 2 hr 30 min

- 2 tablespoons olive or vegetable oil
- 1 large sweet onion (Bermuda, Maui, Spanish or Walla Walla), chopped (2 cups)
- 1 large red onion, chopped (3 cups)
- 1 container (8 ounces) chive-and-onion cream cheese spread
- 1 tablespoon chopped fresh parsley
- 42 slices pumpernickel or rye cocktail bread

1. In 10-inch skillet, heat oil over medium heat. Cook sweet and red onions in oil 20 to 25 minutes, stirring frequently, until tender and caramelized.

2. Stir cream cheese into onions until well mixed. Spoon into small bowl. Cover and refrigerate 2 hours. Sprinkle with parsley. Serve with bread.

14 servings (2 tablespoons spread and 3 slices bread each)
1 Serving: Calories 140 (Calories from Fat 70); Total Fat 7g (Saturated Fat 3.5g); Cholesterol 15mg; Sodium 250mg; Total Carbohydrate 16g (Dietary Fiber 2g; Sugars 4g); Protein 4g
% Daily Value: Vitamin A 6%; Vitamin C 4%; Calcium 4%; Iron 6%
Exchanges: $\frac{1}{2}$ Starch, $1\frac{1}{2}$ Fat
Carbohydrate Choices: 1

KITCHEN TIPS

- Have fresh basil on hand? Try it instead of the parsley for a completely different flavor combo.
- This super-easy spread can be made a day or two before the party; just cover and refrigerate.

Cream Cheese–Onion Spread

Taco Mozzi Sticks

Prep time: 40 min Start to finish: 1 hr 10 min

- 3 tablespoons milk
- 3 tablespoons Gold Medal all-purpose flour
- 1 package (8 ounces) mozzarella string cheese (8 sticks), cut crosswise in half
- 1 egg
- 3 cups cheese-flavored tortilla chips, crushed (³⁄₄ cup crushed)
- 1 tablespoon Old El Paso taco seasoning mix (from 1.25-ounce envelope)
- ³⁄₄ cup vegetable oil
- ¹⁄₃ cup taco sauce, warmed

1. Line 15 × 10 × 1-inch pan with waxed paper. Place milk in shallow bowl. Place flour in another shallow bowl. Dip each stick of string cheese in milk, then coat with flour.

2. Beat egg into remaining milk with fork. In another shallow bowl, mix crushed chips and taco seasoning mix. Dip coated cheese sticks in egg mixture, then coat with chip mixture. Place in pan. Freeze at least 30 minutes but no longer than 8 hours.

3. In 12-inch skillet, heat oil over medium-high heat until 375°F. Cook frozen cheese sticks in oil 1 to 2 minutes on each side, gently turning once or twice, until light golden brown and cheese is warm. Do not overcook or cheese will melt. Serve immediately with warmed taco sauce.

8 servings (2 cheese sticks and 2 teaspoons taco sauce each)
1 Serving: Calories 210 (Calories from Fat 130); Total Fat 14g (Saturated Fat 5g); Cholesterol 40mg; Sodium 380mg; Total Carbohydrate 11g (Dietary Fiber 0g; Sugars 0g); Protein 9g
% Daily Value: Vitamin A 4%; Vitamin C 0%; Calcium 20%; Iron 4%
Exchanges: ¹⁄₂ Starch, 1 Medium-Fat Meat, 2 Fat
Carbohydrate Choices: 1

KITCHEN TIPS

- To keep mess to a minimum, place the tortilla chips in a plastic food-storage bag and crush with a rolling pin.
- For a last-minute appetizer, don't freeze the cheese sticks; just pan-fry them right after coating with the chip mixture.

Taco Mozzi Sticks

Bloody Mary Cocktail Spread

Quick

Prep time: 25 min Start to finish: 25 min

- 1 package (8 ounces) cream cheese, softened
- 2 tablespoons milk
- ³⁄₄ cup chili sauce
- 1¹⁄₂ teaspoons red pepper sauce
- ¹⁄₂ teaspoon celery salt
- ¹⁄₂ teaspoon sugar
- ²⁄₃ cup finely chopped celery
- ¹⁄₂ cup chopped or sliced ripe olives
- ¹⁄₂ cup finely chopped baby dill pickles
  Assorted crackers

1. In medium bowl, beat cream cheese and milk with electric mixer on medium speed until smooth. Spread on 10-inch round serving plate.

2. In small bowl, mix chili sauce, pepper sauce, celery salt and sugar. Pour over cream cheese mixture to within ¹⁄₂ inch of edge. Top with rows of celery, olives and pickles. Serve with crackers.

36 servings (1 tablespoon spread and 2 crackers each)
1 Serving: Calories 60 (Calories from Fat 35); Total Fat 4g (Saturated Fat 2g); Cholesterol 5mg; Sodium 210mg; Total Carbohydrate 5g (Dietary Fiber 0g; Sugars 1g); Protein 1g
% Daily Value: Vitamin A 4%; Vitamin C 0%; Calcium 0%; Iron 2%
Exchanges: ¹⁄₂ Other Carbohydrate, 1 Fat
Carbohydrate Choices: 0

KITCHEN TIPS

- To keep the top of the spread from getting watery, pat the chopped olives and pickles dry between paper towels.
- Make this appetizer several hours ahead; cover tightly with plastic wrap and refrigerate.

Bloody Mary Cocktail Spread

Quick
Grilled Stuffed Pepper Wedges

Prep time: 25 min Start to finish: 25 min

½ cup chive-and-onion cream cheese spread (from 8-ounce container)

1 tablespoon chopped ripe olives

1 medium green bell pepper, cut into 8 wedges

1 medium red bell pepper, cut into 8 wedges

3 tablespoons finely shredded Cheddar-American cheese blend

1. Heat coals or gas grill for direct heat. In small bowl, mix cream cheese and olives.

2. Spread about 2 teaspoons cream cheese mixture inside each pepper wedge. Sprinkle with shredded cheese.

3. Cover and grill, cheese sides up, over medium heat 8 to 10 minutes or until bottoms of peppers are blistered and charred and cheese is melted.

8 servings (2 wedges each)
1 Serving: Calories 60 (Calories from Fat 50); Total Fat 5g (Saturated Fat 3.5g); Cholesterol 15mg; Sodium 150mg; Total Carbohydrate 3g (Dietary Fiber 0g; Sugars 2g); Protein 2g
% Daily Value: Vitamin A 25%; Vitamin C 35%; Calcium 2%; Iron 0%
Exchanges: 1½ Fat
Carbohydrate Choices: 0

KITCHEN TIPS

- Up to 2 hours ahead, spread pepper wedges with cream cheese mixture and refrigerate. Sprinkle with cheese before grilling.

Grilled Stuffed Pepper Wedges

Betty Crocker
IN SEASON

Herbs

These small garden treasures are packed with distinctive flavors and fragrant aromas that make everyday fare simply extraordinary. Here's a sampler of summer herb favorites.

Basil

CHARACTERISTICS

- Intense sweet and spicy flavor, often described as a blend of licorice and cloves.
- Signature herb in Mediterranean and Italian cuisines.
- Available in other varieties, such as lemon, clove, cinnamon and Thai basil.

HERB IDEAS

- Toss chopped basil with mixed salad greens.
- Sprinkle sliced tomatoes with chopped basil, Parmesan cheese and olive oil.

RECIPES TO TRY

- Grilled Margherita Pizza (page 85)
- Mozzarella and Basil with Marinara Sauce (page 28)

Cilantro

CHARACTERISTICS

- Extremely aromatic with a pungent, acidic flavor.
- Sometimes referred to as Mexican parsley or Chinese parsley.
- This flat-leaf parsley look-alike is a global herb used in Mexican, Indian, Middle Eastern and Asian cuisines.

HERB IDEAS

- Stir into sour cream, salsa or dips.
- Add to chicken salad.

RECIPES TO TRY

- Grilled Vegetable Salsa (page 40)
- Caribbean Layered Dip (page 26)

Chives

CHARACTERISTICS

- Bright green with hollow stems.
- Delicate onion flavor.
- Heating chives diminishes their flavor, so add right before serving.

HERB IDEAS

- Sprinkle over grilled or roasted vegetables.
- Stir into cream cheese or cottage cheese.

RECIPE TO TRY

- Cheesy Herb and Turkey Bites (page 50)

Mint

CHARACTERISTICS

- Strong, sweet flavor and cool aftertaste.
- Although "mint" encompasses numerous varieties of this herb, peppermint and spearmint are the most notable.
- Adventurous cooks may want to try chocolate, pineapple and apple mint.
- Peppermint has large, bright green leaves; spearmint has small, dustier gray-green leaves.

HERB IDEAS

- Slightly bruise leaves and add to your favorite beverage (teas, lemonade, sparkling water).
- Stir chopped mint into chocolate sauce or hot fudge sauce and serve over cake or ice cream.

RECIPE TO TRY

- Chicken-Fruit Salad (page 55)

Parsley

CHARACTERISTICS

- Distinctive tangy, peppery flavor.
- Most popular in the United States is curly leaf parsley, which has small, curly, dark green leaves. In most of Europe, however, flat-leaf parsley or Italian parsley, with its flat, dark green leaves, is more popular.

HERB IDEAS

- Stir chopped parsley into tuna salad or egg salad filling for sandwiches.
- Toss with melted butter or olive oil and cooked vegetables.
- Make a parsley pesto by using half basil and half parsley in your favorite pesto recipe.

RECIPE TO TRY

- Cream Cheese–Onion Spread (page 30)

Sage Advice

- Home-grown fresh herbs should be picked early in the morning after the dew has evaporated but before the sun is too strong. Pick the tops of the herbs (about 2 to 3 inches) because those leaves contain the most oils.

- Most fresh herbs can be stored in the refrigerator. Wrap stems of fresh herbs in a damp paper towel, then put the herbs in a plastic bag and refrigerate.

- For herbs like mint, parsley and cilantro, fill a small jar or glass with about 2 inches of water. Place the stems in the water and place a plastic bag over the herbs. Secure with a rubber band around the neck of the jar.

Herb Blends

The best way to combine different herbs is to experiment, starting with two or three and then adding from there, depending on the recipe. Start with these tried-and-true herb mixtures.

FINES HERBES is terrific for delicately flavored foods like green salads, eggs and cream sauces. Make this with equal parts of summer favorites such as chives, chervil, parsley and tarragon.

BOUQUET GARNI is a French-inspired herb combination used to flavor soups, stews, casseroles and even rice and grains. Wrap a whole bay leaf, a thyme sprig and several parsley sprigs in a small piece of cheesecloth or linen and tie with string; simmer in the liquid mixture.

MIXED HERBS are a bit stronger than Fines Herbes and thus are used with more robustly flavored foods like meat, fish and some vegetables. Make with equal parts sage, thyme, marjoram and parsley.

- Experimenting with a new herb or adding fresh herbs to a recipe? Use 1 teaspoon of fresh herbs for every four servings the recipe makes. Taste the recipe to decide if you have enough herbs. If you'd like a little more, add a little at a time until the flavor is right.

- Fresh herbs can't be beat, but if you'd like to (or need to) use dried herbs, substitute in a 3-to-1 ratio. For every 3 teaspoons (1 tablespoon) of fresh herbs, you'll need 1 teaspoon of dried herbs.

Summer Herbs, Winter Flavor

FREEZING

- You can freeze herbs either before or after chopping.

- Herbs such as dill weed, sage, rosemary and thyme can be rinsed, lightly dried and then placed in a heavy plastic freezer bag while still on the stem. When you want to use the herbs, toss them whole into soups or stews or snip the leaves into measuring spoons or directly into recipes.

- Another option is to rinse the herbs, remove the leaves from the stems and dry the leaves thoroughly—several hours on paper towels works well. Freeze in heavy plastic bags.

- You can also chop rinsed herbs and place in small containers or plastic bags. These will freeze in small clusters, so to use, just break off the amount you need.

- If you use an herb blend frequently, mix it and freeze in small containers or bags.

DRYING

- The best way to dry fresh herbs is the old-fashioned method of air drying. The slow removal of moisture leaves the concentrated herb oils behind.

- Herbs with low moisture, such as sage, dill weed, bay leaves, rosemary and marjoram, dry faster and easier and are less susceptible to mold. Higher-moisture herbs, such as basil, mint and tarragon, should be dried in small batches and may take longer.

- To dry, rinse herbs (on stems) with water and dry with paper towels. Cut small holes in a paper bag. Place the herbs, stem end toward the top, in the bag and seal the bag or tie the stems with string. The holes provide air circulation, and the bag keeps out dust and other contaminants. Hang the bag in a warm, airy room for at least two weeks or until the herbs are dry. After they're dry, store up to one year in a covered container.

Sesame Toast–Vegetable Bites

Prep time: 40 min Start to finish: 40 min

1   can (8 ounces) refrigerated crescent dinner rolls (8 rolls)

1   egg, beaten

1   teaspoon sesame seed

4   ounces cream cheese (from 8-ounce package), softened

$\frac{1}{2}$ teaspoon grated lemon peel

$\frac{1}{4}$ teaspoon dried dill weed

12   snap pea pods, cut crosswise in half

$\frac{1}{2}$ medium red bell pepper, cut into 24 strips, $1\frac{1}{2}$ inches long

24   small broccoli florets or cauliflowerets

1   medium carrot, cut lengthwise in half, then cut crosswise into 12 slices (24 pieces)

1. Heat oven to 375°F. Unroll dough into 12 × 8-inch rectangle; press perforations to seal. Brush dough with egg; sprinkle with sesame seed. Cut dough lengthwise into 4 strips. Cut each strip crosswise into 6 pieces. Place pieces 2 inches apart on ungreased cookie sheet.

2. Bake 6 to 8 minutes or until golden brown. Remove from cookie sheet to wire rack. Cool completely, about 10 minutes.

3. Meanwhile, in small bowl, mix cream cheese, lemon peel and dill weed until smooth. Spread cream cheese mixture over cooled toasts. Arrange 1 piece of each vegetable on the toast.

24 servings
1 Serving: Calories 60 (Calories from Fat 35); Total Fat 4g (Saturated Fat 2g); Cholesterol 15mg; Sodium 95mg; Total Carbohydrate 5g (Dietary Fiber 0g; Sugars 1g); Protein 2g
% Daily Value: Vitamin A 15%; Vitamin C 15%; Calcium 0%; Iron 2%
Exchanges: $\frac{1}{2}$ Starch, $\frac{1}{2}$ Fat
Carbohydrate Choices: 0

KITCHEN TIPS

- Use reduced-fat crescent rolls and cream cheese (Neufchâtel) to trim the fat to 3 grams and the calories to 55 per serving.
- A day or two ahead, cut up the veggies, mix the cream cheese spread and bake the toasts, then assemble just before serving.

Grilled Vegetable Salsa

Prep time: 1 hr 10 min Start to finish: 1 hr 25 min

- 2 ears corn, husked, cleaned and broken crosswise in half
- 2 medium zucchini, cut lengthwise in half, then cut crosswise into 1½-inch pieces
- 1 medium red bell pepper, cut into 8 pieces
- 1 medium red onion, cut into wedges, separated
- 2 jalapeño chilies, cut in half, seeded
- 2 tablespoons olive or vegetable oil
- 6 roma (plum) tomatoes, cut lengthwise in half, seeded
- 2 teaspoons grated lime peel
- 2 tablespoons chopped fresh cilantro
- 1 teaspoon salt
  Tortilla chips

1. Heat coals or gas grill for direct heat. In large bowl, toss corn, zucchini, bell pepper, onion and chilies with oil. Place in grill basket (grill "wok").

2. Cover and grill vegetables over medium heat 25 to 30 minutes, shaking basket or stirring occasionally, until vegetables are tender. Add tomatoes to basket; cover and grill 1 to 2 minutes longer or until tomatoes are hot. Remove basket from grill; cool vegetables 15 minutes.

3. Cut corn off cobs (about 1 cup kernels); chop all remaining vegetables into small pieces. In large bowl, mix vegetables, lime peel, cilantro and salt. Serve immediately or cover and refrigerate up to 24 hours. Serve with tortilla chips. Store covered in refrigerator.

24 servings (¼ cup salsa and 6 chips each)
1 Serving: Calories 80 (Calories from Fat 35); Total Fat 4g (Saturated Fat 0.5g); Cholesterol 0mg; Sodium 170mg; Total Carbohydrate 11g (Dietary Fiber 1g; Sugars 1g); Protein 1g
% Daily Value: Vitamin A 10%; Vitamin C 15%; Calcium 0%; Iron 4%
Exchanges: ½ Other Carbohydrate, ½ Vegetable, 1 Fat
Carbohydrate Choices: 1

KITCHEN TIPS

- For salsa with an extra kick, include the seeds of the jalapeño chilies.

Grilled Vegetable Salsa

Zesty Corn Dip

Prep time: 10 min Start to finish: 1 hr 10 min

2 packages (8 ounces each) cream cheese, softened
¼ cup lime juice
1 tablespoon ground red chilies or chili powder
1 tablespoon ground cumin
2 tablespoons vegetable oil
½ teaspoon salt
   Dash of pepper
1 can (7 ounces) Green Giant Niblets whole kernel corn, drained
¼ cup chopped walnuts
1 small onion, chopped (¼ cup)
   Tortilla chips

1. In large bowl, beat cream cheese, lime juice, chilies, cumin, oil, salt and pepper with electric mixer on medium speed until smooth. Stir in corn, walnuts and onion.

2. Refrigerate at least 1 hour. Serve with tortilla chips.

24 servings (about 3 tablespoons dip and 3 chips each)
1 Serving: Calories 120 (Calories from Fat 90); Total Fat 10g (Saturated Fat 4.5g); Cholesterol 20mg; Sodium 150mg; Total Carbohydrate 6g (Dietary Fiber 0g; Sugars 0g); Protein 2g
% Daily Value: Vitamin A 8%; Vitamin C 2%; Calcium 2%; Iron 4%
Exchanges: ½ Starch, 2 Fat
Carbohydrate Choices: ½

KITCHEN TIPS

● Fill hollowed-out large bell peppers with the dip and arrange on a tray lined with corn husks.

Zesty Corn Dip

Ham-Twisted Pretzels with Beer Dip

Prep time: 50 min Start to finish: 50 min

Pretzels

- 1 can (11 ounces) refrigerated breadsticks
- 1 package (2.5 ounces) thinly sliced lean ham
- 1 egg, beaten
- 1 teaspoon coarse salt, if desired

Beer Dip

- 4 ounces cream cheese (from 8-ounce package), softened
- 1/3 cup regular or nonalcoholic beer
- 2 tablespoons mayonnaise or salad dressing
- 1/4 cup finely shredded Cheddar-American cheese blend (1 ounce)

Tie each rope into a loose knot.

1. Heat oven to 375°F. Grease large cookie sheet with shortening or spray with cooking spray. Unroll breadstick dough; separate into 12 breadsticks. Cut each breadstick lengthwise in half.

2. On work surface, roll each piece of dough into 9-inch rope. Cut each slice of ham into 4 equal strips. Wrap 2 pieces ham around each rope (in a candy cane pattern). Tie each rope into a loose knot. Place on cookie sheet. Brush with egg. Sprinkle lightly with salt.

3. Bake 10 to 13 minutes or until light golden brown on top and golden brown on bottom.

4. Meanwhile, in small microwavable bowl, beat cream cheese, beer and mayonnaise with electric mixer on low speed until smooth. Stir in cheese blend. Microwave uncovered on High 1 to 2 minutes, stirring once, until heated through. Serve dip with pretzels.

8 servings (3 pretzels and about 2 tablespoons dip each)
1 Serving: Calories 220 (Calories from Fat 110); Total Fat 12g (Saturated Fat 5g); Cholesterol 50mg; Sodium 490mg; Total Carbohydrate 20g (Dietary Fiber 0g; Sugars 3g); Protein 8g
% Daily Value: Vitamin A 6%; Vitamin C 0%; Calcium 4%; Iron 8%
Exchanges: 1 1/2 Starch, 1/2 High-Fat Meat, 1 1/2 Fat
Carbohydrate Choices: 1

Ham-Twisted Pretzels with Beer Dip

Quick

Cinnamon-Raisin Snack Mix

Prep time: 10 min Start to finish: 10 min

¼ cup sugar

1 teaspoon ground cinnamon

¼ cup butter or margarine

1½ cups Corn Chex® cereal

1½ cups Rice Chex® cereal

1½ cups Wheat Chex® cereal

½ cup raisins, dried cranberries or dried cherries

1. In small bowl, mix sugar and cinnamon; set aside.

2. In large microwavable bowl, microwave butter uncovered on High about 40 seconds or until melted. Stir in cereals until evenly coated. Microwave uncovered 2 minutes, stirring after 1 minute.

3. Sprinkle half of the sugar mixture evenly over cereals; stir. Sprinkle with remaining sugar mixture; stir. Microwave uncovered 1 minute. Stir in raisins. Spread on paper towels to cool.

10 servings (½ cup each)
1 Serving: Calories 140 (Calories from Fat 45); Total Fat 5g (Saturated Fat 2.5g); Cholesterol 10mg; Sodium 180mg; Total Carbohydrate 24g (Dietary Fiber 1g; Sugars 11g); Protein 2g
% Daily Value: Vitamin A 8%; Vitamin C 2%; Calcium 6%; Iron 25%
Exchanges: ½ Starch, 1 Other Carbohydrate, 1 Fat
Carbohydrate Choices: 1½

KITCHEN TIPS

● Scoop portions of this tasty snack mix into small plastic bags and wrap with colorful ribbons, then have on hand to tuck into lunches.

Cinnamon-Raisin Snack Mix

Chili and Garlic Snack Mix

Prep time: 5 min Start to finish: 50 min

3 cups Cheerios® cereal

3 cups corn chips (broken in half, if desired)

1 cup unsalted peanuts

1 cup thin pretzel sticks

$^1/_3$ cup butter or margarine, melted

$^1/_2$ teaspoon chili powder

$^1/_2$ teaspoon garlic powder

14 servings ($^1/_2$ cup each)
1 Serving: Calories 170 (Calories from Fat 110); Total Fat 12g (Saturated Fat 3.5g); Cholesterol 10mg; Sodium 170mg; Total Carbohydrate 12g (Dietary Fiber 2g; Sugars 0g); Protein 4g
% Daily Value: Vitamin A 6%; Vitamin C 2%; Calcium 4%; Iron 10%
Exchanges: 1 Starch, 2 Fat
Carbohydrate Choices: 1

KITCHEN TIPS

● For an anytime snack, prepare this tasty mix up to 1 week before serving and store in an airtight container.

1. Heat oven to 300°F. In large bowl, mix cereal, corn chips, peanuts and pretzels. In small bowl, mix remaining ingredients; pour over cereal mixture. Toss until evenly coated. Spread cereal mixture in ungreased 15 × 10 × 1-inch pan.

2. Bake uncovered 15 minutes, stirring once. Cool completely, about 30 minutes. Store in airtight container.

Chili and Garlic Snack Mix

Citrus-Marinated Shrimp Canapés

Prep time: 40 min Start to finish: 40 min

1/3 cup olive or vegetable oil

1 tablespoon lemon juice

1 tablespoon honey

2 teaspoons grated lime peel

1/4 teaspoon salt

24 uncooked peeled deveined medium shrimp, thawed if frozen, tails peeled

3 tablespoons butter or margarine, softened

1 tablespoon orange marmalade

24 slices French baguette, 1/4 inch thick

Cilantro sprigs

1. In medium bowl, mix oil, lemon juice, honey, lime peel and salt. Add shrimp; toss to coat. Cover and refrigerate at least 30 minutes but no longer than 2 hours, stirring once after half the time.

2. Meanwhile, set oven control to broil. In small bowl, stir butter and marmalade until well mixed. Spread butter over baguette slices.

3. Remove shrimp from marinade; discard marinade. Place shrimp in single layer on rack in broiler pan. Broil with tops 4 to 6 inches from heat 4 to 6 minutes or until shrimp are lightly browned.

4. Place 1 shrimp on each baguette slice. Garnish with cilantro.

24 servings
1 Serving: Calories 140 (Calories from Fat 50); Total Fat 6g (Saturated Fat 1.5g); Cholesterol 15mg; Sodium 230mg; Total Carbohydrate 17g (Dietary Fiber 0g; Sugars 1g); Protein 4g
% Daily Value: Vitamin A 0%; Vitamin C 0%; Calcium 2%; Iron 6%
Exchanges: 1 Starch, 1 1/2 Fat
Carbohydrate Choices: 1

KITCHEN TIPS

● The citrus marinade can break down the shrimp if they marinate longer than 2 hours, resulting in a less firm texture.

Citrus-Marinated Shrimp Canapés

Low-Fat
Smoked Salmon Tarts

Prep time: 15 min Start to finish: 40 min

$1/2$ cup Original Bisquick® mix

$1/2$ cup milk

$1/4$ cup sour cream

$1/2$ teaspoon Worcestershire sauce

2 eggs

$2/3$ cup shredded Cheddar cheese

$1/3$ cup chopped smoked salmon

2 medium green onions, sliced (2 tablespoons)

1. Heat oven to 400°F. Spray 24 mini muffin cups with cooking spray.

2. In small bowl, beat Bisquick mix, milk, sour cream, Worcestershire sauce and eggs with fork until blended. Stir in remaining ingredients. Spoon about 1 tablespoon mixture into each muffin cup.

3. Bake 15 to 20 minutes or until golden. Cool 5 minutes. Loosen sides of tarts from pan; remove from pan. Serve warm.

24 mini tarts
1 Mini Tart: Calories 40 (Calories from Fat 20); Total Fat 2.5g (Saturated Fat 1g); Cholesterol 25mg; Sodium 80mg; Total Carbohydrate 2g (Dietary Fiber 0g; Sugars 0g); Protein 2g
% Daily Value: Vitamin A 0%; Vitamin C 0%; Calcium 4%; Iron 0%
Exchanges: $1/2$ Medium-Fat Meat
Carbohydrate Choices: 0

Smoked Salmon Tarts

KITCHEN TIPS

- Vary the flavor with the cheese you use. Havarti, Colby, mozzarella or Monterey Jack cheese would be delicious.

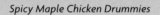

Spicy Maple Chicken Drummies

Grilled Buffalo Chicken Sticks

Spicy Maple
Chicken Drummies

Prep time: 15 min Start to finish: 1 hr 10 min

- ¼ cup real maple syrup or honey
- ¼ cup chili sauce
- 2 tablespoons chopped fresh chives
- 1 tablespoon soy sauce
- ½ teaspoon ground mustard
- ¼ teaspoon ground red pepper (cayenne), if desired
- 2 pounds chicken drummettes (about 20)

1. Heat oven to 375°F. In small bowl, mix all ingredients except chicken. Place chicken in ungreased 15 × 10 × 1-inch pan. Pour syrup mixture over chicken; turn chicken to coat.

2. Bake uncovered 45 to 55 minutes, turning once and brushing with syrup mixture after 30 minutes, until juice of chicken is clear when thickest part is cut to bone (180°F). Serve chicken with syrup mixture.

20 drummies
1 Drummie: Calories 60 (Calories from Fat 30); Total Fat 3.5g (Saturated Fat 1g); Cholesterol 15mg; Sodium 105mg; Total Carbohydrate 3g (Dietary Fiber 0g; Sugars 3g); Protein 5g
% Daily Value: Vitamin A 0%; Vitamin C 0%; Calcium 0%; Iron 0%
Exchanges: ½ Lean Meat, ½ Fat
Carbohydrate Choices: 0

KITCHEN TIPS

- If desired, sprinkle with crumbled blue cheese and serve with blue cheese dressing.

Grilled Buffalo
Chicken Sticks

Prep time: 30 min Start to finish: 1 hr

- 2 tablespoons butter or margarine, melted
- ¼ cup original cayenne pepper sauce or red pepper sauce
- 1 tablespoon honey
- ½ teaspoon celery seed
- ½ teaspoon salt
- 1 package (1 pound) chicken breast tenders (not breaded)
- ½ cup blue cheese dressing

1. In medium bowl, mix butter, pepper sauce, honey, celery seed and salt. Remove 2 tablespoons sauce mixture; set aside. Add chicken to remaining sauce mixture; stir to coat. Cover and refrigerate at least 30 minutes but no longer than 2 hours.

2. Meanwhile, soak ten 10- to 12-inch wooden skewers in water 30 minutes.

3. Brush grill rack with vegetable oil. Heat coals or gas grill for direct heat. Remove chicken from marinade; discard marinade. Thread each chicken tender on a skewer.

4. Cover and grill chicken over medium heat 8 to 10 minutes, turning once and brushing frequently with reserved sauce mixture, until no longer pink in center. Discard any remaining sauce mixture. Serve chicken with blue cheese dressing.

10 servings
1 Serving: Calories 140 (Calories from Fat 80); Total Fat 9g (Saturated Fat 2g); Cholesterol 35mg; Sodium 270mg; Total Carbohydrate 4g (Dietary Fiber 0g; Sugars 3g); Protein 11g
% Daily Value: Vitamin A 30%; Vitamin C 0%; Calcium 2%; Iron 4%
Exchanges: 1½ Very Lean Meat, 2 Fat
Carbohydrate Choices: 0

KITCHEN TIPS

- Soaking wooden skewers in water for at least 30 minutes before using ensures that they don't char during grilling.

Quick & Low Fat
Cheesy Herb and Turkey Bites
Prep time: 15 min Start to finish: 15 min

10   thin slices turkey, about 4 inches in diameter (from 6-ounce package)

¼   cup herb-and-garlic spreadable cheese

¼   cup finely chopped red bell pepper

40   bite-size garlic-flavor or plain bagel chips or round buttery crackers

    Chopped fresh parsley or chives, if desired

1. Unfold each turkey slice so that it is flat. Spread each slice with 1 teaspoon cheese and top with 1 teaspoon bell pepper. Carefully roll up. Cut each roll into 4 pieces.

2. Place each turkey roll on bagel chip. Garnish with parsley. Serve immediately.

40 servings
1 Serving: Calories 10 (Calories from Fat 5); Total Fat 0.5g (Saturated Fat 0g); Cholesterol 0mg; Sodium 40mg; Total Carbohydrate 0g (Dietary Fiber 0g; Sugars 0g); Protein 0g
% Daily Value: Vitamin A 0%; Vitamin C 2%; Calcium 0%; Iron 0%
Exchanges: Free
Carbohydrate Choices: 0

KITCHEN TIPS

● For more intense flavor, use smoked turkey and chopped oil-packed sun-dried tomatoes instead of the bell pepper.

Cheesy Herb and Turkey Bites

Salads
and Soups

Great Dishes for Lunch or Dinner

Grilled Shrimp Louis Salad (page 52)

Italian Meatball Soup (page 78)

Grilled Shrimp Louis Salad

Prep time: 25 min Start to finish: 25 min

Salad

- ¹/₂ pound uncooked peeled deveined medium shrimp, thawed if frozen, tails removed
- 1 teaspoon olive or vegetable oil
- ¹/₈ teaspoon salt
- 4 cups chopped romaine lettuce
- 1 medium stalk celery, finely chopped (¹/₂ cup)
- ¹/₂ cup chopped red bell pepper
- 1 cup grape tomatoes, cut in half

Dressing

- 2 tablespoons reduced-fat mayonnaise
- 1 tablespoon plain yogurt
- 1 tablespoon shrimp cocktail sauce
- ¹/₂ teaspoon grated lemon peel
- ¹/₈ teaspoon salt
- 1 to 2 tablespoons fat-free (skim) milk

1. Heat gas or charcoal grill. On each of two 12-inch metal skewers, thread shrimp, leaving ¹/₄-inch space between the shrimp. Brush with oil. Sprinkle with ¹/₈ teaspoon salt.

2. Cover and grill kabobs over medium heat 4 to 6 minutes, turning once, until shrimp are pink and firm. Remove shrimp from skewers.

3. Place lettuce on 2 serving plates. Top with celery, bell pepper, tomatoes and grilled shrimp.

4. In small bowl, mix all dressing ingredients, adding enough milk for desired consistency. Spoon dressing onto centers of salads.

Grilled Shrimp Louis Salad

2 servings
1 Serving: Calories 210 (Calories from Fat 80); Total Fat 9g (Saturated Fat 1.5g); Cholesterol 165mg; Sodium 740mg; Total Carbohydrate 15g (Dietary Fiber 5g; Sugars 10g); Protein 21g
% Daily Value: Vitamin A 110%; Vitamin C 200%; Calcium 10%; Iron 25%
Exchanges: ¹/₂ Other Carbohydrate, 1 Vegetable, 2¹/₂ Very Lean Meat, 1¹/₂ Fat
Carbohydrate Choices: ¹/₂

KITCHEN TIPS

● Serving the dressing on the side allows each person to use the desired amount.

Quick & Low Fat
Shrimp Paella Salad

Prep time: 20 min Start to finish: 20 min

2 slices bacon, cut up
1 clove garlic, finely chopped
1 cup cooked rice
½ cup Green Giant frozen sweet peas (from 1-pound bag), thawed
2 tablespoons chopped drained roasted red bell peppers (from 7-ounce jar)
1 tablespoon lemon juice
⅛ teaspoon paprika
2 to 3 drops red pepper sauce
6 ounces cooked peeled deveined medium shrimp, thawed if frozen, tails removed
   Lettuce leaves

1. In 10-inch skillet, cook bacon over medium heat, stirring occasionally, until crisp. Drain fat, reserving 1 tablespoon in skillet. Drain bacon on paper towel.

2. In same skillet, cook garlic in bacon fat over medium heat about 1 minute, stirring occasionally, until softened. Stir in bacon and remaining ingredients except lettuce.

3. Serve shrimp mixture on lettuce. Sprinkle with additional paprika if desired.

2 servings
1 Serving: Calories 250 (Calories from Fat 45); Total Fat 5g (Saturated Fat 1.5g); Cholesterol 175mg; Sodium 650mg; Total Carbohydrate 29g (Dietary Fiber 2g; Sugars 3g); Protein 24g
% Daily Value: Vitamin A 25%; Vitamin C 25%; Calcium 6%; Iron 25%
Exchanges: 2 Starch, 2½ Very Lean Meat, ½ Fat
Carbohydrate Choices: 2

KITCHEN TIPS

● Paella is a Spanish dish made from flavored rice, meats and shellfish. This salad is a wonderfully simple version of the traditional dish.

Shrimp Paella Salad

Quick & Low-Fat

Tropical Salsa-Topped Chicken Salad

Prep time: 15 min Start to finish: 30 min

2   cups (4 ounces each) tropical fruit in lightly sweetened juice (from 16-ounce package)

1   teaspoon grated lime peel

¼   teaspoon salt

2   boneless skinless chicken breasts (5 ounces each), cut into 1-inch pieces

½   medium red bell pepper, chopped (½ cup)

2   medium green onions, sliced (2 tablespoons)

1   tablespoon finely chopped fresh cilantro

1   bag (6 ounces) fresh baby spinach leaves

1   tablespoon flaked coconut

1. Drain fruit cups, reserving juice. In small bowl, mix 2 tablespoons reserved juice, the lime peel and salt. Add chicken pieces; toss to coat. Cover and refrigerate 15 minutes, stirring once.

2. Meanwhile, in medium bowl, mix drained fruit, bell pepper, onions and cilantro; set aside.

3. Heat 10-inch nonstick skillet over medium-low heat. Add chicken with marinade. Cook 6 to 8 minutes, stirring frequently, until chicken is brown on outside and no longer pink in center.

4. In large bowl, toss spinach with remaining reserved juice. Arrange spinach on 2 dinner plates. Top with chicken and fruit mixture. Sprinkle with coconut.

2 servings
1 Serving: Calories 230 (Calories from Fat 45); Total Fat 5g (Saturated Fat 2g); Cholesterol 70mg; Sodium 440mg; Total Carbohydrate 21g (Dietary Fiber 5g; Sugars 13g); Protein 28g
% Daily Value: Vitamin A 210%; Vitamin C 80%; Calcium 10%; Iron 20%
Exchanges: 1 Fruit, 1 Vegetable, 3½ Very Lean Meat, ½ Fat
Carbohydrate Choices: 1

KITCHEN TIPS

- Toasting the coconut adds more flavor. Bake in an ungreased shallow pan at 350°F for 5 to 7 minutes, stirring occasionally, until golden brown.

- Buy the tropical fruit in the canned fruit aisle at your grocery store. These individual cups of fruit come in packages of four.

Tropical Salsa-Topped Chicken Salad

Low Fat
Chicken-Fruit Salad

Prep time: 10 min Start to finish: 40 min

- 1/3 cup plain fat-free yogurt
- 2 tablespoons fat-free mayonnaise or salad dressing
- 1 cup cubed cooked chicken breast
- 2/3 cup seedless green grapes
- 1 large peach, chopped (3/4 cup)
- 1 medium stalk celery, diced (1/2 cup)
- 1 teaspoon chopped fresh or 1/2 teaspoon dried mint leaves

1. In medium bowl, mix yogurt and mayonnaise until smooth. Stir in remaining ingredients.

2. Cover and refrigerate at least 30 minutes until chilled.

2 servings
1 Serving: Calories 220 (Calories from Fat 35); Total Fat 4g (Saturated Fat 1.5g); Cholesterol 60mg; Sodium 230mg; Total Carbohydrate 23g (Dietary Fiber 3g; Sugars 16g); Protein 24g
% Daily Value: Vitamin A 6%; Vitamin C 20%; Calcium 10%; Iron 6%
Exchanges: 1 Fruit, 1/2 Other Carbohydrate, 3 1/2 Very Lean Meat
Carbohydrate Choices: 1 1/2

KITCHEN TIPS

- Place Bibb lettuce leaves in the bowls before dishing up each serving of this fresh salad.
- Bake two frozen Pillsbury Oven Baked crusty dinner rolls while the salad is chilling.

Chicken-Fruit Salad

Quick & Low-Fat

Pineapple Fruit and Rice Salad

Prep time: 20 min Start to finish: 20 min

1 cup uncooked instant rice

½ cup Yoplait Original 99% Fat Free pineapple or piña colada yogurt (from two 6-ounce containers)

¼ teaspoon ground cinnamon

1 cup frozen (thawed) whipped topping

1 medium unpeeled eating apple, coarsely chopped

1 medium unpeeled pear, coarsely chopped

1 cup seedless grape halves

1. Cook rice as directed on package. Place cooked rice in wire mesh strainer or colander with small holes. Rinse with cold water to chill; drain well.

2. In large bowl, mix yogurt and cinnamon. Fold in whipped topping. Gently stir in rice and remaining ingredients.

6 servings

1 Serving: Calories 170 (Calories from Fat 25); Total Fat 3g (Saturated Fat 2g); Cholesterol 0mg; Sodium 230mg; Total Carbohydrate 35g (Dietary Fiber 2g); Protein 3g
% Daily Value: Vitamin A 0%; Vitamin C 10%; Calcium 4%; Iron 6%
Exchanges: 1 Starch, 1 Fruit, ½ Fat
Carbohydrate Choices: 2

KITCHEN TIPS

● Sprinkle with walnuts for added crunch.

Pineapple Fruit and Rice Salad

Winter Fruit Waldorf Salad

Prep Time: 25 min Start to Finish: 25 min

2 medium unpeeled red apples, diced

2 medium unpeeled pears, diced

$^1/_2$ cup thinly sliced celery

$^1/_2$ cup golden raisins

$^1/_2$ cup chopped dates

$^1/_4$ cup mayonnaise or salad dressing

$^1/_4$ cup Yoplait Original 99% Fat Free orange crème yogurt (from 6-ounce container)

2 tablespoons frozen orange juice concentrate

8 cups shredded lettuce

Walnut halves, if desired

1. In a large bowl, mix apples, pears, celery, raisins and dates.

2. In small bowl, mix mayonnaise, yogurt and juice concentrate until well blended. Add to fruit; toss to coat. (Salad can be refrigerated up to 1 hour.) Serve on lettuce. Garnish with walnut halves.

16 servings (1 cup each)
1 Serving: Calories 90 (Calories from Fat 25); Total Fat 3g (Saturated Fat 0g); Cholesterol 0mg; Sodium 30mg; Total Carbohydrate 16g (Dietary Fiber 2g; Sugars 12g); Protein 0g
% Daily Value: Vitamin A 2%; Vitamin C 10%; Calcium 2%; Iron 2%
Exchanges: 1 Fruit, 1$^1/_2$ Fat
Carbohydrate Choices: 1

KITCHEN TIPS

- This refreshing salad is perfect for a holiday meal. Serve it in your prettiest glass bowl, and garnish with orange peel curls.
- You can substitute or add regular raisins or dried cranberries if you like.

Winter Fruit Waldorf Salad

Pomegranate and Citrus Broccoli Salad

Prep time: 20 min Start to finish: 20 min

- $^1/_2$ cup mayonnaise or salad dressing
- $^1/_4$ cup orange juice
- 1 teaspoon sugar
- $^1/_2$ teaspoon salt
  Dash of pepper
- 3 cups coarsely chopped broccoli florets (about 8 ounces)
- 1 medium orange, peeled, cut into bite-size chunks (about 1 cup)
- $^3/_4$ cup pomegranate seeds (from 1 pomegranate) or sweetened dried cranberries
- $^1/_3$ cup roasted salted sunflower nuts
- 2 tablespoons sliced red onion

1. In large serving bowl, mix mayonnaise, orange juice, sugar, salt and pepper.

2. Add remaining ingredients; toss until well coated. Store covered in refrigerator.

9 servings ($^1/_2$ cup each)
1 Serving: Calories 150 (Calories from Fat 110); Total Fat 13g (Saturated Fat 2g); Cholesterol 5mg; Sodium 240mg; Total Carbohydrate 7g (Dietary Fiber 2g; Sugars 4g); Protein 2g
% Daily Value: Vitamin A 8%; Vitamin C 60%; Calcium 2%; Iron 4%
Exchanges: $^1/_2$ Other Carbohydrate, 2$^1/_2$ Fat
Carbohydrate Choices: $^1/_2$

KITCHEN TIPS

● Make the salad a day ahead—it'll taste just as good!

Low Fat

Citrus Pasta Salad

Prep time: 20 min Start to finish: 1 hr 20 min

- 1 box (9 ounces) Green Giant frozen cut broccoli
- $^1/_4$ cup fat-free mayonnaise or salad dressing
- 1 teaspoon grated orange peel
- 1 tablespoon orange juice
- $^1/_4$ teaspoon salt
- $^3/_4$ cup cooked medium pasta shells
- 2 large radishes, sliced
- 1 medium orange, peeled, sectioned and seeded

1. Cook and drain broccoli as directed on package. Rinse with cold water to cool; drain.

2. In medium bowl, mix mayonnaise, orange peel, orange juice and salt. Stir in pasta, radishes, orange sections and broccoli.

3. Cover and refrigerate at least 1 hour until chilled.

2 servings
1 Serving: Calories 160 (Calories from Fat 15); Total Fat 1.5g (Saturated Fat 0.5g); Cholesterol 0mg; Sodium 620mg; Total Carbohydrate 34g (Dietary Fiber 7g; Sugars 11g); Protein 7g
% Daily Value: Vitamin A 40%; Vitamin C 70%; Calcium 8%; Iron 8%
Exchanges: 1$^1/_2$ Starch, $^1/_2$ Fruit, 1 Vegetable
Carbohydrate Choices: 2

KITCHEN TIPS

● If you aren't a fan of radishes, use $^1/_2$ cup chopped cucumber instead.

Citrus Pasta Salad

Pomegranate and Citrus Broccoli Salad

Spring Vegetable Pasta Salad

Prep time: 40 min Start to finish: 1 hr 40 min

1 package (16 ounces) medium pasta shells

1½ pounds asparagus, cut into 2-inch pieces

1 pound snap pea pods, strings removed

1 cup mayonnaise or salad dressing

½ cup plain fat-free yogurt

¼ cup fat-free (skim) milk

3 tablespoons chopped fresh or 1 tablespoon dried tarragon leaves

1 tablespoon sugar

2 tablespoons lemon juice

1½ teaspoons salt

1 medium yellow bell pepper, coarsely chopped (1 cup)

8 medium green onions, sliced (½ cup)

1. In 6-quart Dutch oven or stockpot, cook pasta as directed on package, adding asparagus and pea pods for last 2 minutes of cooking; drain. Rinse with cold water; drain.

2. Meanwhile, in small bowl, mix mayonnaise, yogurt, milk, tarragon, sugar, lemon juice and salt; set aside.

3. In very large (1-gallon) bowl, mix pasta, asparagus, pea pods, bell pepper and onions. Stir in mayonnaise mixture until well mixed. Cover and refrigerate 1 to 2 hours until chilled.

12 servings

1 Serving: Calories 310 (Calories from Fat 140); Total Fat 16g (Saturated Fat 2.5g); Cholesterol 10mg; Sodium 560mg; Total Carbohydrate 37g (Dietary Fiber 4g); Protein 8g
% Daily Value: Vitamin A 10%; Vitamin C 40%; Calcium 6%; Iron 15%
Exchanges: 2 Starch, 1 Vegetable, 3 Fat
Carbohydrate Choices: 2½

KITCHEN TIPS

● If you're lucky enough to have leftover pasta salad, toss in some cooked chicken for a delicious main-dish salad.

Spring Vegetable Pasta Salad

Layered Ranch Salad

Prep time: 35 min Start to finish: 35 min

- 6 cups shredded romaine lettuce
- 1 can (15 ounces) Green Giant garbanzo beans, drained, rinsed
- 1 medium yellow bell pepper, chopped (1 cup)
- 1/2 cup chopped red onion
- 2 cups broccoli coleslaw blend (from 16-ounce bag)
- 3 medium roma (plum) tomatoes, chopped (1 1/2 cups)
- 1/4 cup finely chopped fresh parsley
- 1/2 cup mayonnaise or salad dressing
- 1/2 cup ranch dressing
- 1 1/2 cups Parmesan-flavored croutons

Layered Ranch Salad

1. In 3-quart clear bowl, layer all ingredients except mayonnaise, dressing and croutons in order listed. In small bowl, mix mayonnaise and dressing; spread over top. Cover; refrigerate until ready to serve.

2. Just before serving, sprinkle with croutons. If desired, toss to mix.

10 servings (3/4 cup each)
1 Serving: Calories 260 (Calories from Fat 150); Total Fat 17g (Saturated Fat 2.5g); Cholesterol 10mg; Sodium 250mg; Total Carbohydrate 20g (Dietary Fiber 5g; Sugars 4g); Protein 6g
% Daily Value: Vitamin A 35%; Vitamin C 100%; Calcium 6%; Iron 10%
Exchanges: 1 Starch, 1 Vegetable, 3 1/2 Fat
Carbohydrate Choices: 1

KITCHEN TIPS

- To decrease the fat a bit, use reduced-fat mayonnaise and ranch dressing instead of the regular types.
- You can cut the romaine yourself or for convenience, look for packages of ready-to-eat romaine in the produce department.

Italian New Potato Salad

Prep time: 30 min Start to finish: 30 min

³/₄ pound green beans

10 to 12 new potatoes (1¹/₂ pounds), cut into fourths

¹/₄ cup water

¹/₂ cup Italian dressing or balsamic vinaigrette

¹/₄ cup chopped red onion

1 can (2.25 ounces) sliced ripe olives, drained

1. Cut beans in half if desired. In 2-quart microwavable casserole, place beans, potatoes and water. Cover and microwave on High 10 to 12 minutes, rotating dish ¹/₂ turn every 4 minutes, until potatoes are tender; drain.

2. In large glass or plastic bowl, place beans and potatoes. Pour dressing over vegetables; toss. Add onion and olives; toss.

8 servings
1 Serving: Calories 140 (Calories from Fat 60); Total Fat 7g (Saturated Fat 0.5g); Cholesterol 0mg; Sodium 210mg; Total Carbohydrate 19g (Dietary Fiber 3g); Protein 3g
% Daily Value: Vitamin A 6%; Vitamin C 8%; Calcium 6%; Iron 8%
Exchanges: 1 Starch, 1 Fat
Carbohydrate Choices: 1

KITCHEN TIPS

● It's easy to tell when the potatoes are done: you should be able to easily pierce them with a fork.

Italian New Potato Salad

Fresh Tomato and Cucumber Salad

Prep time: 10 min Start to finish: 15 min

2	medium tomatoes, cut into 6 slices each
1/2	cup chopped cucumber
1/8	teaspoon salt
1 1/2	teaspoons finely chopped fresh basil leaves
1	teaspoon grated lemon peel
1	teaspoon sugar
1	tablespoon balsamic vinegar

1. On 2 salad plates, arrange tomato slices in a circle, slightly overlapping. Top with cucumber. Sprinkle salt over tomatoes and cucumber.

2. In small bowl, mix basil, lemon peel and sugar; sprinkle over salads. Drizzle with vinegar. Let stand 5 minutes before serving.

2 servings
1 Serving: Calories 25 (Calories from Fat 0); Total Fat 0g (Saturated Fat 0g); Cholesterol 0mg; Sodium 150mg; Total Carbohydrate 6g (Dietary Fiber 1g; Sugars 4g); Protein 0g
% Daily Value: Vitamin A 10%; Vitamin C 25%; Calcium 0%; Iron 2%
Exchanges: 1 Vegetable
Carbohydrate Choices: 1 1/2

KITCHEN TIPS

● You can easily replace the basil with fresh parsley.

Fresh Tomato and Cucumber Salad

Fire-Roasted Tomato Basil Soup

Prep time: 30 min Start to finish: 30 min

-   1 tablespoon olive or vegetable oil
-   1 large onion, chopped (1 cup)
-   2 medium carrots, chopped (1 cup)
-   2 cans (14.5 ounces each) fire-roasted diced tomatoes, undrained
-   2 cans (14 ounces each) chicken broth
-   1 cup water
-   1 teaspoon red pepper sauce
-   $1/2$ cup uncooked orzo pasta
-   1 teaspoon dried basil leaves

1. In 4-quart saucepan, heat oil over medium heat. Add onion and carrots. Cook 2 to 3 minutes, stirring occasionally, until softened.

2. Stir in tomatoes, broth, water and pepper sauce. Heat to boiling. Stir in pasta. Heat to boiling; reduce heat to medium. Cook uncovered 10 to 15 minutes, stirring occasionally, until pasta and carrots are tender.

3. Stir in basil. Cook about 1 minute, stirring constantly.

5 servings (1$1/2$ cups each)
1 Serving: Calories 160 (Calories from Fat 40); Total Fat 4g (Saturated Fat 0.5g); Cholesterol 0mg; Sodium 990mg; Total Carbohydrate 23g (Dietary Fiber 4g; Sugars 7 g); Protein 7g
% Daily Value: Vitamin A 110%; Vitamin C 25%; Calcium 8%; Iron 10%
Exchanges: 1$1/2$ Starch, 1 Vegetable, $1/2$ Fat
Carbohydrate Choices: 1$1/2$

KITCHEN TIPS

-   Serve this slightly smoky-flavored soup with grilled cheese sandwiches.

Cheddar Cheese and Broccoli Soup

Prep time: 30 min Start to finish: 30 min

-   2 cans (10$3/4$ ounces each) condensed Cheddar cheese soup
-   2 cups water
-   1 bag (14 ounces) Green Giant Select® frozen broccoli florets
-   2 cups milk
-   $1/2$ teaspoon ground mustard
-   $1/4$ teaspoon salt
-   $1/4$ teaspoon garlic powder
-   $1/8$ teaspoon pepper
-   2 cups shredded Cheddar cheese (8 ounces)

1. In 4-quart saucepan, mix soup and water. Heat over high heat, stirring constantly, until boiling and smooth.

2. Add broccoli. Heat to boiling; reduce heat to medium. Cover; cook 8 to 10 minutes, stirring occasionally, until broccoli is tender.

3. Stir in milk, mustard, salt, garlic powder and pepper. Cook uncovered 3 to 5 minutes, stirring occasionally, until thoroughly heated. Stir in cheese until melted.

6 servings (1$1/3$ cups each)
1 Serving: Calories 340 (Calories from Fat 200); Total Fat 22g (Saturated Fat 13g); Cholesterol 60mg; Sodium 1300mg; Total Carbohydrate 16g (Dietary Fiber 2g; Sugars 7g); Protein 18g
% Daily Value: Vitamin A 70%; Vitamin C 20%; Calcium 40%; Iron 6%
Exchanges: $1/2$ Starch, $1/2$ Other Carbohydrate, 2$1/2$ High-Fat Meat, $1/2$ Fat
Carbohydrate Choices: 1

KITCHEN TIPS

-   Be sure to stir in the cheese just until melted and serve the soup right away to help prevent curdling.

Fire-Roasted Tomato Basil Soup

Cheddar Cheese and Broccoli Soup

Top 10 tips for cooking in a slow cooker. . .

1. **Use the size of slow cooker called for in each recipe.** It's best if the cooker is two-thirds to three-fourths full, but using it half full will also work. Slow cookers range in size from 1 quart to 6 quarts. The recipes in this book call for the cooker size that works best for each recipe.

2. **Don't lift the lid during cooking.** Each time the cooker is uncovered, 15 to 20 minutes of cooking time must be added. The recipes do not require stirring during the long cook time.

3. **Browning meats before placing them in a slow cooker is often recommended** for better color of the meat, as well as to lower fat and improve the flavor and overall appearance of the entire recipe.

4. **Prevent darkening of peeled potatoes** by covering them with a liquid in the slow cooker.

5. **Do not add extra liquids to recipes** prepared in a slow cooker, because no evaporation takes place. Ingredients may appear dry before cooking, but be sure to follow the recipe.

6. **When there is a cook time range,** such as 8 to 10 hours, foods cooked for 8 hours will be different than if they were cooked for 10 hours. After 8 hours of cooking, large pieces of meat can still usually be sliced, but after 10 hours, the meat will shred.

7. **Add tender vegetables** that require short cooking times, such as fresh tomatoes, mushrooms and zucchini, at the end of the recipe cook time to retain their color, texture and flavor.

8. **Because many of the liquids** that remain in a slow cooker after the meat and vegetables are removed are very thin, they may require thickening before being served. This usually takes only 10 to 15 minutes, and the results are worth the time. Be sure to use the amount of flour stated in the recipe and cook for the recommended time to remove the raw flour taste.

9. **Frozen foods, such as vegetables,** should usually be thawed before adding them to a slow cooker unless they are added near the end of the cook time.

10. **For food safety, never reheat foods in a slow cooker.** Leftovers should be placed in shallow containers and refrigerated within 2 hours of cooking.

Cheesy Potato Soup

Prep Time: 15 min Start to Finish: 6 hr 45 min

1 bag (32 ounces) frozen Southern-style diced hash brown potatoes, thawed

½ cup frozen chopped onion (from 12-ounce bag), thawed

1 medium stalk celery, diced (½ cup)

2 cans (14 ounces each) chicken broth

1 cup water

3 tablespoons Gold Medal all-purpose flour

1 cup milk

1 bag (8 ounces) shredded American-Cheddar cheese blend (2 cups)

¼ cup real bacon pieces (from 2.8-ounce package)

4 medium green onions, sliced (¼ cup)

1. In 3- to 4-quart slow cooker, mix potatoes, onion, celery, broth and water.

2. Cover; cook on Low heat setting 6 to 8 hours.

3. In small bowl, mix flour into milk; stir into potato mixture. Increase heat setting to High. Cover; cook 20 to 30 minutes or until mixture thickens. Stir in cheese until melted. Garnish individual servings with bacon and green onions. Sprinkle with pepper if desired.

6 servings (1½ cups each)
1 Serving: Calories 410 (Calories from Fat 140); Total Fat 15g (Saturated Fat 9g, Trans Fat 0g); Cholesterol 45mg; Sodium 1210mg; Total Carbohydrate 50g (Dietary Fiber 5g; Sugars 5g); Protein 19g
% Daily Value: Vitamin A 10%; Vitamin C 15%; Calcium 25%; Iron 10%
Exchanges: 3½ Starch, 1 High-Fat Meat, 1 Fat
Carbohydrate Choices: 3

KITCHEN TIPS

- Instead of using purchased bacon pieces, cook 2 slices of bacon until crisp, then drain and crumble.
- Southern-style hash brown potatoes are diced instead of shredded. These work best in this recipe.

Cheesy Potato Soup

Low Fat
Three-Bean Christmas Chili

Prep time: 20 min Start to finish: 55 min

1   can (28 ounces) whole tomatoes, undrained

1   can (15 ounces) Progresso dark red kidney beans, drained

1   can (15 ounces) Green Giant garbanzo beans, drained

1   can (15.5 ounces) Green Giant butter beans, drained

1   can (15 ounces) tomato sauce

3   small red, orange or yellow bell peppers, cut into 1-inch pieces

1   Anaheim or jalapeno chili, seeded, chopped

1   to 2 tablespoons chili powder

2   teaspoons ground cumin

1/4   teaspoon pepper

1/2   cup sour cream

3   tablespoons Old El Paso® Thick 'n Chunky salsa

    Chopped fresh cilantro, if desired

1. Pour can of tomatoes into 4-quart Dutch oven; break up tomatoes with spoon. Stir in remaining ingredients except sour cream, salsa and cilantro. Heat to boiling; reduce heat. Cover and simmer 30 to 35 minutes or until bell peppers are tender.

2. In small bowl, mix sour cream and salsa. Serve chili with sour cream mixture. Sprinkle with cilantro.

6 servings (1¼ cups each)
1 Serving: Calories 380 (Calories from Fat 60); Total Fat 7g (Saturated Fat 2.5g); Cholesterol 15mg; Sodium 1070mg; Total Carbohydrate 60g (Dietary Fiber 16g; Sugars 10g); Protein 19g
% Daily Value: Vitamin A 70%; Vitamin C 100%; Calcium 15%; Iron 40%
Exchanges: 2½ Starch, 1 Other Carbohydrate, 2 Vegetable, 1 Very Lean Meat, 1 Fat
Carbohydrate Choices: 4

KITCHEN TIPS

● Beef it up with a pound of ground beef, cooked and drained.

Three-Bean Christmas Chili

Low Fat

Red and White Turkey Chili

Prep time: 30 min Start to finish: 9 hr

1 medium onion, chopped (1/2 cup)

1 clove garlic, finely chopped

2 teaspoons ground cumin

1/8 teaspoon ground red pepper (cayenne)

1 can (15.5 ounces) Green Giant great northern beans, drained

1 can (15 ounces) Progresso dark red kidney beans, drained

2 cans (4.5 ounces each) Old El Paso chopped green chilies, undrained

2 cans (14 ounces each) chicken broth

2 pounds turkey thighs, skin removed

1 cup Green Giant Select frozen shoepeg white corn (from 1-pound bag), thawed

2 tablespoons Gold Medal all-purpose flour

1/4 cup water

1 lime, cut into wedges, if desired

1. In 4- to 5-quart slow cooker, mix all ingredients except turkey, corn, flour, water and lime. Place turkey on bean mixture.

2. Cover; cook on Low heat setting 8 to 10 hours.

3. Place turkey on cutting board. Remove meat from bones; discard bones. Cut turkey into bite-size pieces. Add turkey and corn to cooker. In small bowl, mix flour and water; stir into turkey mixture. Increase heat setting to High. Cover; cook 20 to 30 minutes or until thoroughly heated and slightly thickened. Serve individual servings with lime wedges for squeezing juice over chili.

Red and White Turkey Chili

6 servings (1 1/2 cups each)
1 Serving: Calories 370 (Calories from Fat 45); Total Fat 5g (Saturated Fat 1.5g; Trans Fat 0g); Cholesterol 95mg; Sodium 970mg; Total Carbohydrate 40g (Dietary Fiber 9g; Sugars 2g); Protein 40g
% Daily Value: Vitamin A 0%; Vitamin C 10%; Calcium 15%; Iron 40%
Exchanges: 2 1/2 Starch, 4 1/2 Very Lean Meat, 1/2 Fat
Carbohydrate Choices: 2 1/2

KITCHEN TIPS

● For those who prefer a spicier flavor, place a bottle of red pepper sauce on the table and let diners add the amount they like.

Low Fat
Easy Chicken Chili

Prep time: 40 min Start to finish: 40 min

1 tablespoon olive or vegetable oil

1 medium onion, chopped (1/2 cup)

1/2 cup chopped red bell pepper

1 can (10 3/4 ounces) condensed cream of chicken soup

1 can (14 ounces) chicken broth

1 cup water

2 cups diced rotisserie-cooked chicken

2 cans (15.5 ounces each) Green Giant great northern beans, drained, rinsed

1 can (4.5 ounces) Old El Paso chopped green chilies, undrained

1/2 teaspoon dried oregano leaves

1/2 teaspoon ground cumin

1/2 cup sour cream, if desired

Chopped fresh cilantro, if desired

1. In 4-quart saucepan, heat oil over medium-high heat. Add onion and bell pepper. Cook 2 to 3 minutes, stirring frequently, until tender.

2. Stir in soup, broth and water. Cook 1 to 2 minutes, stirring frequently, until smooth and well blended. Stir in chicken, beans, chilies, oregano and cumin. Heat to boiling; reduce heat to medium-low. Cook uncovered 10 to 15 minutes, stirring occasionally, until thoroughly heated.

3. Top each serving with sour cream and cilantro.

6 servings (1 1/3 cups each)
1 Serving: Calories 360 (Calories from Fat 90); Total Fat 10g (Saturated Fat 2.5g); Cholesterol 45mg; Sodium 860mg; Total Carbohydrate 39g (Dietary Fiber 9g, Sugars 2g); Protein 28g
% Daily Value: Vitamin A 20%; Vitamin C 25%; Calcium 15%; Iron 30%
Exchanges: 2 1/2 Starch, 3 Very Lean Meat, 1 1/2 Fat
Carbohydrate Choices: 2 1/2

KITCHEN TIPS

● If you are pressed for time, use 1 cup frozen bell pepper and onion stir-fry (from 1-pound bag) instead of the fresh onion and bell pepper.

Easy Chicken Chili

Low-Fat

Italian Chicken Noodle Soup

Prep time: 35 min Start to finish: 35 min

1   tablespoon olive or vegetable oil

2   boneless skinless chicken breasts (about ½ pound), cut into ½-inch pieces

1   medium onion, chopped (½ cup)

2   cans (14 ounces each) chicken broth

2   cups water

3   medium carrots, sliced (1½ cups)

2   cups broccoli florets

1½ cups uncooked medium egg noodles

1   teaspoon dried basil leaves

½   teaspoon garlic-pepper blend

¼   cup shredded Parmesan cheese

1. In 4-quart saucepan, heat oil over medium heat. Add chicken. Cook 4 to 6 minutes, stirring occasionally, until no longer pink in center. Stir in onion. Cook 2 to 3 minutes, stirring occasionally, until onion is tender.

2. Stir in broth, water and carrots. Heat to boiling. Cook 5 minutes over medium heat. Stir in broccoli, noodles, basil and garlic pepper. Heat to boiling; reduce heat. Simmer uncovered 8 to 10 minutes, stirring occasionally, until vegetables and noodles are tender.

3. Top each serving with cheese.

6 servings (1½ cups each)
1 Serving: Calories 170 (Calories from Fat 50); Total Fat 6g (Saturated Fat 2g); Cholesterol 35mg; Sodium 710mg; Total Carbohydrate 13g (Dietary Fiber 2g; Sugars 3g); Protein 15g
% Daily Value: Vitamin A 120%; Vitamin C 20%; Calcium 10%; Iron 8%
Exchanges: 1 Starch, 1½ Very Lean Meat, 1 Fat
Carbohydrate Choices: 1

KITCHEN TIPS

- You can substitute chicken thighs for part or all of the chicken breasts. Usually, two boneless thighs will equal one breast half.
- Fresh vegetables are used to make this colorful soup, but you can use frozen vegetables if you like.

Italian Chicken Noodle Soup

Spicy Chicken and Sausage Soup

Prep time: 20 min Start to finish: 8 hr 35 min

1	package (20 ounces) boneless skinless chicken thighs, cubed
1	can (14.5 ounces) diced tomatoes, undrained
1	can (14 ounces) chicken broth
1	cup water
½	teaspoon red pepper sauce
½	pound cooked kielbasa, sliced
1	cup frozen bell pepper and onion stir-fry (from 1-pound bag), thawed
½	cup uncooked instant white rice

6 servings (1⅓ cups each)
1 Serving: Calories 330 (Calories from Fat 170); Total Fat 19g (Saturated Fat 6g; Trans Fat 0g); Cholesterol 80mg; Sodium 810mg; Total Carbohydrate 14g (Dietary Fiber 1g; Sugars 3g); Protein 27g % Daily Value: Vitamin A 6%; Vitamin C 15%; Calcium 6%; Iron 15% Exchanges: ½ Starch, 1 Vegetable, 3½ Lean Meat, 1½ Fat Carbohydrate Choices: 1

KITCHEN TIPS

- Sizes of packaged chicken can vary. You can use a 1- to 1½-pound package in this recipe.
- Season this soup to suit your family. For a spicier flavor, increase the amount of red pepper sauce.

1. In 3- to 3½-quart slow cooker, mix chicken, tomatoes, broth, water and red pepper sauce.

2. Cover; cook on Low heat setting 8 to 10 hours.

3. Stir in kielbasa, stir-fry vegetables and rice. Increase heat setting to High. Cover; cook 10 to 15 minutes or until rice is tender.

Spicy Chicken and Sausage Soup

Low Fat

Dijon Steak and Potato Stew

Prep time: 20 min Start to finish: 45 min

1 pound boneless beef sirloin, cut into ¹/₂-inch pieces

¹/₂ teaspoon peppered seasoned salt

2 jars (12 ounces each) home-style beef gravy

1 cup water

2 tablespoons Dijon mustard

¹/₄ teaspoon dried thyme leaves

4 unpeeled small red potatoes, cut into ¹/₂- to ³/₄-inch cubes (about 2 cups)

1¹/₂ cups Green Giant frozen cut green beans (from 1-pound bag)

2 medium carrots, sliced (1 cup)

1. Sprinkle beef with peppered seasoned salt. In 4-quart Dutch oven or 12-inch nonstick skillet, cook beef over medium-high heat about 4 minutes, stirring frequently, until brown.

2. Stir in gravy, water, mustard and thyme until well blended. Stir in potatoes, green beans and carrots. Heat to boiling; reduce heat to medium-low. Cover and cook 20 to 22 minutes, stirring occasionally, until potatoes and beans are tender.

4 servings (1¹/₄ cups each)
1 Serving: Calories 300 (Calories from Fat 70); Total Fat 8g (Saturated Fat 3g); Cholesterol 65mg; Sodium 1370mg; Total Carbohydrate 28g (Dietary Fiber 5g; Sugars 3g); Protein 32g
% Daily Value: Vitamin A 120%; Vitamin C 10%; Calcium 6%; Iron 30%
Exchanges: 1¹/₂ Starch, 1 Vegetable, 3¹/₂ Very Lean Meat, 1 Fat
Carbohydrate Choices: 1¹/₂

KITCHEN TIPS

● If you have baby-cut carrots on hand, use them instead of the sliced carrots.

Dijon Steak and Potato Soup

Savory Beef Stew

Prep time: 15 min Start to finish: 3 hr 45 min

- 1 1/2 pounds beef stew meat
- 1 medium onion, cut into 8 wedges
- 1 can (14.5 ounces) stewed tomatoes, undrained
- 1 1/2 teaspoons seasoned salt
- 1/2 teaspoon pepper
- 1 dried bay leaf
- 2 cups water
- 2 tablespoons Gold Medal all-purpose flour
- 12 small red potatoes (1 1/2 pounds), cut in half
- 1 bag (8 ounces) baby-cut carrots (about 30)

1. Heat oven to 325°F. In ovenproof 4-quart Dutch oven, mix beef, onion, tomatoes, seasoned salt, pepper and bay leaf. In small bowl, mix water and flour; stir into beef mixture.

2. Cover and bake 2 hours, stirring once.

3. Stir in potatoes and carrots. Cover and bake 1 hour to 1 hour 30 minutes longer or until beef and vegetables are tender. Remove bay leaf.

6 servings (1 1/3 cups each)
1 Serving: Calories 350 (Calories from Fat 120); Total Fat 13g (Saturated Fat 5g); Cholesterol 70mg; Sodium 610mg; Total Carbohydrate 33g (Dietary Fiber 5g; Sugars 7g); Protein 26g
% Daily Value: Vitamin A 140%; Vitamin C 20%; Calcium 6%; Iron 30%
Exchanges: 2 Starch, 1 Vegetable, 2 1/2 Lean Meat, 1 Fat
Carbohydrate Choices: 2

KITCHEN TIPS

- Add a bit of rich flavor, if you have the time, by browning the beef in a little oil before assembling the stew.
- Purchase small red potatoes that are bright in color, firm and of uniform size. If yours are larger, you can cut them into fourths.

Bacon-Chili Beef Stew

Prep time: 1 hr 50 min Start to finish: 1 hr 50 min

- 4 slices bacon, cut into 1/2-inch pieces
- 1 1/2 pounds lean beef stew meat (1/2-inch pieces)
- 1 medium onion, chopped (1/2 cup)
- 1/2 teaspoon seasoned salt
- 1/8 teaspoon pepper
- 2 cans (14.5 ounces each) diced tomatoes with mild green chilies, undrained
- 1 jar (12 ounces) home-style beef gravy
- 2 tablespoons chili sauce
- 4 unpeeled small red potatoes, diced (2 cups)
- 2 medium carrots, sliced (1 cup)
- 1 cup Green Giant Niblets frozen whole kernel corn (from 1-pound bag)

1. In 4-quart saucepan, cook bacon over medium heat 3 to 4 minutes, stirring frequently, until cooked but not crisp. Drain all but 2 tablespoons bacon fat from saucepan.

2. Add beef and onion to bacon; sprinkle with seasoned salt and pepper. Cook 4 to 6 minutes, stirring frequently, until beef is beginning to brown and onion is tender.

3. Stir in tomatoes, gravy and chili sauce. Heat to boiling. Add potatoes and carrots. Cover; cook over medium-low heat 50 to 60 minutes, stirring occasionally, until beef is tender.

4. Stir in corn. Cook uncovered 10 to 15 minutes longer, stirring occasionally, until corn is tender.

6 servings (1 1/2 cups each)
1 Serving: Calories 430 (Calories from Fat 190); Total Fat 22g (Saturated Fat 8g); Cholesterol 80mg; Sodium 1070mg; Total Carbohydrate 28g (Dietary Fiber 5g; Sugars 9g); Protein 31g
% Daily Value: Vitamin A 90%; Vitamin C 15%; Calcium 8%; Iron 25%
Exchanges: 1 Starch, 1/2 Other Carbohydrate, 1 Vegetable, 3 1/2 Lean Meat, 2 Fat
Carbohydrate Choices: 2

KITCHEN TIPS

- Like your chili spicy? Use tomatoes labeled "hot" instead of the mild variety.
- Serve the stew with warm rolled flour tortillas and a tossed green salad.

Savory Beef Stew

Bacon-Chili Beef Stew

Beef Stroganoff Stew

Prep Time: 20 min Start to Finish: 5 hr 50 min

- 1 medium onion, chopped ($\frac{1}{2}$ cup)
- 1 clove garlic, finely chopped
- 1 pound boneless beef tip steak, cut into $\frac{1}{2}$-inch pieces
- 2 cans (18 ounces each) Progresso® Vegetable Classics creamy mushroom soup
- $\frac{1}{2}$ cup water
- $2\frac{1}{2}$ cups uncooked wide egg noodles (4 ounces)
- 1 cup sour cream
- 2 tablespoons chopped fresh parsley, if desired

5 servings (1$\frac{1}{2}$ cups each)
1 Serving: Calories 430 (Calories from Fat 220); Total Fat 25g (Saturated Fat 12g; Trans Fat 0g); Cholesterol 125mg; Sodium 880mg; Total Carbohydrate 29g (Dietary Fiber 1g; Sugars 6g); Protein 24g
% Daily Value: Vitamin A 15%; Vitamin C 0%; Calcium 8%; Iron 15%
Exchanges: 2 Starch, 2$\frac{1}{2}$ Lean Meat, 3 Fat
Carbohydrate Choices: 2

KITCHEN TIPS

- To save precious minutes in the morning, use minced garlic in a jar. You could also cut up the beef the night before and refrigerate.

1. In 3$\frac{1}{2}$- to 4-quart slow cooker, layer onion, garlic and beef. Pour soup and water over beef.

2. Cover; cook on Low heat setting 5 to 7 hours.

3. Stir noodles into mixture. Increase heat setting to High. Cover; cook 20 to 30 minutes or until noodles are tender. Stir in sour cream. Garnish individual servings with parsley.

Beef Stroganoff Stew

Beefy Vegetable-Barley Soup

Prep Time: 20 min Start to Finish: 8 hr 50 min

1½ pounds beef stew meat

½ cup frozen chopped onion (from 12-ounce bag), thawed

½ cup uncooked medium barley

2 cans (14 ounces each) beef broth

1 cup water

1 teaspoon dried thyme leaves

¼ teaspoon dried marjoram leaves

½ teaspoon salt

¼ teaspoon pepper

2 cups Green Giant frozen mixed vegetables (from 1-pound bag), thawed

1. Cut beef into bite-size pieces if desired. In 3½- to 4-quart slow cooker, mix all ingredients except vegetables.

2. Cover; cook on Low heat setting 8 to 10 hours.

3. Add vegetables. Increase heat setting to High. Cover; cook 20 to 30 minutes or until vegetables are crisp-tender.

6 servings (1⅓ cups each)
1 Serving: Calories 330 (Calories from Fat 120); Total Fat 14g (Saturated Fat 5g; Trans Fat 0g); Cholesterol 70mg; Sodium 880mg; Total Carbohydrate 22g (Dietary Fiber 6g; Sugars 3g); Protein 28g
% Daily Value: Vitamin A 60%; Vitamin C 2%; Calcium 4%; Iron 20%
Exchanges: 1½ Starch, 3½ Lean Meat, ½ Fat
Carbohydrate Choices: 1½

KITCHEN TIPS

● Stew meat pieces vary in size from store to store. If the pieces are large, cut them in half.

● Purchase a bag of chopped onions to keep in the freezer. Take out just what you need to save chopping time on a busy morning.

Beefy Vegetable-Barley Soup

Italian Meatball Soup

Prep Time: 10 min Start to Finish: 8 hr 10 min

1 bag (16 ounces) frozen cooked Italian meatballs, thawed

1 can (14 ounces) beef broth

1 cup water

1 can (14.5 ounces) diced tomatoes with basil, garlic and oregano, undrained

1 can (19 ounces) Progresso cannellini beans, drained

1/3 cup shredded Parmesan cheese

1. In 3- to 4-quart slow cooker, mix all ingredients except cheese.

2. Cover; cook on Low heat setting 8 to 10 hours.

3. Garnish individual servings with cheese.

5 servings (1 1/2 cups each)
1 Serving: Calories 410 (Calories from Fat 140); Total Fat 15g (Saturated Fat 6g; Trans Fat 1g); Cholesterol 100mg; Sodium 1540mg; Total Carbohydrate 38g (Dietary Fiber 6g; Sugars 8g); Protein 31g
% Daily Value: Vitamin A 6%; Vitamin C 10%; Calcium 25%; Iron 30%
Exchanges: 2 Starch, 1/2 Other Carbohydrate, 3 1/2 Lean Meat, 1/2 Fat
Carbohydrate Choices: 2 1/2

KITCHEN TIPS

● Purchase crisp Italian breadsticks instead of crackers to serve with this soup.

● Place the package of meatballs in your refrigerator the night before, and they will be thawed in the morning.

Italian Meatball Soup

Low Fat
Slow Cooker Beef-Tortellini Soup

Prep time: 20 min Start to finish: 8 hr 50 min

1 lb beef stew meat

1 large onion, chopped (³⁄₄ cup)

1 large carrot, chopped (³⁄₄ cup)

1 medium stalk celery, chopped (¹⁄₂ cup)

2 cloves garlic, finely chopped

2 teaspoons sugar

1 can (14.5 oz) diced tomatoes, undrained

2 cans (10¹⁄₂ oz each) condensed beef consomme

1 teaspoon dried basil leaves

2 cups frozen cheese-filled tortellini (from 1-lb 3-oz bag)

1 cup Green Giant® frozen cut green beans (from 1-lb bag)

1. In 3¹⁄₂- to 4-quart slow cooker, place beef, onion, carrot, celery, garlic, sugar, tomatoes and beef consomme in order listed.

2. Cover; cook on low heat setting 8 to 9 hours.

3. Stir in basil, frozen tortellini and green beans. Increase heat setting to high. Cover; cook 25 to 30 minutes or until beans are tender.

6 servings (1¹⁄₂ cups each)
1 serving: Calories 310 (Calories from Fat 120); Total Fat 14g (Saturated Fat 5g); Cholesterol 100mg; Sodium 710mg; Total Carbohydrate 22g (Dietary Fiber 3g; Sugars 6g); Protein 26g
% Daily Value: Vitamin A 70%; Vitamin C 15%; Calcium 10%; Iron 20%
Exchanges: 1 Starch, 1 Vegetable, 3 Lean Meat, 1 Fat
Carbohydrate Choices: 1¹⁄₂

KITCHEN TIPS

● For a special touch, top each serving with a teaspoon of refrigerated basil pesto.

Slow Cooker Beef-Tortellini Soup

Italian Seafood Stew with Garlic-Herb Croutons

Italian Seafood Stew with Garlic-Herb Croutons

Prep time: 1 hr Start to finish: 1 hr 30 min

12 fresh clams in shells
2 tablespoons white vinegar
12 fresh mussels in shells
2 bottles (8 ounces each) clam juice
2 cans (14.5 ounces each) diced tomatoes, undrained
2 cans (15 ounces each) tomato sauce
1 cup dry white wine or water
1 container (7 ounces) refrigerated pesto
1 pound cod fillets, cut into bite-size pieces
$\frac{1}{2}$ pound uncooked peeled deveined medium shrimp (about 16), thawed if frozen, tails removed
$\frac{1}{2}$ pound uncooked sea scallops (about 16), thawed if frozen
3 tablespoons butter or margarine, softened
16 slices French bread, $\frac{1}{2}$ inch thick

1. Discard any broken-shell or open (dead) clams. Place remaining clams in large container. Cover with $1\frac{1}{2}$ cups water and the vinegar. Let stand 30 minutes; drain. Scrub clams in cold water.

2. Meanwhile, discard any broken-shell or open (dead) mussels. Scrub remaining mussels in cold water, removing any barnacles with dull paring knife. Pull beard by giving it a tug (using a kitchen towel may help). If you have trouble removing it, use pliers to grip and pull gently. Place mussels in large container. Cover with cool water. Agitate water with hand, then drain and discard water. Repeat several times until water runs clear; drain.

3. Heat oven to 350°F. In 4-quart Dutch oven, mix clam juice, tomatoes, tomato sauce, wine and $\frac{1}{2}$ cup of the pesto. Layer cod, shrimp, scallops, mussels and clams in Dutch oven. Heat to boiling over medium-high heat; reduce heat. Cover and simmer 15 to 20 minutes or until mussel and clam shells have opened.

4. Meanwhile, in small bowl, mix butter and remaining pesto until well blended. Spread on both sides of bread. Place bread in single layer on ungreased cookie sheet. Bake 10 to 15 minutes, turning once, until toasted on both sides.

5. Discard any mussels or clams that don't open. Spoon stew into soup bowls; top with croutons.

8 servings ($1\frac{3}{4}$ cups each)
1 Serving: Calories 450 (Calories from Fat 190); Total Fat 21g (Saturated Fat 5g); Cholesterol 110mg; Sodium 1590mg; Total Carbohydrate 33g (Dietary Fiber 4g; Sugars 7g); Protein 32g
% Daily Value: Vitamin A 35%; Vitamin C 30%; Calcium 25%; Iron 60%
Exchanges: 2 Starch, 1 Vegetable, $3\frac{1}{2}$ Very Lean Meat, $3\frac{1}{2}$ Fat
Carbohydrate Choices: 2

KITCHEN TIPS

- Double up on frozen seafood and fish if fresh is hard to come by.
- Have all the ingredients assembled on a tray or cookie sheet in your refrigerator so you can whip this up in minutes on Christmas Eve.

Slow Cooker Southwestern Pork Stew

Prep time: 20 min Start to finish: 8 hr 50 min

- 1   medium onion, chopped ($\frac{1}{2}$ cup)
- 3   large cloves garlic, finely chopped
- 2   pounds boneless pork shoulder, trimmed of fat, cut into 1$\frac{1}{2}$-inch pieces
- $\frac{1}{4}$ cup cornmeal
- 2   teaspoons ground cumin
- $\frac{1}{2}$ teaspoon dried oregano leaves
- $\frac{1}{2}$ teaspoon salt
- 1   can (15 to 16 ounces) chili beans in sauce, undrained
- 1   can (14.5 ounces) diced tomatoes with mild green chilies, undrained
- 1   cup chicken broth
- 2   cups Green Giant Niblets frozen whole kernel corn (from 1-pound bag)

Slow Cooker Southwestern Pork Stew

1. In 3$\frac{1}{2}$- to 4-quart slow cooker, place onion and garlic. Top with pork. In small bowl, mix cornmeal, cumin, oregano and salt; sprinkle over pork and mix well. Add beans, tomatoes and broth; mix well.

2. Cover; cook on Low heat setting 8 to 10 hours.

3. Stir in corn. Cover; cook on Low heat setting about 30 minutes or until corn is tender.

6 servings
1 Serving: Calories 460 (Calories from Fat 170); Total Fat 19g (Saturated Fat 7g); Cholesterol 95mg; Sodium 1140mg; Total Carbohydrate 31g (Dietary Fiber 6g; Sugars 6g); Protein 40g
% Daily Value: Vitamin A 10%; Vitamin C 15%; Calcium 6%; Iron 20%
Exchanges: 2 Starch, 5 Lean Meat, $\frac{1}{2}$ Fat
Carbohydrate Choices: 2

KITCHEN TIPS

- The cornmeal used in this tasty stew not only adds a unique flavor but also acts as a thickener.

Pizzas, Sandwiches and Burgers

Fun Meals Anytime

Grilled Margherita Pizza (page 85)

Grilled Open-Face Pork Sandwiches (page 96)

Ranch Turkey Pizza

Prep time: 20 min Start to finish: 35 min

1   package (14 ounces) prebaked original Italian pizza crust (12 inch)

2   tablespoons ranch dressing

1½ cups diced cooked turkey

1   cup baby spinach leaves

1   cup chopped roma (plum) tomatoes (3 medium)

2   tablespoons chopped red onion, if desired

½   teaspoon Italian seasoning

1½ cups shredded mozzarella cheese (6 ounces)

6 servings
1 Serving: Calories 360 (Calories from Fat 130); Total Fat 15g (Saturated Fat 6g); Cholesterol 55mg; Sodium 560mg; Total Carbohydrate 32g (Dietary Fiber 2g; Sugars 1g); Protein 25g
% Daily Value: Vitamin A 20%; Vitamin C 6%; Calcium 25%; Iron 15%
Exchanges: 2 Starch, 2½ Lean Meat, 1½ Fat
Carbohydrate Choices: 2

KITCHEN TIPS

● Any texture and thickness of prebaked pizza crust will work in this recipe, so use your favorite brand.

1. Heat oven to 450°F. Place pizza crust on ungreased cookie sheet. Spread dressing over crust. Top with turkey, spinach, tomatoes, onion, Italian seasoning and cheese.

2. Bake 10 to 15 minutes or until thoroughly heated and cheese is melted.

Ranch Turkey Pizza

Grilled Margherita Pizza

Prep time: 25 min Start to finish: 25 min

2 cloves garlic, finely chopped

1 teaspoon olive or vegetable oil

1 teaspoon dried oregano leaves

1 package (14 ounces) prebaked original Italian pizza crust (12 inch)

1 medium roma (plum) tomato, thinly sliced

2 tablespoons coarsely chopped fresh basil leaves

1 cup finely shredded Italian cheese blend (4 ounces)

1. Heat coals or gas grill for direct heat. In small bowl, mix garlic, oil and oregano; brush over pizza crust. Top with tomato, basil and cheese.

2. Cover and grill over medium-low heat 7 to 9 minutes, moving pizza around grill every 2 minutes to prevent bottom from burning, until cheese is melted.

3. Cut pizza into 36 squares. Serve immediately.

9 servings (4 pieces each)
1 Serving: Calories 170 (Calories from Fat 60); Total Fat 7g (Saturated Fat 3g); Cholesterol 15mg; Sodium 340mg; Total Carbohydrate 20g (Dietary Fiber 1g; Sugars 0g); Protein 8g
% Daily Value: Vitamin A 6%; Vitamin C 0%; Calcium 10%; Iron 8%
Exchanges: 1½ Starch, ½ Medium-Fat Meat, ½ Fat
Carbohydrate Choices: 1

KITCHEN TIPS

- Finely shredded mozzarella cheese can be used instead of the Italian blend.
- To bake the pizza, heat oven to 450°F. Bake on an ungreased cookie sheet for 8 to 10 minutes.

Grilled Margherita Pizza

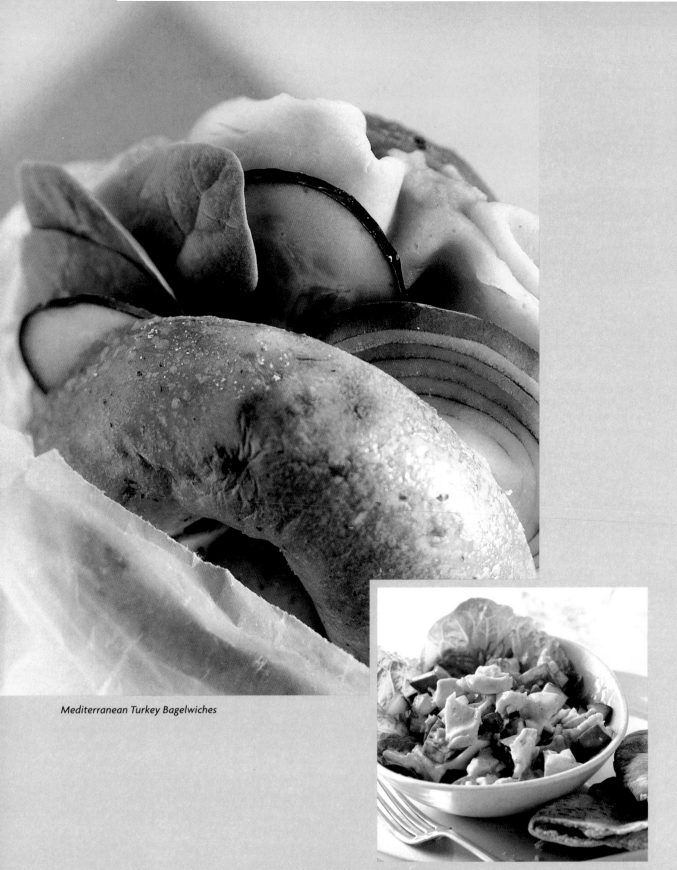

Mediterranean Turkey Bagelwiches

Chicken Salad Pita Sandwiches

Chicken Salad Pita Sandwiches

Prep time: 15 min Start to finish: 45 min

- 1 cup chopped cooked chicken breast
- ¼ cup fat-free honey Dijon dressing
- ¼ cup chopped cucumber
- ¼ cup chopped tomato
- 1 tablespoon finely chopped cashews
- 2 whole wheat pita breads (6 inch), cut in half to form pockets
- 2 tablespoons fat-free mayonnaise or salad dressing

1. In small bowl, mix chicken, dressing, cucumber, tomato and cashews. Cover and refrigerate at least 30 minutes until chilled.

2. Just before serving, spread insides of pita pockets with mayonnaise. Fill pockets with chicken mixture.

2 sandwiches (2 halves each)
1 Sandwich: Calories 360 (Calories from Fat 70); Total Fat 7g (Saturated Fat 2g); Cholesterol 60mg; Sodium 830mg; Total Carbohydrate 50g (Dietary Fiber 6g; Sugars 12g); Protein 28g
% Daily Value: Vitamin A 6%; Vitamin C 8%; Calcium 2%; Iron 20%
Exchanges: 2½ Starch, 1 Other Carbohydrate, 3 Very Lean Meat, ½ Fat
Carbohydrate Choices: 3

KITCHEN TIPS

- Serve this healthy chicken salad on top of a lettuce leaf. Omit the mayonnaise and serve pita wedges on the side. (See image at left.)
- Tuck chopped lettuce into the pita pockets with the chicken mixture for an easy sandwich topper.

Quick & Low Fat

Mediterranean Turkey Bagelwiches

Prep time: 5 min Start to finish: 5 min

- 2 tablespoons hummus (from 5-ounce container)
- 2 bagels, cut horizontally in half
- 3 ounces sliced smoked turkey
- ½ medium cucumber, thinly sliced
- ½ small red onion, thinly sliced
- 8 spinach leaves

1. Spread about 1 tablespoon hummus over each of 2 bagel halves.

2. Layer turkey, cucumber, onion and spinach on bagel halves with hummus. Top with remaining bagel halves.

2 sandwiches
1 Serving: Calories 240 (Calories from Fat 35); Total Fat 4g (Saturated Fat 0.5g); Cholesterol 20mg; Sodium 900mg; Total Carbohydrate 39g (Dietary Fiber 5g; Sugars 6g); Protein 16g
% Daily Value: Vitamin A 80%; Vitamin C 15%; Calcium 10%; Iron 25%
Exchanges: 2 Starch, 1 Vegetable, 1 Very Lean Meat, ½ Fat
Carbohydrate Choices: 2

KITCHEN TIPS

- Try any flavor of refrigerated hummus. Besides plain hummus, you can buy roasted red pepper hummus, garlic hummus and many other flavors.

Quick

Philly Turkey Panini

Prep time: 10 min Start to finish: 10 min

2 tablespoons butter or margarine, softened

8 slices rye or pumpernickel bread, ½ inch thick

½ pound thinly sliced cooked deli turkey or chicken

4 slices (1 ounce each) mozzarella cheese

1. Spread butter on one side of each bread slide. In 12-inch skillet, place 4 bread slices, buttered sides down; top with turkey and cheese. Top with remaining bread slices, buttered sides up.

2. Cover; cook sandwiches over medium heat 4 to · 5 minutes, turning once, until bread is crisp and cheese is melted.

4 sandwiches
1 Sandwich: Calories 330 (Calories from Fat 130); Total Fat 15g (Saturated Fat 7g); Cholesterol 60mg; Sodium 1200mg; Total Carbohydrate 27g (Dietary Fiber 2g; Sugars 3g); Protein 22g
% Daily Value: Vitamin A 8%; Vitamin C 0%; Calcium 25%; Iron 10%
Exchanges: 2 Starch, 2½ Lean Meat, 1 Fat
Carbohydrate Choices: 2

KITCHEN TIPS

● Add slices of green bell pepper or tomato to this hearty sandwich.

Philly Turkey Panini

Tartar-Topped Salmon Burgers

Prep time: 20 Start to finish: 1 hr 20 min

Salmon Burgers

- 1 can (7½ ounces) red salmon, drained
- ⅓ cup Progresso dry bread crumbs
- 2 tablespoons finely chopped green bell pepper
- 3 tablespoons plain yogurt
- 1 tablespoon lemon juice
- 1 egg white
- ⅛ teaspoon pepper

Tartar Sauce

- 2 tablespoons reduced-fat mayonnaise
- 1 teaspoon dill pickle relish
- ⅛ teaspoon grated lime peel
- ⅛ teaspoon dried dill weed

1. In small bowl, mix salmon, bread crumbs and bell pepper, breaking up salmon with spoon. Stir in remaining burger ingredients until well mixed.

2. Line cookie sheet with waxed paper. Shape salmon mixture into 4 patties, each about ½ inch thick.

Place on waxed paper. Refrigerate 1 hour. Meanwhile, in small bowl, mix all tartar sauce ingredients. Refrigerate until ready to serve.

3. Spray grill rack with cooking spray. Heat gas or charcoal grill. Cover and grill burgers over medium heat 6 to 8 minutes, turning once, until heated through. Serve with tartar sauce.

2 servings (2 burgers each)
1 Serving: Calories 290 (Calories from Fat 100); Total Fat 12g (Saturated Fat 2.5g); Cholesterol 50mg; Sodium 850mg; Total Carbohydrate 24g (Dietary Fiber 0g; Sugars 4g); Protein 22g
% Daily Value: Vitamin A 2%; Vitamin C 8%; Calcium 30%; Iron 15%
Exchanges: 1½ Starch, 2½ Lean Meat, 1 Fat
Carbohydrate Choices: 1½

KITCHEN TIPS

- Serve these flavor-packed burgers on top of Boston lettuce and credit yourself with eating an extra vegetable—you won't miss the bun.

Tartar-Topped Salmon Burgers

Lemon-Pepper Fish Fillet Sandwiches

Prep time: 15 min Start to finish: 15 min

2 tablespoons yellow cornmeal

2 tablespoons Gold Medal all-purpose flour

1 teaspoon seasoned salt

$\frac{1}{2}$ teaspoon lemon-pepper seasoning

1 tablespoon vegetable oil

2 walleye fillets (about 6 ounces each), each cut crosswise in half

$\frac{1}{4}$ cup tartar sauce

4 whole-grain or rye sandwich buns, toasted

1 cup shredded lettuce

1. In shallow bowl, mix cornmeal, flour, seasoned salt and lemon-pepper seasoning.

2. In 12-inch nonstick skillet, heat oil over medium-high heat. Coat fish fillets with flour mixture. Cook in oil 4 to 6 minutes, turning once, until fish flakes easily with fork.

3. Spread tartar sauce on cut sides of toasted buns. Layer lettuce and fish fillets in buns.

4 sandwiches

1 Sandwich: Calories 310 (Calories from Fat 130); Total Fat 14g (Saturated Fat 2g); Cholesterol 55mg; Sodium 870mg; Total Carbohydrate 25g (Dietary Fiber 2g; Sugars 2g); Protein 21g
% Daily Value: Vitamin A 2%; Vitamin C 0%; Calcium 4%; Iron 10%
Exchanges: 1$\frac{1}{2}$ Starch, 2$\frac{1}{2}$ Lean Meat, 1 Fat
Carbohydrate Choices: 1$\frac{1}{2}$

KITCHEN TIPS

- Why not try another type of fish instead of the walleye? Tilapia is another mild white fish and is delicious cooked this way.
- Be sure to have the buns and lettuce ready to go when the fish is done so that you can serve the sandwiches while warm.

Lemon-Pepper Fish Fillet Sandwiches

Grilled Stuffed Tuna Melts

Prep time: 30 min Start to finish: 30 min

1 can (6 ounces) tuna packed in water, drained
2 tablespoons finely chopped onion
2 tablespoons finely chopped green bell pepper
1 tablespoon finely chopped dill pickles
2 tablespoons creamy Dijon mustard
¼ cup shredded Cheddar cheese (1 ounce)
4 slices whole-grain bread

1. Heat gas or charcoal grill for indirect grilling as directed in owner's manual. Cut two 12-inch square pieces of heavy-duty foil. In small bowl, mix tuna, onion, bell pepper and pickles. Stir in mustard and cheese.

2. Spoon tuna mixture on 2 bread slices; top with remaining bread slices. Place each sandwich on center of foil piece. Fold foil over sandwich so edges meet. Seal edges, making tight ½-inch fold; fold again. Allow space on sides for circulation and expansion.

3. Place packets over unheated area on grill. Cover and grill 12 to 15 minutes or until sandwiches are heated through.

2 servings
1 Serving: Calories 350 (Calories from Fat 80); Total Fat 9g (Saturated Fat 4g); Cholesterol 40mg; Sodium 970mg; Total Carbohydrate 39g (Dietary Fiber 2g; Sugars 1g); Protein 31g
% Daily Value: Vitamin A 6%; Vitamin C 8%; Calcium 15%; Iron 20%
Exchanges: 2 Starch, ½ Other Carbohydrate, 3½ Very Lean Meat, 1 Fat
Carbohydrate Choices: 2½

Grilled Stuffed Tuna Melts

KITCHEN TIPS

- Add crunch to your lunch. Serve carrot and celery sticks plus veggie chips with these sandwiches.
- Avoid grilling these foil-wrapped sandwiches over direct heat. The bread can burn quickly inside the foil.

Quick
Ranch Tuna Melt Wedges

Prep time: 15 min Start to finish: 25 min

1½ cups Original Bisquick mix

⅓ cup boiling water

1 can (12 ounces) chunk light tuna in water, well drained

¼ cup ranch dressing

3 tablespoons finely chopped green onions

1 small tomato, cut into 6 slices

3 slices American cheese, cut in half diagonally

1. Heat oven to 450°F. In medium bowl, stir Bisquick mix and boiling water until soft dough forms. Gather dough into a ball.

2. Place dough on surface lightly dusted with Bisquick mix. Roll dough into 13-inch round. Place on ungreased 12-inch pizza pan; pinch edge to form ½-inch rim. Bake 6 to 8 minutes or until light brown.

3. Meanwhile, in medium bowl, mix tuna, dressing and onions. Spread tuna mixture over crust. Arrange tomato and cheese slices alternately in a pinwheel pattern on tuna mixture. Bake 1 to 2 minutes or until cheese is melted. Cut into wedges.

6 servings
1 Serving: Calories 260 (Calories from Fat 120); Total Fat 13g (Saturated Fat 4g); Cholesterol 25mg; Sodium 810mg; Total Carbohydrate 20g (Dietary Fiber 0g; Sugars 3g); Protein 16g
% Daily Value: Vitamin A 6%; Vitamin C 4%; Calcium 10%; Iron 10%
Exchanges: 1½ Starch, 1½ Very Lean Meat, 2 Fat
Carbohydrate Choices: 1

KITCHEN TIPS

● Add a salad tossed with ranch dressing and glasses of sparkling mineral water garnished with orange wedges.

Ranch Tuna Melt Wedges

Quick & Low Fat
Tex-Mex Veggie Burgers

Prep time: 25 min Start to finish: 25 min

1/2 cup Green Giant Niblets frozen whole kernel corn (from 1-pound bag)

1/4 cup finely chopped red bell pepper

1 tablespoon cider vinegar

1/4 teaspoon chili powder

1/8 teaspoon ground cumin

2 frozen vegetable burgers

2 whole wheat pita breads (6 inch), cut in half to form pockets

2 tablespoons reduced-fat sour cream

1. Heat gas or charcoal grill. In 1-quart saucepan, mix corn, bell pepper, vinegar, chili powder and cumin. Heat to boiling; reduce heat to medium-low. Cook about 5 minutes or until vegetables are crisp-tender.

2. Cover and grill burgers over medium heat 8 to 12 minutes, turning once, until heated through.

3. Cut burgers in half. Place each burger half in pita bread pocket. Top with corn mixture and sour cream.

2 servings
1 Serving: Calories 320 (Calories from Fat 50); Total Fat 6g (Saturated Fat 2g); Cholesterol 5mg; Sodium 930mg; Total Carbohydrate 53g (Dietary Fiber 9g; Sugars 10g); Protein 18g
% Daily Value: Vitamin A 25%; Vitamin C 35%; Calcium 4%; Iron 15%
Exchanges: 3 Starch, 1/2 Other Carbohydrate, 1 Lean Meat
Carbohydrate Choices: 3

KITCHEN TIPS

● To complete this meal, serve these Tex-Mex burgers with a hearty side salad topped with low-fat dressing.

Tex-Mex Veggie Burgers

Quick & Low-Fat

Hawaiian Quesadillas

Prep time: 15 min Start to finish: 20 min

- 4 flour tortillas (7 inch)
- 2 teaspoons fat-free mayonnaise
- 3 ounces thinly sliced cooked ham, cut into strips
- 1 can (8 ounces) crushed pineapple, well drained
- 1/2 cup chopped green bell pepper
- 1/4 cup finely shredded mozzarella cheese (1 ounce)

1. Place tortilla in 12-inch nonstick skillet. Spread with 1 teaspoon mayonnaise. Top with half of the ham, pineapple and bell pepper and a second tortilla.

2. Cook over medium heat 2 to 4 minutes, turning once, until lightly browned. Remove from skillet.

3. Repeat to make second quesadilla.

2 servings
1 Serving: Calories 390 (Calories from Fat 90); Total Fat 10g (Saturated Fat 4g); Cholesterol 30mg; Sodium 940 mg; Total Carbohydrate 57g (Dietary Fiber 4g; Sugars 18g); Protein 19g
% Daily Value: Vitamin A 6%; Vitamin C 35%; Calcium 20%; Iron 20%
Exchanges: 3 Starch, 1 Fruit, 1 1/2 Lean Meat, 1/2 Fat
Carbohydrate Choices: 4

KITCHEN TIPS

- Brighten up the plate by adding wedges of cantaloupe.
- Give your quesadillas an extra Hawaiian touch by adding 1 teaspoon flaked coconut to the filling for each quesadilla.

Hawaiian Quesadillas

Ham and String Cheese Roll-Ups

Prep time: 20 min Start to finish: 50 min

- 2 cups Original Bisquick mix
- 2 tablespoons water
- 1 egg
- 2 teaspoons honey mustard
- 4 sticks (1 ounce each) mozzarella string cheese
- 8 slices (about 8 ounces) thinly sliced cooked ham (from deli)
- 2 tablespoons milk

1. Heat oven to 375°F. In medium bowl, stir Bisquick mix, water and egg until dough forms. On surface sprinkled with Bisquick mix, knead dough about 10 times. Divide dough into fourths.

2. For each sandwich, place one-fourth of dough on surface sprinkled with Bisquick mix; roll in Bisquick mix to coat. Press or roll dough into $6\frac{1}{2} \times 4\frac{1}{2}$-inch rectangle, $\frac{1}{4}$ inch thick. Spread rectangle with $\frac{1}{2}$ teaspoon mustard. Wrap each cheese stick with 2 slices of ham. Place ham and cheese bundle in center of dough. Roll up dough, enclosing filling. Pinch ends and tuck under. Place rolls seam side down on ungreased cookie sheet. Brush with milk.

3. Bake 18 to 23 minutes or until crust is golden brown. Let stand 5 minutes before serving.

4 servings
1 Serving: Calories 430 (Calories from Fat 170); Total Fat 19g (Saturated Fat 7g); Cholesterol 100mg; Sodium 1720mg; Total Carbohydrate 40g (Dietary Fiber 0g; Sugars 8g); Protein 25g
% Daily Value: Vitamin A 4%; Vitamin C 0%; Calcium 35%; Iron 15%
Exchanges: 2 Starch, $\frac{1}{2}$ Other Carbohydrate, $2\frac{1}{2}$ Lean Meat, 2 Fat
Carbohydrate Choices: $2\frac{1}{2}$

KITCHEN TIPS

- Try one of the newer flavors of string cheese in place of the mozzarella.
- For a special touch, sprinkle $\frac{1}{4}$ teaspoon sesame seed on each roll-up before baking.

Quick & Low Fat
Grilled Open-Face Pork Sandwiches

Prep time: 25 min Start to finish: 25 min

- $\frac{1}{4}$ cup orange marmalade
- 2 tablespoons Dijon mustard
- 1 teaspoon olive or vegetable oil
- 1 pork tenderloin (about $\frac{1}{2}$ pound)
- 4 diagonally cut slices French bread, $\frac{1}{2}$ inch thick
  Lettuce leaves

1. Heat gas or charcoal grill. In small bowl, mix marmalade and 1 tablespoon of the mustard.

2. Brush oil over pork. Cover and grill pork over medium heat 15 to 20 minutes, turning occasionally, until pork has slight blush of pink in center and meat thermometer inserted in center reads 160°F. Lightly brush 1 tablespoon marmalade mixture over pork for last few minutes of grilling.

3. Spread remaining 1 tablespoon mustard on one side of bread slices. Place 2 bread slices, mustard sides up, on each plate. Cut pork into thin slices. Place lettuce and pork on bread slices. Heat remaining marmalade mixture to boiling; drizzle over pork.

2 servings (2 sandwiches each)
1 Serving: Calories 350 (Calories from Fat 70); Total Fat 8g (Saturated Fat 2g); Cholesterol 70mg; Sodium 560mg; Total Carbohydrate 40g (Dietary Fiber 1g; Sugars 20g); Protein 28g
% Daily Value: Vitamin A 0%; Vitamin C 4%; Calcium 4%; Iron 15%
Exchanges: $1\frac{1}{2}$ Starch, 1 Other Carbohydrate, $3\frac{1}{2}$ Very Lean Meat, 1 Fat
Carbohydrate Choices: $2\frac{1}{2}$

KITCHEN TIPS

- High-sugar glazes, such as this orange marmalade mixture, can cause burning if applied too soon or if the meat is not turned frequently after the glaze is brushed on.

Grilled Open-Face Pork Sandwiches

Ham and String Cheese Roll-Ups

Quick
Onion and Bacon Cheese Sandwiches

Prep time: 25 min Start to finish: 25 min

4   slices bacon, cut into ½-inch pieces
1   medium onion, thinly sliced
8   slices (¾ ounce each) Cheddar cheese
8   slices Vienna bread, ½ inch thick

1. In 12-inch nonstick skillet, cook bacon over medium heat about 4 minutes, stirring occasionally, until almost cooked. Add onion. Cook 2 to 3 minutes, turning occasionally, until tender. Remove bacon and onion from skillet. Reserve 1 tablespoon drippings in skillet.

2. To make each sandwich, layer cheese, bacon and onion between 2 bread slices. Place 2 sandwiches in drippings in skillet. Cover and cook over medium-low heat 3 to 5 minutes, turning once, until bread is crisp and golden brown, and cheese is melted. Repeat with remaining sandwiches.

4 sandwiches
1 Sandwich: Calories 380 (Calories from Fat 180); Total Fat 20g (Saturated Fat 11g); Cholesterol 50mg; Sodium 740mg; Total Carbohydrate 32g (Dietary Fiber 2g; Sugars 3g); Protein 19g
% Daily Value: Vitamin A 10%; Vitamin C 2%; Calcium 25%; Iron 10%
Exchanges: 2 Starch, 2 High-Fat Meat, ½ Fat
Carbohydrate Choices: 2

KITCHEN TIPS

- You can use any good bread such as sourdough or Italian to make these delicious sandwiches.
- Make it a hearty supper by heating up a favorite family soup to serve with these sandwiches.

Onion and Bacon Cheese Sandwiches

Layered Italian Sandwiches

Prep time: 5 min Start to finish: 1 hr 5 min

1 round focaccia bread (about 8 inches)
1 container (7 ounces) refrigerated basil pesto
4 ounces sliced hard salami
6 lettuce leaves
4 roma (plum) tomatoes, sliced
6 ounces thinly sliced smoked turkey
4 ounces sliced provolone cheese

6 sandwiches
1 Sandwich: Calories 480 (Calories from Fat 310); Total Fat 34g (Saturated Fat 10g); Cholesterol 45mg; Sodium 1500mg; Total Carbohydrate 25g (Dietary Fiber 2g); Protein 21g
% Daily Value: Vitamin A 15%; Vitamin C 15%; Calcium 30%; Iron 15%
Exchanges: 1$\frac{1}{2}$ Starch, 2$\frac{1}{2}$ High-Fat Meat, 2$\frac{1}{2}$ Fat
Carbohydrate Choices: 1$\frac{1}{2}$

KITCHEN TIPS

- This sandwich can be made up to 6 hours ahead of time. Cut into wedges just before serving.

1. Cut focaccia horizontally in half. Spread pesto on both cut sides of focaccia.

2. Layer salami, lettuce, tomatoes, turkey and cheese on bottom of focaccia. Add top of focaccia. Wrap in plastic wrap and refrigerate at least 1 hour to blend flavors. Cut into 6 wedges.

Layered Italian Sandwiches

Sweet Onion-Topped Caesar Burgers

Ranch Cheeseburgers

Sweet Onion-Topped Caesar Burgers

Prep time: 30 min Start to finish: 30 min

1 pound lean (at least 80%) ground beef
2 tablespoons chopped fresh parsley
1/2 cup Caesar dressing
1/2 teaspoon peppered seasoned salt
1 small sweet onion (such as Bermuda, Maui, Spanish or Walla Walla), cut into 1/4- to 1/2-inch slices
1 1/2 cups shredded romaine lettuce
2 tablespoons freshly shredded Parmesan cheese
4 sandwich buns, split

1. Heat coals or gas grill for direct heat. In medium bowl, mix beef, parsley, 2 tablespoons of the dressing and the seasoned salt. Shape mixture into 4 patties, about 1/2 inch thick.

2. Cover and grill patties over medium heat 12 to 15 minutes, turning once, until meat thermometer inserted in center reads 160°F and patties are no longer pink in center. Add onion slices for last 8 to 10 minutes of grilling, brushing with 2 tablespoons of the dressing and turning once, until crisp-tender.

3. In small bowl, toss romaine, remaining 1/4 cup dressing and the cheese. Layer romaine, burger and onion in each bun.

4 sandwiches
1 Sandwich: Calories 490 (Calories from Fat 300); Total Fat 33g (Saturated Fat 9g); Cholesterol 75mg; Sodium 840mg; Total Carbohydrate 25g (Dietary Fiber 2g); Protein 26g
% Daily Value: Vitamin A 15%; Vitamin C 8%; Calcium 15%; Iron 20%
Exchanges: 1 1/2 Starch, 3 Medium-Fat Meat, 3 1/2 Fat
Carbohydrate Choices: 1 1/2

KITCHEN TIPS

● For the juiciest burgers, avoid overmixing the ground beef mixture. If you moisten your hands with water before shaping the patties, the meat won't stick to them.

● Also, don't press the patties with a spatula while they are cooking; you'll squeeze out the flavorful juices.

Ranch Cheeseburgers

Prep time: 20 min Start to finish: 20 min

1 pound lean (at least 80%) ground beef
1/4 cup finely chopped onion
1/4 cup chopped fresh parsley
1/3 cup ranch dressing
1/4 teaspoon coarse ground pepper
4 slices (about 3/4 ounce each) Cheddar or American cheese
4 whole-grain sandwich buns, split
12 dill pickle slices

1. Heat closed medium-size contact grill for 5 minutes. In medium bowl, mix beef, onion, parsley, 3 tablespoons of the dressing and the pepper. Shape mixture into 4 patties, about 3/4 inch thick.

2. Place patties on grill; close grill. Grill 4 to 6 minutes or until meat thermometer inserted in center of patties reads 160°F and patties are no longer pink in center. Top each patty with cheese slice. Let stand on grill about 3 minutes or until cheese is melted.

3. Spread remaining ranch dressing on cut sides of buns. Place cheese-topped patties and pickles in buns.

4 sandwiches
1 Sandwich: Calories 490 (Calories from Fat 280); Total Fat 32g (Saturated Fat 11g); Cholesterol 100mg; Sodium 840mg; Total Carbohydrate 23g (Dietary Fiber 4g); Protein 30g
% Daily Value: Vitamin A 15%; Vitamin C 6%; Calcium 20%; Iron 25%
Exchanges: 1 1/2 Starch, 3 1/2 Medium-Fat Meat, 2 1/2 Fat
Carbohydrate Choices: 1 1/2

KITCHEN TIPS

● To keep the ground beef from sticking to your hands when working with it, wet your hands before shaping the patties.

● These burgers are perfect for year-round picnics! Just serve them with your favorite picnic side dishes—potato salad, baked beans, coleslaw and chips.

Barbecued Chili Beef and Cheddar Sandwiches

Prep time: 5 min Start to finish: 8 hr 5 min

3   pound beef chuck roast
1   package (1$^3/_8$ ounces) chili seasoning mix
$^1/_2$ cup barbecue sauce
10   onion kaiser rolls, split
10   slices (1 ounce each) Cheddar cheese

1. Place beef roast in 3$^1/_2$- to 4-quart slow cooker. Sprinkle seasoning mix (dry) over beef; drizzle with barbecue sauce.

2. Cover and cook on Low heat setting 8 to 10 hours (chili seasoning will appear black when done).

3. Remove beef from cooker; place on cutting board. Skim fat from top of juices in cooker. Shred beef, using 2 forks. Stir shredded beef into juices in cooker. To serve, fill each roll with $^1/_2$ cup beef and top with cheese.

10 sandwiches

1 Sandwich: Calories 540 (Calories from Fat 250); Total Fat 27g (Saturated Fat 12g); Cholesterol 115mg; Sodium 760mg; Total Carbohydrate 33g (Dietary Fiber 2g); Protein 40g
% Daily Value: Vitamin A 15%; Vitamin C 0%; Calcium 20%; Iron 90%
Exchanges: 2 Starch, 5 Lean Meat, 2 Fat
Carbohydrate Choices: 2

Barbcued Chili Beef and Cheddar Sandwiches

KITCHEN TIPS

● Keep the meat mixture warm on the Low heat setting of the slow cooker for up to 2 hours so guests can make sandwiches when desired.

Seafood and Meatless Main Dishes

Something New for Your Table

Margarita Shrimp Stir-Fry (page 109)

Zucchini and Tomato Skillet Dinner (page 122)

Low Fat
Skewered Shrimp with Apricot-Curry Glaze

Prep time: 30 min Start to finish: 1 hr

3   tablespoons vegetable oil
3   tablespoons apricot preserves
1½   tablespoons white wine vinegar
2¼   teaspoons Dijon mustard
2¼   teaspoons curry powder
1¼   teaspoons finely chopped garlic
1½   pounds uncooked peeled deveined large
     shrimp, thawed if frozen
     Shredded lettuce, if desired
     Lemon wedges, if desired

1. In shallow glass or plastic dish, mix oil, preserves, vinegar, mustard, curry powder and garlic. Add shrimp; turn to coat with glaze. Cover and refrigerate 15 to 30 minutes.

2. Heat coals or gas grill for direct heat. Remove shrimp from glaze; reserve glaze. Thread shrimp on six 10- to 12-inch skewers leaving ¼-inch space between shrimp. (If using bamboo skewers, soak in water 30 minutes before using.)

3. Cover and grill kabobs over medium heat 6 to 8 minutes, brushing several times with glaze and turning once, until shrimp are pink and firm. Discard any remaining glaze.

4. Place shredded lettuce on platter; arrange kabobs on top. Garnish with lemon wedges.

6 servings
1 Serving: Calories 80 (Calories from Fat 20); Total Fat 2.5g (Saturated Fat 0g); Cholesterol 105mg; Sodium 135mg; Total Carbohydrate 3g (Dietary Fiber 0g); Protein 12g
% Daily Value: Vitamin A 4%; Vitamin C 4%; Calcium 2%; Iron 10%
Exchanges: 1½ Very Lean Meat, ½ Fat
Carbohydrate Choices: 0

KITCHEN TIPS

● Pair these shrimp kabobs with rice pilaf and a fresh fruit salad.
● Make the glaze ahead of time, then refrigerate until it's time to grill.

Skewered Shrimp with Apricot-Curry Glaze

Quick & Low Fat

Lemon-Pesto Shrimp and Scallops

Prep time: 25 min Start to finish: 25 min

1 pound uncooked peeled deveined large shrimp, thawed if frozen, tails removed

1 pound uncooked sea scallops

1/4 cup refrigerated basil pesto (from 7-ounce container)

1 teaspoon grated lemon peel

1/4 teaspoon salt

1/4 teaspoon coarse ground pepper

6 servings
1 Serving: Calories 150 (Calories from Fat 60); Total Fat 7g (Saturated Fat 1.5g); Cholesterol 130mg; Sodium 410mg; Total Carbohydrate 0g (Dietary Fiber 0g); Protein 21g
% Daily Value: Vitamin A 6%; Vitamin C 0%; Calcium 10%; Iron 15%
Exchanges: 3 Very Lean Meat, 1 Fat
Carbohydrate Choices: 0

KITCHEN TIPS

● If you don't have a grill basket, double a sheet of heavy-duty foil and poke several holes in it. Then grill this dish according to the recipe.

1. Heat coals or gas grill for direct heat. In large bowl, mix all ingredients. Place seafood mixture in grill basket (grill "wok").

2. Cover and grill seafood mixture over medium heat 10 to 12 minutes, shaking basket or stirring seafood mixture occasionally, until shrimp are pink and firm and scallops are white.

Lemon-Pesto Shrimp and Scallops

Betty . . .
ON BASICS

Quick & Low-Fat

Jamaican Jerk Seasoning

Prep time: 5 min Start to finish: 5 min

4   teaspoons dried thyme leaves
2   teaspoons onion powder
2   teaspoons ground allspice
2   teaspoons black pepper
1   teaspoon salt
1   teaspoon ground cinnamon
1/2 teaspoon ground red pepper (cayenne)

1. In storage container with tight-fitting lid, mix all ingredients.

2. Store in cool, dry place up to 6 months. Stir before each use.

About 1/4 cup seasoning.
1 Teaspoon Dry Seasoning: Calories 5 (Calories from Fat 0); Total Fat 0g (Saturated Fat 0g); Cholesterol 0mg; Sodium 200mg; Total Carbohydrate 1g (Dietary Fiber 0g); Protein 0g
% Daily Value: Vitamin A 0%; Vitamin C 0%; Calcium 0%; Iron 4%
Exchanges: Free
Carbohydrate Choices: 0

Quick & Low-Fat

Jamaican Jerk Shrimp Kabobs

Prep time: 20 min Start to finish: 20 min

2 medium mangoes, peeled, finely chopped (2 cups)

½ medium jalapeño chili, seeded, finely chopped

3 tablespoons chopped fresh cilantro

2 tablespoons lime juice

4 teaspoons Jamaican Jerk Seasoning (left)

1 pound uncooked peeled deveined shrimp, thawed if frozen, tails removed

1 tablespoon olive or vegetable oil

1. Heat closed medium-size contact grill for 5 minutes. In medium bowl, mix mangoes, chili, cilantro, lime juice and 1 teaspoon of the Jamaican Jerk Seasoning. Cover and refrigerate until serving.

2. Brush shrimp with oil; in medium bowl, toss with remaining 3 teaspoons Jamaican Jerk Seasoning. Thread shrimp on eight 6-inch metal skewers, leaving space between shrimp. Place kabobs crosswise on grill. Close grill. Grill 4 to 6 minutes or until shrimp are pink and firm. Serve mango mixture with shrimp.

4 servings
1 Serving: Calories 190 (Calories from Fat 40); Total Fat 4.5g (Saturated Fat 1g); Cholesterol 160mg; Sodium 390mg; Total Carbohydrate 19g (Dietary Fiber 2g); Protein 18g
% Daily Value: Vitamin A 25%; Vitamin C 30%; Calcium 6%; Iron 20%
Exchanges: 1 Fruit, 2½ Very Lean Meat, ½ Fat
Carbohydrate Choices: 1

KITCHEN TIPS

● Score the mango with a very sharp paring knife, then peel it like a banana. Carefully cut slices from either side of the large flat seed in the center of the fruit.

Jamaican Jerk Shrimp Kabobs

Low Fat

Citrus Shrimp and Rice

Prep time: 35 min Start to finish: 35 min

- 2 tablespoons butter or margarine
- 1 package (6.2 ounces) rice and vermicelli mix with almonds and Oriental seasonings
- 2 cups water
- 2 tablespoons orange marmalade
- 1 teaspoon grated lemon peel
- 1 pound uncooked peeled deveined medium shrimp, thawed if frozen, tails removed
- 1½ cups Green Giant Select frozen sugar snap pea pods

1. In 12-inch nonstick skillet, cook butter, rice and vermicelli mix and contents of seasoning packet over medium heat about 2 minutes, stirring frequently, until rice and vermicelli are light golden brown.

2. Stir in water. Heat to boiling; reduce heat to low. Cover and cook about 15 minutes or until most of liquid is absorbed.

3. Stir in marmalade, lemon peel and shrimp. Cover and cook 5 to 6 minutes, stirring occasionally, until shrimp are pink and firm. Stir in pea pods. Cover and cook 3 to 4 minutes or until pea pods are crisp-tender.

4 servings (1¼ cups each)
1 Serving: Calories 220 (Calories from Fat 60); Total Fat 7g (Saturated Fat 3.5g); Cholesterol 175mg; Sodium 400mg; Total Carbohydrate 20g (Dietary Fiber 1g; Sugars 6g); Protein 20g
% Daily Value: Vitamin A 10%; Vitamin C 10%; Calcium 6%; Iron 20%
Exchanges: 1 Starch, ½ Other Carbohydrate, 2½ Very Lean Meat, 1 Fat
Carbohydrate Choices: 1

KITCHEN TIPS

- You could use peach or apricot preserves instead of the orange marmalade.

Citrus Shrimp and Rice

Low-Fat

Margarita Shrimp Stir-Fry

Prep time: 15 min Start to finish: 45 min

¹/₂ cup frozen (thawed) margarita mix
1 teaspoon grated lime peel
¹/₂ pound uncooked peeled deveined medium shrimp, thawed if frozen, tails removed
1 tablespoon butter or margarine
¹/₂ medium green bell pepper, cut into thin strips
¹/₂ medium red bell pepper, cut into thin strips
1 tablespoon finely chopped fresh cilantro
1 cup uncooked instant white rice
1 cup water

1. In small bowl, stir margarita mix and lime peel. Reserve 2 tablespoons mixture. Add shrimp to remaining mixture; toss to coat. Cover and refrigerate 30 minutes.

2. In 10-inch nonstick skillet, melt butter over medium-high heat. Cook green and red bell peppers in butter 2 to 4 minutes, stirring occasionally, until crisp-tender.

3. Remove shrimp from marinade; discard marinade. Stir shrimp into mixture in skillet. Cook 1 to 2 minutes, stirring occasionally, until shrimp are pink and firm. Stir in reserved 2 tablespoons sauce and the cilantro. Cook until heated through.

4. Meanwhile, cook rice in water as directed on package. Serve stir-fry over rice.

2 servings
1 Serving: Calories 380 (Calories from Fat 70); Total Fat 7g (Saturated Fat 3.5g); Cholesterol 175mg; Sodium 860mg; Total Carbohydrate 59g (Dietary Fiber 2g; Sugars 10g); Protein 22g
% Daily Value: Vitamin A 45%; Vitamin C 70%; Calcium 6%; Iron 25%
Exchanges: 3 Starch, ¹/₂ Other Carbohydrate, 1 Vegetable, 1¹/₂ Very Lean Meat, 1 Fat
Carbohydrate Choices: 4

Margarita Shrimp Stir-Fry

KITCHEN TIPS

● Chicken is a great substitute for the shrimp in this recipe. Use ¹/₂ pound boneless skinless chicken breasts, cut into 1-inch pieces.

● Try basmati or jasmine rice with this stir-fry. Start the rice before you start cooking the peppers, preparing as directed on the package.

Betty Crocker
IN SEASON

Bell Peppers

Where once only green bell peppers were available, there is now a rainbow of peppers, from dusty chocolate to bright yellow and orange, fiery red to creamy ivory. Bell peppers are mildly flavored compared to their more heat-intense cousins, chili peppers. Although not hot, bell peppers can add color, crunch and sweetness to almost every dish.

Color Power

Green peppers are the most common and widely used bell peppers. But as the interest in peppers continues to increase, so do the colors and varieties available. Green peppers are unripened peppers; they have not yet turned into another color. They have a sharp, strong pepper taste. Left to fully ripen, those green peppers will turn red or another color, the sugar content will increase, and the flavor will mellow and become increasingly sweet. Some varieties, like ivory and yellow peppers, however, are never green, and their color develops in the unripened vegetable.

- Red, orange and yellow varieties will keep their color when cooked.

- Chocolate-hued peppers are brown on the outside and green on the inside, and they will turn green when cooked.

- As a rule, the more colorful, sweeter peppers are better for eating raw; green peppers, with their less sweet taste, are better for cooking.

- Purple peppers when fully ripe are a deep purple color. Depending on the variety, they may start out green or white and change to purple. If not harvested when purple, they will change to red. These are terrific raw, and they also turn green when cooked.

CHOOSE

Peppers should be bright, shiny and firm. They should not have wrinkled skin, soft spots, cuts or moldy stems. Green peppers are available year-round. Other colors peak from July to October, so watch the produce aisle for the colorful varieties.

STORE

Refrigerate unwashed peppers in a plastic bag; store green peppers for up to one week and colored peppers for several days. Colored peppers have a higher sugar content so will not last as long. Wash peppers before using.

PREPARE

Starting at the stem, cut vertically all the way around the pepper. Break the halves apart, and the seeds will pop out and be easy to remove. Be sure to also remove the thick membranes, which can be bitter. It's easiest to cut peppers from the flesh side, with the skin side on the cutting board.

FREEZE

Peppers can be halved, chopped or cut into strips before freezing. If you like, freeze in single-portion amounts in freezer bags or containers for up to six months. Frozen peppers will lose their crisp texture when thawed, so they're best used in soups, stew, stir-fries and casseroles.

NUTRITION HIGHLIGHTS

Every sweet, crisp bell pepper is a nutritional star. Each offers a unique mix of the nutrients listed below, including a variety of phytonutrients such as phenols and carotenoids. These substances are thought to protect the cells in your body from damage caused by free radicals.

- Vitamin C (an excellent source—red and yellow bell peppers have 3 times as much vitamin C as oranges do; green bell peppers have $1\frac{1}{2}$ times as much)

- Beta-carotene (especially red bell peppers)

WHAT THAT MIGHT MEAN FOR YOUR HEALTH

Some of the nutrients in bell peppers are linked to a lower risk of:

- Certain cancers
- Age-related macular degeneration (loss of eyesight)

The rich vitamin C content of bell peppers can help improve the body's absorption of iron from grains, legumes and other vegetables—a nutritional bonus for those who don't eat meat.

IDEAS FOR ADDING BELL PEPPERS TO YOUR PLATE

- Add slices to sandwiches.
- Dice and toss into lettuce salads or favorite soups.
- Use as a colorful garnish.
- Partner with other vegetable crudités for dipping.
- Hollow out and steam, then stuff with rice or another grain pilaf.

How to Roast Peppers

You can roast peppers under the broiler or over a gas stove-top. Use whichever method works best for you. After roasting, place peppers in a paper or plastic bag and close tightly. Allow to steam about 20 minutes or until skins are easy to remove. Then remove the skin, stem, seeds and membrane, if necessary. Cut pepper as desired.

BROILER

Cut peppers into halves or fourths; remove stem, seeds and membranes. Place skin sides up on a cookie sheet. Broil 5 to 10 minutes until the skin is blistered and evenly browned (some spots may blacken).

GAS STOVE-TOP

Spear a whole pepper on a long-handled metal fork with a heatproof handle (a grilling fork works well) and hold it about 5 inches from the gas flame. Turn the pepper frequently so it roasts evenly. Roast about 5 minutes until the skin is blistered and evenly browned (some spots may blacken).

Seafood Enchiladas

Seafood Enchiladas

Prep time: 30 min Start to finish: 1 hr 5 min

2 tablespoons butter or margarine

1 medium onion, chopped ($^1/_2$ cup)

2 cloves garlic, finely chopped

3 tablespoons Gold Medal all-purpose flour

1 can (14 ounces) chicken broth

1 container (8 ounces) sour cream

2 cups shredded Mexican cheese blend (8 ounces)

1 can (4.5 ounces) Old El Paso chopped green chilies, undrained

3 cans (6 ounces each) crabmeat, drained, rinsed

1 package (8 ounces) frozen cooked peeled shrimp, thawed (45 to 50 count)

1 package (11.5 ounces) Old El Paso flour tortillas for burritos (8 tortillas)

1 ripe avocado, pitted, peeled and chopped

2 tablespoons fresh lime juice

1 small roma (plum) tomato, chopped ($^1/_3$ cup)

3 tablespoons chopped fresh cilantro

1. Heat oven to 350°F. In 2-quart saucepan, melt butter over medium-high heat. Cook onion and garlic in butter 3 to 4 minutes, stirring frequently, until softened. Stir in flour until all flour is blended with butter. Stir in broth and sour cream until smooth. Heat to boiling; cook about 2 minutes, stirring constantly, until sauce is thickened. Remove from heat. Stir in cheese until melted. Stir in chilies.

2. In medium bowl, mix 1 cup cheese sauce, the crabmeat and shrimp. Spoon 1 cup of the cheese sauce over bottom of 13 x 9-inch (3-quart) glass baking dish. Spoon about $^1/_2$ cup seafood mixture onto each tortilla. Roll up tortillas; place seam sides down on sauce in dish. Pour remaining sauce over enchiladas.

3. Cover baking dish with foil. Bake 30 to 35 minutes or until bubbly.

4. In medium bowl, toss remaining ingredients. Just before serving, spoon avocado mixture down center of enchiladas.

8 servings
1 Serving: Calories 480 (Calories from Fat 240); Total Fat 26g (Saturated Fat 13g); Cholesterol 155mg; Sodium 1050mg; Total Carbohydrate 29g (Dietary Fiber 2g; Sugars 3g); Protein 30g
% Daily Value: Vitamin A 15%; Vitamin C 10%; Calcium 35%; Iron 15%
Exchanges: 2 Starch, $3^1/_2$ Lean Meat, 3 Fat
Carbohydrate Choices: 2

KITCHEN TIPS

- Use Cheddar or Monterey Jack instead of the cheese blend if you prefer.
- Assemble the enchiladas the night before; cover and refrigerate until ready to bake. Wait to prepare the avocado-tomato topping until just before serving.

Quick

Shrimp Alfredo Primavera

Prep time: 20 min Start to finish: 20 min

3 cups uncooked bow-tie (farfalle) pasta (8 ounces)

2 slices bacon, cut into $1/2$-inch pieces

$1^1/_2$ cups Green Giant frozen sweet peas (from 1-pound bag)

$1/_4$ cup water

1 pound uncooked peeled deveined medium shrimp, thawed if frozen, tails removed

$3/_4$ cup refrigerated Alfredo sauce (from 10-ounce container)

2 tablespoons chopped fresh chives

1. Cook and drain pasta as directed on package.

2. Meanwhile, in 12-inch nonstick skillet, cook bacon over medium heat 4 to 5 minutes, stirring occasionally, until crisp. Stir in peas; cook 2 minutes, stirring occasionally. Add water; cover and cook 3 to 5 minutes or until peas are tender and water has evaporated. Add shrimp; cook 2 to 3 minutes, stirring occasionally, until shrimp are pink and firm.

3. Stir in Alfredo sauce and pasta. Cook over medium-low heat, stirring occasionally, until thoroughly heated. Sprinkle with chives.

4 servings ($1^1/_2$ cups each)
1 Serving: Calories 510 (Calories from Fat 180); Total Fat 20g (Saturated Fat 10g); Cholesterol 215mg; Sodium 720mg; Total Carbohydrate 54g (Dietary Fiber 5g; Sugars 4g); Protein 32g
% Daily Value: Vitamin A 25%; Vitamin C 6%; Calcium 20%; Iron 30%
Exchanges: 3 Starch, 1 Vegetable, 3 Very Lean Meat, $3^1/_2$ Fat
Carbohydrate Choices: 3

KITCHEN TIPS

- You can use rotini or penne pasta instead of the bow-ties if you like.
- Frozen shrimp can be used, but be sure to thaw them before adding to the skillet.

Shrimp Alfredo Primavera

Cajun Halibut

Prep time: 25 min Start to finish: 25 min

Relish

1	can (7 ounces) Green Giant Niblets whole kernel corn, drained
1	medium roma (plum) tomato, chopped ($^1/_3$ cup)
2	medium green onions, chopped (2 tablespoons)
1	tablespoon cider vinegar
2	teaspoons honey
$^3/_4$	teaspoon dried oregano leaves
$^1/_4$	teaspoon ground red pepper (cayenne)
$^1/_4$	teaspoon salt

Fish

4	halibut steaks (about 6 ounces each)
2	tablespoons Worcestershire sauce
$^1/_2$	teaspoon coarse ground pepper
$^1/_4$	teaspoon dried oregano leaves

1. Heat coals or gas grill for direct heat. In small bowl, mix all relish ingredients; set aside.

2. Brush halibut with Worcestershire sauce; sprinkle with pepper and oregano.

3. Cover and grill fish over medium heat 10 to 15 minutes, turning once or twice, until fish flakes easily with fork. Serve fish with relish.

4 servings
1 Serving: Calories 220 (Calories from Fat 25); Total Fat 2.5g (Saturated Fat 0.5g); Cholesterol 90mg; Sodium 480mg; Total Carbohydrate 15g (Dietary Fiber 1g); Protein 34g
% Daily Value: Vitamin A 6%; Vitamin C 8%; Calcium 4%; Iron 10%
Exchanges: 1 Starch, 4$^1/_2$ Very Lean Meat
Carbohydrate Choices: 1

Cajun Halibut

KITCHEN TIPS

- Halibut is a mild, firm, white fish from northern Pacific or Atlantic waters. This flatfish ranges in weight from 50 to as much as 1,000 pounds!
- Keep a spray bottle filled with water near the grill. Use it to douse any flare-ups that might occur.

Garlic and Herb Halibut and Vegetables

Prep time: 10 min Start to finish: 45 min

- ⅓ cup zesty Italian dressing
- ½ teaspoon salt
- ½ teaspoon garlic-pepper blend
- ½ teaspoon dried basil leaves
- 4 halibut fillets, about ¾ inch thick (about 2 pounds)
- 2 cups refrigerated cooked new potato wedges (from 1-pound 4-ounce bag)
- 1 medium zucchini, cut into ½-inch pieces (1 cup)
- 1 cup small whole fresh mushrooms

1. Heat oven to 425°F. Spray 15 × 10 × 1-inch pan with cooking spray.

2. In small bowl, mix dressing, salt, garlic pepper and basil. Place fish and vegetables in pan. Drizzle with dressing mixture, turning fish and vegetables to coat.

3. Bake uncovered 30 to 35 minutes, turning vegetables once or twice, until fish flakes easily with fork and vegetables are tender.

4 servings

1 Serving: Calories 350 (Calories from Fat 100); Total Fat 11g (Saturated Fat 1.5g); Cholesterol 125mg; Sodium 850mg; Total Carbohydrate 18g (Dietary Fiber 3g; Sugars 3g); Protein 46g
% Daily Value: Vitamin A 6%; Vitamin C 10%; Calcium 8%; Iron 15%
Exchanges: 1 Starch, 6 Very Lean Meat, 1½ Fat
Carbohydrate Choices: 1

KITCHEN TIPS

- The size of halibut fillets will vary, so allow less or more time depending on the thickness of the pieces that you have.
- Halibut is a large flatfish that is usually found in northern ocean waters. It's rich, mild, meaty and fairly low in fat.

Garlic and Herb Halibut and Vegetables

Quick & Low-Fat
Basil Salmon and Julienne Vegetables

Prep time: 15 min Start to finish: 25 min

- 1 tablespoon butter or margarine
- 1 bag (1 pound) frozen bell pepper and onion stir-fry
- 1 medium zucchini, cut into julienne (matchstick-size) strips
- 4 salmon fillets (4 to 5 ounces each)
- 2 tablespoons chopped fresh basil leaves
- $\frac{1}{2}$ teaspoon seasoned salt
- 1 teaspoon lemon-pepper seasoning
- $\frac{1}{4}$ cup chicken broth

1. In 12-inch nonstick skillet, melt butter over medium heat. Add bell pepper stir-fry. Cook and stir 2 minutes. Stir in zucchini.

2. Place salmon, skin side down, in skillet, pushing down into vegetables if necessary. Sprinkle salmon and vegetables with basil, seasoned salt and lemon-pepper seasoning. Pour broth over salmon and vegetables.

3. Cover and cook over medium-low heat 8 to 10 minutes or until salmon flakes easily with fork. Remove salmon and vegetables from skillet with slotted spoon.

4 servings
1 Serving: Calories 240 (Calories from Fat 90); Total Fat 10g (Saturated Fat 3.5g); Cholesterol 80mg; Sodium 410mg; Total Carbohydrate 11g (Dietary Fiber 2g; Sugars 3g); Protein 26g
% Daily Value: Vitamin A 15%; Vitamin C 45%; Calcium 4%; Iron 8%
Exchanges: $\frac{1}{2}$ Starch, 1 Vegetable, 3 Lean Meat
Carbohydrate Choices: 1

Basil Salmon and Julienne Vegetables

KITCHEN TIPS

- If you don't have the bell pepper stir-fry mixture, use 2 cups mixed cut-up fresh bell peppers and onions.
- If you purchase one large salmon fillet, just cut it into serving-size pieces before cooking. You can leave the skin on if you like. You could also use salmon steaks.

Quick & Low-Fat
Lemon and Herb Salmon Packets

Prep time: 30 min Start to finish: 30 min

1	cup uncooked instant white rice
1	cup reduced-sodium chicken broth
1/2	cup matchstick-cut carrots (from 10-ounce bag)
2	salmon fillets (4 to 6 ounces each)
1/2	teaspoon lemon-pepper seasoning
2	tablespoons chopped fresh chives
1/2	medium lemon, cut into 1/4-inch slices

1. Heat gas or charcoal grill. Cut two 18 × 22-inch pieces of heavy-duty foil. Spray with cooking spray.

2. In small bowl, mix rice and broth. Let stand about 5 minutes or until most of broth is absorbed. Stir in carrots.

3. Place salmon fillet on center of each foil piece. Sprinkle with lemon-pepper seasoning; top with chives. Arrange lemon slices over salmon. Spoon rice mixture around each fillet. Fold foil over salmon and rice so edges meet. Seal edges, making tight 1/2-inch fold; fold again. Allow space on side for circulation and expansion.

4. Cover and grill packets over low heat 11 to 14 minutes or until salmon flakes easily with fork. Place packets on plates. Cut large X across top of each packet; fold back foil.

2 servings
1 Serving: Calories 430 (Calories from Fat 80); Total Fat 9g (Saturated Fat 2.5g); Cholesterol 95mg; Sodium 710mg; Total Carbohydrate 52g (Dietary Fiber 2g; Sugars 2g); Protein 37g
% Daily Value: Vitamin A 110%; Vitamin C 10%; Calcium 6%; Iron 20%
Exchanges: 3 Starch, 1 Vegetable, 3 1/2 Lean Meat
Carbohydrate Choices: 3 1/2

KITCHEN TIPS

- Don't have matchstick-cut carrots on hand? Chop up baby-cut carrots or regular carrots to use in their place.

Quick & Low-Fat
Broccoli and Tuna Shortcakes

Prep time: 20 min Start to finish: 30 min

2 1/4	cups Original Bisquick mix
2 2/3	cups milk
1/4	cup grated Parmesan cheese
1	can (12 ounces) chunk light tuna in water, drained
1/8	teaspoon pepper
2	cups Green Giant frozen broccoli cuts (from 1-pound bag)

1. Heat oven to 450°F. In medium bowl, stir 2 cups of the Bisquick mix and 2/3 cup of the milk until soft dough forms. Drop dough by 6 spoonfuls on ungreased cookie sheet. Bake 8 to 10 minutes or until tops are golden brown.

2. Meanwhile, in 2-quart saucepan, stir remaining 2 cups milk and 1/4 cup Bisquick mix with wire whisk until completely smooth. Cook over medium heat 9 to 11 minutes, stirring constantly, until sauce thickens. Gently stir in cheese, tuna and pepper. Cook 1 to 2 minutes, stirring constantly, until hot.

3. Cook broccoli as directed on package; drain.

4. To serve, split each shortcake; arrange bottoms on serving plate. Top each with slightly less than 1/2 cup tuna mixture and 1/4 cup broccoli. Top with shortcake tops.

6 servings
1 Serving: Calories 310 (Calories from Fat 90); Total Fat 10g (Saturated Fat 3.5g); Cholesterol 25mg; Sodium 920mg; Total Carbohydrate 34g (Dietary Fiber 2g; Sugars 9g); Protein 21g
% Daily Value: Vitamin A 15%; Vitamin C 10%; Calcium 25%; Iron 15%
Exchanges: 1 1/2 Starch, 1/2 Other Carbohydrate, 2 1/2 Very Lean Meat, 1 1/2 Fat
Carbohydrate Choices: 2

KITCHEN TIPS

- Sliced cucumbers and tomato wedges make a colorful side for the shortcakes.

Lemon and Herb Salmon Packets

Broccoli and Tuna Shortcakes

Fresh Tomato and Garlic Penne

Light and Creamy Mac and Cheese

Quick & Low-Fat
Fresh Tomato and Garlic Penne

Prep time: 25 min Start to finish: 25 min

- 1¼ cups uncooked penne pasta (4 ounces)
- 2 teaspoons olive or vegetable oil
- 2 cloves garlic, finely chopped
- 1 pound roma (plum) tomatoes (6 medium), coarsely chopped
- 1 tablespoon chopped fresh basil leaves
- ¼ teaspoon salt
- ⅛ teaspoon freshly ground pepper

1. Cook and drain pasta as directed on package, omitting salt.

2. Meanwhile, in 10-inch skillet, heat oil over medium-high heat. Cook garlic in oil 30 seconds, stirring frequently. Stir in tomatoes. Cook 5 to 8 minutes, stirring frequently, until tomatoes are soft and sauce is slightly thickened. Stir in basil, salt and pepper. Cook 1 minute. Serve sauce over pasta.

2 servings
1 Serving: Calories 300 (Calories from Fat 60); Total Fat 6g (Saturated Fat 1g); Cholesterol 0mg; Sodium 320mg; Total Carbohydrate 55g (Dietary Fiber 6g; Sugars 4g); Protein 9g
% Daily Value: Vitamin A 35%; Vitamin C 35%; Calcium 2%; Iron 20%
Exchanges: 3 Starch, 1 Vegetable, 1 Fat
Carbohydrate Choices: 3

KITCHEN TIPS

- Add chicken to this pasta dish. After cooking the garlic, add about ½ pound cubed boneless skinless chicken; cook until no longer pink in center.
- A crusty French baguette is a nice addition and adds a different texture to this meal.

Quick & Low-Fat
Light and Creamy Mac and Cheese

Prep time: 10 min Start to finish: 10 min

- 1 cup uncooked jumbo elbow macaroni (3 ounces)
- ⅓ cup Green Giant frozen sweet peas (from 1-pound bag)
- ⅔ cup fat-free (skim) milk
- 1 ounce reduced-fat cream cheese (Neufchâtel), cut into small pieces, softened
- 2 slices (¾ ounce each) process American cheese
- 2 tablespoons crushed fat-free herb-seasoned croutons

1. Cook and drain macaroni as directed on package, omitting salt and adding peas for the last 5 minutes of cooking.

2. Meanwhile, in 10-inch nonstick skillet, heat milk, cream cheese and American cheese over medium-low heat, stirring carefully with wire whisk, until cheese is melted.

3. Add cooked macaroni and peas to cheese sauce; stir to coat. Let stand 2 to 3 minutes or until slightly thickened. Serve topped with croutons.

2 servings
1 Serving: Calories 390 (Calories from Fat 100); Total Fat 8g (Saturated Fat 5g); Cholesterol 20mg; Sodium 300mg; Total Carbohydrate 56g (Dietary Fiber 4g; Sugars 5g); Protein 18g
% Daily Value: Vitamin A 10%; Vitamin C 0%; Calcium 25%; Iron 15%
Exchanges: 3½ Starch, 1 Medium-Fat Meat, 1 Fat
Carbohydrate Choices: 4

KITCHEN TIPS

- Using a wire whisk helps make stirring the cream cheese into the milk easier.

Low Fat
Zucchini and Tomato Skillet Dinner

Prep time: 20 min Start to finish: 35 min

1   teaspoon olive or vegetable oil

¹/₃ cup chopped onion

1   medium zucchini, cut lengthwise in half,
     then cut crosswise into slices (2 cups)

1   can (15 ounces) ready-to-serve creamy
     tomato soup with 30% less sodium

¹/₂ cup water

1   teaspoon red pepper sauce

1   cup uncooked instant brown rice

1   medium tomato, chopped (³/₄ cup)

¹/₃ cup shredded mozzarella cheese

1. In 10-inch nonstick skillet, heat oil over medium
heat. Cook onion in oil, stirring occasionally, until
tender. Stir in zucchini. Cook 4 to 6 minutes, stirring
occasionally, until crisp-tender. Remove from heat.

2. Carefully stir in soup, water, pepper sauce and rice.
Heat to boiling; reduce heat to low. Cover and cook
13 to 15 minutes or until rice is tender.

3. Stir in tomato. Sprinkle with cheese. Cover and cook
about 2 minutes or until cheese is melted.

2 servings
1 Serving: Calories 410 (Calories from Fat 90); Total Fat 10g
(Saturated Fat 3g); Cholesterol 10mg; Sodium 520mg; Total
Carbohydrate 70g (Dietary Fiber 8g; Sugars 10g); Protein 13g
% Daily Value: Vitamin A 35%; Vitamin C 35%; Calcium 20%; Iron 10%
Exchanges: 3 Starch, 1 Other Carbohydrate, 2 Vegetable, 1¹/₂ Fat
Carbohydrate Choices: 4

Zucchini and Tomato Skillet Dinner

KITCHEN TIPS

● Add a little more spice to this entrée by increasing the
red pepper sauce to 1 tablespoon.

Poultry
Main Dishes
A Twist on the Traditional

Dijon and Herb Turkey Breast with Mushroom Gravy (page 141)

Green Chili–Turkey Enchiladas (page 150)

Baked Spicy Chicken

Prep time: 20 min Start to finish: 1 hr 20 min

2 cups bite-size round tortilla chips, crushed (1 cup)

1 teaspoon dried oregano leaves

1 teaspoon paprika

$\frac{1}{2}$ teaspoon dried thyme leaves

$\frac{1}{2}$ teaspoon seasoned salt

$\frac{1}{4}$ teaspoon garlic powder

$\frac{1}{4}$ teaspoon ground red pepper (cayenne)

1 egg

2 tablespoons milk

1 cut-up whole chicken (3 to 3$\frac{1}{2}$ pounds), skin removed if desired

2 tablespoons butter or margarine, melted

1. Heat oven to 400°F. Line 15 × 10 × 1-inch pan with foil; spray foil with cooking spray. In shallow bowl, mix crushed chips, oregano, paprika, thyme, seasoned salt, garlic powder and red pepper. In another shallow bowl, beat egg and milk.

2. Coat chicken pieces lightly with egg mixture, then coat lightly with crumb mixture. Place in pan, skin sides up. Sprinkle with any remaining crumb mixture. Drizzle with melted butter.

3. Bake uncovered 50 to 60 minutes or until juice of chicken is clear when thickest piece is cut to bone (170°F for breasts; 180°F for thighs and legs).

4 servings

1 Serving: Calories 520 (Calories from Fat 290); Total Fat 32g (Saturated Fat 10g); Cholesterol 195mg; Sodium 470mg; Total Carbohydrate 14g (Dietary Fiber 1g; Sugars 0g); Protein 43g
% Daily Value: Vitamin A 20%; Vitamin C 0%; Calcium 6%; Iron 15%
Exchanges: 1 Starch, 5$\frac{1}{2}$ Lean Meat, 3 Fat
Carbohydrate Choices: 1

KITCHEN TIPS

● If your family prefers white meat, substitute 4 chicken breast halves for the cut-up whole chicken.

Baked Spicy Chicken

Chicken and Noodles Romanoff

Prep time: 25 min Start to finish: 5 hr 55 min

¼ cup chopped onion

1 package (20 ounces) boneless skinless chicken thighs, cut into ¾-inch pieces

⅛ teaspoon ground red pepper (cayenne)

1 container (12 ounces) small-curd cottage cheese

1½ cups sour cream (from 16-ounce container)

½ cup grated Parmesan cheese

2 tablespoons Gold Medal all-purpose flour

2 cups uncooked wide egg noodles (about 3 ounces)

1 cup Green Giant frozen sweet peas (from 1-pound bag), thawed

2 tablespoons chopped fresh chives, if desired

1. Spray 3- to 4-quart slow cooker with cooking spray. Mix onion, chicken and red pepper in cooker. In large bowl, mix cottage cheese, sour cream, Parmesan cheese and flour; pour over chicken.

2. Cover; cook on Low heat setting 5 to 6 hours.

3. Stir mixture; stir in noodles and peas. Increase heat setting to High. Cover; cook 20 to 30 minutes or until noodles are tender. Garnish with chives.

6 servings (1 cup each)
1 Serving: Calories 430 (Calories from Fat 210); Total Fat 23g (Saturated Fat 12g; Trans Fat 0.5g); Cholesterol 120mg; Sodium 480mg; Total Carbohydrate 19g (Dietary Fiber 1g; Sugars 6g); Protein 36g
% Daily Value: Vitamin A 15%; Vitamin C 2%; Calcium 25%; Iron 15%
Exchanges: 1 Starch, 4½ Lean Meat, 2 Fat
Carbohydrate Choices: 1

KITCHEN TIPS

● Be sure to layer the cottage cheese mixture over the chicken. This protects it from direct heat on the bottom of the slow cooker and prevents curdling.

Chicken and Noodles Romanoff

Chicken and Pinto Tostadas

Prep time: 20 min Start to finish: 8 hr 40 min

1 package (20 ounces) boneless skinless chicken thighs

$\frac{1}{2}$ cup Old El Paso Thick 'n Chunky salsa

$\frac{1}{4}$ cup water

2 tablespoons Old El Paso taco seasoning mix (from 1.25-ounce package)

1 can (15 ounces) Progresso pinto beans, drained

8 Old El Paso tostada shells (from 4.5-ounce package), heated if desired

1 cup shredded lettuce

$\frac{1}{2}$ cup sour cream

$\frac{1}{2}$ cup refrigerated guacamole (from 12-ounce container)

1. Place chicken in 3- to $3\frac{1}{2}$-quart slow cooker. In small bowl, mix salsa, water and taco seasoning mix; pour over chicken.

2. Cover; cook on Low heat setting 8 to 10 hours.

3. Remove chicken from cooker; place on cutting board. Using 2 forks, pull into shreds. Return chicken to juices in cooker. Stir in beans. Increase heat setting to High. Cover; cook 15 to 20 minutes or until thoroughly heated.

4. Spoon chicken mixture over tostada shells. Top with lettuce, sour cream and guacamole.

8 servings
1 Serving: Calories 290 (Calories from Fat 120); Total Fat 13g (Saturated Fat 4.5g; Trans Fat 0g); Cholesterol 55mg; Sodium 570mg; Total Carbohydrate 24g (Dietary Fiber 5g; Sugars 2g); Protein 20g
% Daily Value: Vitamin A 6%; Vitamin C 6%; Calcium 6%; Iron 15%
Exchanges: $1\frac{1}{2}$ Starch, 2 Lean Meat, 1 Fat
Carbohydrate Choices: $1\frac{1}{2}$

KITCHEN TIPS

● If you don't have tostada shells, just break taco shells in half. Place the halves on each plate and top with the chicken and bean mixture.

Chicken and Pinto Tostadas

Ranch Oven-Fried Chicken with Warm Corn Relish

Prep time: 15 min Start to finish: 45 min

- ¾ cup Original Bisquick mix
- ¼ teaspoon pepper
- ¾ cup reduced-fat ranch dressing
- 4 boneless skinless chicken breasts (about 1¼ pounds)
- 2 tablespoons butter or margarine, melted
- 2 cups Green Giant Niblets frozen corn (from 1-pound bag)

1. Heat oven to 425°F. Spray 13 x 9-inch pan with cooking spray.

2. In shallow dish, mix Bisquick mix and pepper. Into another shallow dish, pour ½ cup of the dressing. Coat chicken with dressing, then coat with Bisquick mixture, pressing so coating sticks to chicken. Place in pan. Drizzle with butter.

3. Bake uncovered about 30 minutes or until juice of chicken is clear when center of thickest part is cut (170°F).

4. Meanwhile, cook corn as directed on bag; drain. Stir remaining ¼ cup dressing into corn. Spoon warm corn relish onto serving plate. Arrange chicken on corn.

4 servings
1 Serving: Calories 480 (Calories from Fat 200); Total Fat 22g (Saturated Fat 6g); Cholesterol 110mg; Sodium 870mg; Total Carbohydrate 37g (Dietary Fiber 3g; Sugars 5g); Protein 35g
% Daily Value: Vitamin A 8%; Vitamin C 2%; Calcium 10%; Iron 15%
Exchanges: 2½ Starch, 4 Very Lean Meat, 3½ Fat
Carbohydrate Choices: 2½

KITCHEN TIPS

- Betty Crocker roasted garlic mashed potatoes and sliced tomatoes would be tasty additions to this comforting meal.
- Use regular ranch dressing if you like.

Ranch Oven-Fried Chicken with Warm Corn Relish

Mustardy Chicken and Dumplings

Mustardy Chicken and Dumplings

Prep time: 15 min Start to finish: 35 min

1 tablespoon vegetable oil

4 boneless skinless chicken breasts (about 1¼ pounds), cut into bite-size pieces

1 medium onion, chopped (½ cup)

2 cups milk

2 cups Green Giant frozen mixed vegetables (from 1-pound bag)

1 can (10¾ ounces) condensed cream of chicken soup

1 tablespoon yellow mustard

1½ cups Original Bisquick mix

1. In 4-quart Dutch oven, heat oil over medium-high heat. Cook chicken and onion in oil 6 to 8 minutes, stirring occasionally, until chicken is no longer pink in center and onion is tender.

2. Stir in 1½ cups of the milk, the mixed vegetables, soup and mustard. Heat to boiling.

3. In small bowl, stir Bisquick mix and remaining ½ cup milk until soft dough forms. Drop dough by 6 spoonfuls onto chicken mixture; reduce heat to low. Cover and cook 20 minutes.

6 servings
1 Serving: Calories 390 (Calories from Fat 130); Total Fat 15g (Saturated Fat 4g); Cholesterol 65mg; Sodium 930mg; Total Carbohydrate 36g (Dietary Fiber 3g; Sugars 10g); Protein 29g
% Daily Value: Vitamin A 60%; Vitamin C 20%; Calcium 20%; Iron 15%
Exchanges: 2 Starch, ½ Other Carbohydrate, 3 Very Lean Meat, 2½ Fat
Carbohydrate Choices: 2½

KITCHEN TIPS

- Serve this creamy dish with a broccoli salad. Who could resist chocolate cupcakes for dessert?
- Sprinkle with chopped fresh parsley just before serving.

Low Fat
Spanish Chicken Supper

Prep time: 1 hr 5 min Start to finish: 1 hr 5 min

3 medium unpeeled baking potatoes, cut into $\frac{1}{2}$-inch cubes (4 cups)

2 medium green or red bell peppers, chopped (2 cups)

1 large onion, coarsely chopped (1 cup)

12 large pimiento-stuffed olives, coarsely chopped

1 can (14.5 ounces) diced tomatoes with roasted garlic, undrained

1 tablespoon Gold Medal all-purpose flour

3 teaspoons chili powder

1 teaspoon salt

$1\frac{1}{2}$ pounds chicken breast tenders (not breaded)

Spanish Chicken Supper

1. Heat coals or gas grill for direct heat. In large bowl, mix potatoes, bell peppers, onion, olives and tomatoes. Stir in flour, 2 teaspoons of the chili powder and $\frac{1}{2}$ teaspoon of the salt. Spoon mixture into large heavy-duty foil bag.

2. Sprinkle remaining 1 teaspoon chili powder and $\frac{1}{2}$ teaspoon salt over chicken. Arrange chicken on top of vegetables. Double-fold open end of bag. Slide foil bag onto cookie sheet to carry to grill.

3. Slide foil bag onto grill. Cover and grill over medium-high heat 30 to 35 minutes, rotating bag $\frac{1}{2}$ turn after 15 minutes, until potatoes are tender and chicken is no longer pink in center.

6 servings

1 Serving: Calories 260 (Calories from Fat 50); Total Fat 6g (Saturated Fat 1.5g); Cholesterol 70mg; Sodium 720mg; Total Carbohydrate 28g (Dietary Fiber 5g); Protein 29g
% Daily Value: Vitamin A 20%; Vitamin C 50%; Calcium 6%; Iron 15%
Exchanges: $1\frac{1}{2}$ Starch, 1 Vegetable, 3 Very Lean Meat, $\frac{1}{2}$ Fat
Carbohydrate Choices: $1\frac{1}{2}$

KITCHEN TIPS

- If you can't find the tomatoes with roasted garlic, use plain diced tomatoes and add 2 cloves of chopped regular or roasted garlic.
- To make your own foil bag, cut two 18 × 15-inch pieces of heavy-duty foil. Layer food on one piece, then cover with remaining piece and tightly seal.

Chicken Risotto

Prep time: 15 min Start to finish: 6 hr 30 min

1¼ pounds boneless skinless chicken breasts, cut into ¾-inch cubes

½ cup finely chopped onion

½ cup shredded carrot

1 clove garlic, finely chopped

2 cups water

2 cups uncooked instant white rice

2 tablespoons butter or margarine

1 can (10¾ ounces) condensed cream of chicken soup

½ cup grated Parmesan cheese

4 servings (1½ cups each)
1 Serving: Calories 580 (Calories from Fat 180); Total Fat 20g (Saturated Fat 8g; Trans Fat 0.5g); Cholesterol 115mg; Sodium 900mg; Total Carbohydrate 57g (Dietary Fiber 2g; Sugars 2g); Protein 43g
% Daily Value: Vitamin A 60%; Vitamin C 2%; Calcium 20%; Iron 20%
Exchanges: 3½ Starch, 4½ Very Lean Meat, 3 Fat
Carbohydrate Choices: 4

KITCHEN TIPS

- Serve this rice casserole immediately. Rice continues to absorb moisture as it stands, so the casserole will lose some of its creaminess.
- If you are watching your sodium intake, use reduced-sodium cream of chicken soup.

1. In 3- to 4-quart slow cooker, mix chicken, onion, carrot, garlic and water.

2. Cover; cook on Low heat setting 6 to 7 hours.

3. Stir in rice and butter. Increase heat setting to High. Cover; cook 5 minutes until rice is tender. Stir in soup and cheese. Cover; cook 10 to 15 minutes or until thoroughly heated. Serve immediately.

Chicken Risotto

Chicken Shepherd's Pie

Alfredo Chicken Bake

Chicken Shepherd's Pie

Prep time: 20 min Start to finish: 55 min

- 1 pouch Betty Crocker roasted garlic mashed potatoes (from 7.2-ounce box)
- 1 cup hot water
- 1/2 cup milk
- 3 tablespoons butter or margarine
- 1 pound boneless skinless chicken breasts, cut into 1/2-inch pieces
- 1 medium onion, chopped (1/2 cup)
- 1 1/2 cups Green Giant frozen mixed vegetables (from 1-pound bag)
- 1 jar (12 ounces) home-style chicken gravy
- 2 1/4 teaspoons paprika
- 1/2 cup sour cream

1. Heat oven to 350°F. Spray 2-quart shallow casserole or 8-inch square glass baking dish with cooking spray. Make mashed potatoes as directed on box for 4 servings—except use the hot water, milk and 2 tablespoons of the butter.

2. Meanwhile, in 12-inch nonstick skillet, melt remaining 1 tablespoon butter over medium-high heat. Cook chicken and onion in butter 4 to 6 minutes, stirring frequently, until chicken is no longer pink in center. Stir in mixed vegetables, gravy and 2 teaspoons of the paprika. Cover; cook over medium-low heat 5 minutes, stirring frequently to prevent sticking.

3. Stir in sour cream. Spoon into casserole. Spoon or pipe potatoes in 8 mounds around edge of casserole. Sprinkle potatoes with remaining paprika.

4. Bake uncovered 25 to 35 minutes or until mixture bubbles around edge of casserole.

4 servings
1 Serving: Calories 500 (Calories from Fat 230); Total Fat 25g (Saturated Fat 11g); Cholesterol 115mg; Sodium 1000mg; Total Carbohydrate 36g (Dietary Fiber 5g; Sugars 8g); Protein 33g
% Daily Value: Vitamin A 90%; Vitamin C 4%; Calcium 10%; Iron 15%
Exchanges: 2 Starch, 1/2 Other Carbohydrate, 4 Very Lean Meat, 4 Fat
Carbohydrate Choices: 2 1/2

KITCHEN TIPS

- To add a slightly smoky flavor to the casserole, add about 1/4 pound sliced smoked kielbasa sausage when you stir in the vegetables.

Alfredo Chicken Bake

Prep time: 15 min Start to finish: 40 min

- 1 package (9 ounces) fresh diced cooked chicken breast, thawed (about 2 cups)
- 1/2 cup Green Giant Select LeSueur® frozen baby sweet peas (from 1-pound bag)
- 1/2 cup shredded Swiss cheese (2 ounces)
- 3/4 cup Alfredo pasta sauce
- 2 tablespoons slivered almonds
- 1 cup Original Bisquick mix
- 1/3 cup milk

1. Heat oven to 425°F. In 1 1/2-quart saucepan, mix chicken, peas, cheese, Alfredo sauce and almonds. Heat to boiling over medium-high heat. Pour into ungreased 1 1/2-quart casserole.

2. In small bowl, stir Bisquick mix and milk until soft dough forms. Drop dough by about 12 spoonfuls onto chicken mixture.

3. Bake uncovered 20 to 25 minutes or until golden brown.

4 servings
1 Serving: Calories 460 (Calories from Fat 250); Total Fat 27g (Saturated Fat 13g); Cholesterol 105mg; Sodium 1050mg; Total Carbohydrate 26g (Dietary Fiber 1g; Sugars 5g); Protein 28g
% Daily Value: Vitamin A 15%; Vitamin C 0%; Calcium 35%; Iron 8%
Exchanges: 1 1/2 Starch, 3 1/2 Very Lean Meat, 5 Fat
Carbohydrate Choices: 2

KITCHEN TIPS

- For a great side dish, add fresh orange segments to a simple tossed salad and dress with your favorite vinaigrette.
- The creamy chicken mixture must be hot before you drop on the biscuit topping. The heat helps cook the bottom of the biscuits.

Layered Chili-Chicken Enchilada Casserole

Prep time: 25 min Start to finish: 1 hr 30 min

- 2 cups diced cooked chicken
- 3 cups shredded Colby-Monterey Jack cheese (12 ounces)
- 1 can (4.5 ounces) Old El Paso chopped green chilies, undrained
- ³⁄₄ cup sour cream
- 1 package (11.5 ounces) Old El Paso flour tortillas for burritos (8 tortillas)
- 1 can (16 ounces) Old El Paso refried beans
- 1 can (10 ounces) Old El Paso enchilada sauce
- 4 medium green onions, sliced (¹⁄₄ cup)
- 1 cup shredded lettuce
- 1 medium tomato, chopped (³⁄₄ cup)

1. Heat oven to 350°F. Spray 13 x 9-inch (3-quart) glass baking dish with cooking spray. In medium bowl, mix chicken, 1¹⁄₂ cups of the cheese, the green chilies and sour cream.

2. Layer 3 tortillas in baking dish, overlapping as necessary and placing slightly up sides of dish (cut third tortilla in half). Spread about half of the beans over tortillas. Top with about half of the chicken mixture and half of the enchilada sauce. Layer with 3 more tortillas and remaining beans and chicken mixture. Place remaining 2 tortillas over chicken mixture, overlapping slightly (do not place up sides of dish). Pour remaining enchilada sauce over top. Sprinkle with remaining 1¹⁄₂ cups cheese. Cover baking dish with foil.

3. Bake 45 to 55 minutes or until bubbly and thoroughly heated. Let stand 5 to 10 minutes before cutting. Garnish casserole or individual servings with onions, lettuce and tomato.

8 servings

1 Serving: Calories 470 (Calories from Fat 220); Total Fat 25g (Saturated Fat 13g); Cholesterol 85mg; Sodium 1080mg; Total Carbohydrate 34g (Dietary Fiber 3g; Sugars 3g); Protein 27g
% Daily Value: Vitamin A 15%; Vitamin C 6%; Calcium 45%; Iron 15%
Exchanges: 2¹⁄₂ Starch, 2¹⁄₂ Medium-Fat Meat, 2 Fat
Carbohydrate Choices: 2

KITCHEN TIPS

● Make this casserole up to 8 hours in advance, then cover and refrigerate until it's time to bake it.

Layered Chili-Chicken Enchilada Casserole

Chicken and Wild Rice Casserole

Prep time: 25 min Start to finish: 55 min

3 tablespoons butter or margarine

1 medium onion, chopped ($^1/_2$ cup)

3 tablespoons Gold Medal all-purpose flour

3 cups half-and-half

1$^1/_2$ cups water

2 tablespoons dry sherry, if desired

1 package (6.2 ounces) fast-cooking long-grain and wild rice mix

2 packages (9 ounces each) frozen diced cooked chicken breast, thawed

8 slices white sandwich bread, crusts removed, cut into $^1/_2$-inch cubes (about 4 cups)

1 cup sliced almonds

$^1/_4$ cup butter or margarine, melted

Chopped fresh parsley, if desired

1. Heat oven to 350°F. Spray 13 × 9-inch (3-quart) glass baking dish with cooking spray. In 3-quart saucepan, melt 3 tablespoons butter over medium heat. Cook onion in butter 2 to 3 minutes, stirring occasionally, until crisp-tender but not brown.

2. Stir in flour, mixing well. Stir in half-and-half, water, sherry and seasoning packet from rice mix. Cook 5 to 6 minutes, stirring constantly, until bubbly. Stir in rice and chicken. Cook 3 to 4 minutes, stirring frequently, until mixture is thickened. Pour into baking dish.

3. Meanwhile, in large bowl, toss bread cubes and almonds with $^1/_4$ cup melted butter, using spoon. Sprinkle evenly over casserole.

4. Bake uncovered 20 to 30 minutes or until topping is golden brown. Let stand 5 minutes before serving. Sprinkle with parsley.

8 servings (1 cup each)
1 Serving: Calories 550 (Calories from Fat 270); Total Fat 31g (Saturated Fat 13g); Cholesterol 115mg; Sodium 580mg; Total Carbohydrate 38g (Dietary Fiber 2g; Sugars 6g); Protein 30g
% Daily Value: Vitamin A 15%; Vitamin C 2%; Calcium 20%; Iron 15%
Exchanges: 2$^1/_2$ Starch, 3 Very Lean Meat, 5$^1/_2$ Fat
Carbohydrate Choices: 2$^1/_2$

Chicken and Wild Rice Casserole

KITCHEN TIPS

● Make the casserole (without the topping) up to a day ahead; cover and refrigerate. Remove from the refrigerator 45 minutes before serving, add the topping and bake as directed.

Mexican Chicken–Sour Cream Lasagna

Prep time: 30 min Start to finish: 1 hr 45 min

12 uncooked lasagna noodles

2 cans (10¾ ounces each) condensed cream of chicken soup

1 container (8 ounces) sour cream

¼ cup milk

1¼ teaspoons ground cumin

½ teaspoon garlic powder

3 cups cubed cooked chicken

1 can (4.5 ounces) Old El Paso chopped green chilies, drained

8 to 10 medium green onions, sliced (about ½ cup)

½ cup chopped fresh cilantro or parsley

3 cups finely shredded Mexican-style Cheddar-Monterey Jack cheese blend (12 ounces)

1 large red bell pepper, chopped (1 cup)

1 can (2.25 ounces) sliced ripe olives, drained

1 cup crushed nacho cheese-flavored tortilla chips

Additional chopped or whole fresh cilantro leaves, if desired

1. Heat oven to 350°F. Spray bottom and sides of 13 × 9-inch (3-quart) glass baking dish with cooking spray. Cook and drain noodles as directed on package. Meanwhile, in large bowl, mix soup, sour cream, milk, cumin, garlic powder, chicken and chilies.

2. Spread about 1¼ cups of the chicken mixture in baking dish. Top with 4 noodles. Spread 1¼ cups chicken mixture over noodles; sprinkle with onions and cilantro. Sprinkle with 1 cup of the cheese.

3. Top with 4 noodles. Spread 1¼ cups chicken mixture over noodles; sprinkle with bell pepper and olives. Sprinkle with 1 cup of the cheese. Top with 4 noodles; spread with remaining chicken mixture.

4. Bake uncovered 30 minutes; sprinkle with tortilla chips and remaining 1 cup cheese. Bake 15 to 30 minutes longer or until bubbly and hot in center. Sprinkle with additional cilantro. Let stand 15 minutes before cutting.

8 servings
1 Serving: Calories 570 (Calories from Fat 280); Total Fat 32g (Saturated Fat 15g); Cholesterol 110mg; Sodium 1150mg; Total Carbohydrate 41g (Dietary Fiber 3g; Sugars 4g); Protein 33g
% Daily Value: Vitamin A 45%; Vitamin C 35%; Calcium 35%; Iron 20%
Exchanges: 2½ Starch, 3½ Lean Meat, 4 Fat
Carbohydrate Choices: 3

KITCHEN TIPS

- The nacho cheese tortilla chips add color and flavor, but you can also use regular tortilla chips for the topping.
- Spoon your favorite salsa over servings of lasagna for a touch of color.

Mexican Chicken–Sour Cream Lasagna

Crispy Chicken and Fettuccine

Prep time: 20 min Start to finish: 20 min

1   package (12 ounces) frozen Southern-style chicken nuggets
1   package (9 ounces) refrigerated fettuccine
1   can (14.5 ounces) Italian-seasoned diced tomatoes, undrained
1   can (15 ounces) tomato sauce
2   tablespoons chopped fresh parsley
2   tablespoons shredded Parmesan cheese

1. Heat oven to 400°F. Bake chicken nuggets as directed on package.

2. Meanwhile, cook and drain fettuccine as directed on package. Leave fettuccine in colander after draining. In same saucepan, heat tomatoes and tomato sauce over medium heat, stirring occasionally, until thoroughly heated.

3. Add fettuccine, chicken and parsley to tomato sauce; toss to coat. (If desired, cut chicken nuggets in half.) Sprinkle with cheese.

4 servings (1¹⁄₂ cups each)
1 Serving: Calories 520 (Calories from Fat 210); Total Fat 24g (Saturated Fat 5g); Cholesterol 45mg; Sodium 1550mg; Total Carbohydrate 57g (Dietary Fiber 5g; Sugars 7g); Protein 21g
% Daily Value: Vitamin A 25%; Vitamin C 25%; Calcium 10%; Iron 15%
Exchanges: 3 Starch, ¹⁄₂ Other Carbohydrate, 1 Vegetable, 1¹⁄₂ Lean Meat, 3¹⁄₂ Fat
Carbohydrate Choices: 3¹⁄₂

KITCHEN TIPS

- If you've purchased breaded chicken fillets instead of the nuggets, bake them, then cut into pieces just before tossing with the fettuccine.
- Refrigerated pasta cooks more quickly than the dried variety, so follow the directions on the package carefully.

Crispy Chicken and Fettuccine

Quick & Low Fat
Glazed Lemon Chicken and Rice

Prep time: 20 min Start to finish: 20 min

1/3 cup water

1 tablespoon fresh lemon juice

2 teaspoons cornstarch

2 tablespoons honey

1 teaspoon grated lemon peel

1 cup uncooked instant white rice

1 cup water

1 teaspoon olive or vegetable oil

1/2 pound boneless skinless chicken breasts, cut into 1-inch pieces

1/2 teaspoon salt

3 green onions, cut into 1-inch pieces

1 small orange bell pepper, cut into 1-inch pieces

1. In 2-cup measuring cup, stir 1/3 cup water, the lemon juice, cornstarch, honey and lemon peel until corn-starch is dissolved; set aside.

2. Cook rice in 1 cup water as directed on package; keep warm.

3. Meanwhile, in 10-inch nonstick skillet, heat oil over medium-high heat. Add chicken; sprinkle with salt. Cook 2 to 3 minutes, stirring frequently, until chicken is brown. Stir in onions and bell pepper. Cook 2 to 4 minutes, stirring frequently, until chicken is no longer pink in center. Reduce heat to low.

4. Stir lemon juice mixture in measuring cup. Pour into skillet; stir to coat chicken mixture. Cook until slightly thickened. Serve chicken mixture over rice.

2 servings
1 Serving: Calories 460 (Calories from Fat 60); Total Fat 6g (Saturated Fat 1.5g); Cholesterol 70mg; Sodium 660mg; Total Carbohydrate 71g (Dietary Fiber 2g; Sugars 21g); Protein 30g
% Daily Value: Vitamin A 45%; Vitamin C 60%; Calcium 6%; Iron 20%
Exchanges: 3 Starch, 1 1/2 Other Carbohydrate, 3 Very Lean Meat, 1/2 Fat
Carbohydrate Choices: 5

KITCHEN TIPS

● Purchase chicken breast tenders for a quick alternative to boneless skinless chicken breasts.

● Garnish this entrée with a sprig of parsley and a lemon twist.

Glazed Lemon Chicken and Rice

Classic Roast Turkey

Prep time: 25 min Start to finish: 4 hr 10 min

Mushroom Stuffing (page 220)
8- to 12- pound turkey, thawed if frozen
2 tablespoons butter or margarine, melted

1. Heat oven to 325°F. Make Mushroom Stuffing. Stuff turkey just before roasting, not ahead of time. Fill neck cavity lightly with stuffing; fasten neck skin to back of turkey with skewer. Fold wings across back of turkey so tips are touching. Fill body cavity lightly with stuffing. (Do not pack stuffing because it will expand during roasting.) Tuck legs under band of skin at tail or tie together with heavy string, then tie to tail.

2. Place turkey, breast side up, on rack in shallow roasting pan. Brush butter over turkey. Insert oven-proof meat thermometer so tip is in thickest part of inside thigh and does not touch bone. (Do not add water or cover turkey.)

3. Roast uncovered 3 hours to 3 hours 30 minutes. After about 2 hours, when turkey begins to turn golden, cut band of skin or remove tie holding drumsticks to allow inside of thighs to cook through, then place a tent of foil loosely over turkey.

4. Turkey is done when thermometer reads 180°F and legs move easily when lifted or twisted. Thermometer placed in center of stuffing will read 165°F when done. If meat thermometer is not used, begin testing for doneness after about 2 hours 30 minutes. Place turkey on warm platter; cover with foil to keep warm. Let stand 15 minutes for easiest carving. Cover and refrigerate any remaining turkey and stuffing separately.

8 to 12 servings
1 Serving: Calories 680 (Calories from Fat 390); Total Fat 44g (Saturated Fat 17g); Cholesterol 195mg; Sodium 790mg; Total Carbohydrate 22g (Dietary Fiber 1g; Sugars 2g); Protein 48g
% Daily Value: Vitamin A 20%; Vitamin C 2%; Calcium 8%; Iron 20%
Exchanges: 1½ Starch, 6 Lean Meat, 5 Fat
Carbohydrate Choices: 1½

KITCHEN TIPS

- To thaw an 8- to 12-pound turkey, leave it in the original wrapping and place in a pan in the refrigerator for about 2 days.

- Letting the turkey stand covered for 15 to 20 minutes before carving helps the juices set up so the sliced meat is more juicy and flavorful.

Classic Roast Turkey

Dijon and Herb Turkey Breast with Mushroom Gravy

Prep time: 25 min Start to finish: 3 hr 15 min

1	tablespoon Dijon mustard
1	tablespoon butter or margarine, softened
$\frac{1}{2}$	teaspoon dried thyme leaves
$\frac{1}{2}$	teaspoon dried marjoram leaves
$\frac{1}{2}$	teaspoon salt
$\frac{1}{4}$	teaspoon coarse ground pepper
5- to 6-	pound bone-in whole turkey breast, thawed if frozen
1	can (14 ounces) chicken broth
8	ounces small fresh whole mushrooms
1	medium onion, cut into 12 wedges
$\frac{1}{4}$	cup Gold Medal all-purpose flour
$\frac{1}{4}$	cup cold water
	Salt and pepper to taste, if desired

Dijon and Herb Turkey Breast with Mushroom Gravy

1. Heat oven to 325°F. In small bowl, mix mustard, butter, thyme, marjoram, $\frac{1}{2}$ teaspoon salt and $\frac{1}{4}$ teaspoon pepper.

2. Place turkey breast, skin side up, In shallow roasting pan. Brush with mustard mixture. Place $\frac{1}{2}$ cup of the broth in bottom of pan; refrigerate remaining broth. Insert ovenproof meat thermometer so tip is in thickest part of turkey breast and does not touch bone. Spray piece of foil with cooking spray; cover turkey. (Foil does not need to tightly cover turkey; secure foil to each end of pan.)

3. Bake 1 hour. Add mushrooms and onion to pan; spoon pan drippings over top. Bake uncovered 1 hour to 1 hour 30 minutes longer or until thermometer reads 170°F. Place turkey on platter; cover with foil to keep warm. Let stand 15 minutes for easiest carving.

4. Pour pan drippings (without vegetables) into measuring cup. Add remaining broth to drippings to equal $1\frac{1}{2}$ cups; pour into 2-quart saucepan. In small bowl, mix flour and cold water until smooth; stir into drippings in saucepan. Heat to boiling over medium-high heat, stirring constantly with wire whisk. Boil and stir about 1 minute or until mixture thickens. Stir in mushrooms and onion from pan. Simmer 5 minutes, stirring occasionally. Stir in salt and pepper to taste. Serve gravy with turkey.

8 servings
1 Serving: Calories 400 (Calories from Fat 150); Total Fat 17g (Saturated Fat 5g); Cholesterol 150mg; Sodium 550mg; Total Carbohydrate 6g (Dietary Fiber 0g; Sugars 1g); Protein 56g
% Daily Value: Vitamin A 4%; Vitamin C 0%; Calcium 4%; Iron 15%
Exchanges: $\frac{1}{2}$ Starch, $7\frac{1}{2}$ Very Lean Meat, $2\frac{1}{2}$ Fat
Carbohydrate Choices: $\frac{1}{2}$

KITCHEN TIPS

- For food safety, always refrigerate leftover turkey and gravy immediately after the meal.
- Side dishes that go well with the turkey are Roasted Butternut Squash Combo (page 201), and fresh green beans.

Turkey Breast with Chili-Cumin Rub

Turkey Breast with Chili-Cumin Rub

Prep time: 10 min Start to finish: 3 hr 20 min

2 tablespoons packed brown sugar

2 teaspoons paprika

1 teaspoon chili powder

1 teaspoon ground cumin

1/2 teaspoon ground mustard

1/2 teaspoon ground ginger

1/2 teaspoon garlic-pepper blend

1/2 teaspoon salt

5- to 6- pound bone-in whole turkey breast, thawed if frozen

2 tablespoons firm butter or margarine

1. If using charcoal grill, place drip pan with 1/2 inch water directly under grilling area and arrange coals around edge of firebox. Heat coals or gas grill for indirect heat.

2. In small bowl, mix all ingredients except turkey and butter. Loosen skin on turkey breast in 4 or 5 places. Cut butter into small slices; place randomly under skin of turkey. Rub chili powder mixture over entire outside of turkey. Insert barbecue meat thermometer so tip is in thickest part of turkey and does not touch bone.

3. Place turkey, skin side down, on grill over drip pan or over unheated side of gas grill. Cover and grill over medium heat 30 minutes; turn turkey. Cover and grill 1 hour 30 minutes to 2 hours longer or until thermometer reads 170°F and juice of turkey is no longer pink when center is cut.

4. Remove turkey from grill; cover with foil. Let stand 10 minutes before slicing.

8 servings

1 Serving: Calories 390 (Calories from Fat 160); Total Fat 18g (Saturated Fat 6g); Cholesterol 155mg; Sodium 290mg; Total Carbohydrate 4g (Dietary Fiber 0g); Protein 54g
% Daily Value: Vitamin A 15%; Vitamin C 0%; Calcium 4%; Iron 15%
Exchanges: 7 1/2 Very Lean Meat, 3 Fat
Carbohydrate Choices: 0

KITCHEN TIPS

- Whole turkey breasts grill beautifully. Because they're available in different sizes, adjust the grilling time as needed and check the meat thermometer for doneness.

- This spice rub is a grilling basic you'll want to keep on hand for chicken and pork, too. Make a double batch and store in a tightly sealed container.

Honey-Mustard Turkey Breast

Prep time: 10 min Start to finish: 3 hr 50 min

$^1/_2$ teaspoon dried basil leaves

$^1/_2$ teaspoon dried rosemary leaves, crumbled

$^1/_2$ teaspoon salt

$^1/_4$ teaspoon coarse ground pepper

5- to 6- pound bone-in whole turkey breast, thawed if frozen

$^1/_4$ cup honey-mustard dressing

1. If using charcoal grill, place drip pan with $^1/_2$ inch water directly under grilling area and arrange coals around edge of firebox. Heat coals or gas grill for indirect heat.

2. In small bowl, mix basil, rosemary, salt and pepper. Rub basil mixture over all sides of turkey. Insert barbecue meat thermometer so tip is in thickest part of turkey and does not touch bone.

3. Place turkey, skin side down, on grill over drip pan or over unheated side of gas grill. Brush with dressing. Cover and grill over medium heat 30 minutes. Turn turkey; brush with dressing. Cover and grill 2 to 3 hours longer, brushing occasionally with dressing, until thermometer reads 170°F and juice of turkey is no longer pink when center is cut.

4. Remove turkey from grill; cover with foil. Let stand 10 minutes before slicing.

8 servings
1 Serving: Calories 360 (Calories from Fat 140); Total Fat 16g (Saturated Fat 4.5g); Cholesterol 145mg; Sodium 290mg; Total Carbohydrate 0g (Dietary Fiber 54g); Protein 54g
% Daily Value: Vitamin A 4%; Vitamin C 0%; Calcium 2%; Iron 10%
Exchanges: 7$^1/_2$ Very Lean Meat, 2$^1/_2$ Fat
Carbohydrate Choices: 0

KITCHEN TIPS

- Thaw a frozen turkey breast in the refrigerator for 1 to 2 days.
- Cut any leftover turkey breast into chunks and use it in a turkey–grape–wild rice salad. Or slice the breast for delicious turkey sandwiches the next day.

Honey-Mustard Turkey Breast

Quick & Low Fat

Buffalo-Style Turkey Tenderloin

Prep time: 10 min Start to finish: 25 min

1 teaspoon olive or vegetable oil

½ pound turkey breast tenderloin

1 cup refrigerated cooked new potato wedges (from 1-pound 4-ounce bag)

1 medium onion, chopped (½ cup)

½ medium red bell pepper, chopped (½ cup)

2 tablespoons reduced-fat blue cheese dressing

1 to 3 teaspoons cayenne pepper sauce
Chopped fresh parsley, if desired

1. In 12-inch nonstick skillet, heat oil over medium-low heat. Add turkey; cover and cook 10 minutes, turning after about 5 minutes. Add potatoes, onion and bell pepper; cook uncovered about 5 minutes longer, stirring occasionally and adding 1 to 2 tablespoons water if needed, until juice of turkey is clear when center of thickest part is cut (170°F) and potatoes are tender.

2. Meanwhile, in small bowl, mix dressing and pepper sauce. Pour sauce over turkey mixture, stirring to coat. Reduce heat to low. Cook until sauce is heated through. Sprinkle with parsley.

2 servings
1 Serving: Calories 230 (Calories from Fat 40); Total Fat 4.5g (Saturated Fat 1g); Cholesterol 75mg; Sodium 270mg; Total Carbohydrate 20g (Dietary Fiber 3g; Sugars 5g); Protein 29g
% Daily Value: Vitamin A 45%; Vitamin C 70%; Calcium 6%; Iron 15%
Exchanges: 1 Starch, 1 Vegetable, 3 Very Lean Meat, ½ Fat
Carbohydrate Choices: 1

KITCHEN TIPS

● The heat and the depth of flavor vary by brand of pepper sauce. The original cayenne pepper sauce has a sweet flavor, perfect for this buffalo-style entrée.

Buffalo-Style Turkey Tenderloin

Garlic and Lemon Roasted Turkey Breast

Prep time: 15 min Start to finish: 3 hr 45 min

3 cloves garlic, finely chopped

1 tablespoon grated lemon peel

¼ cup chopped fresh parsley

1 teaspoon salt

⅛ teaspoon pepper

5- to 6- lb bone-in whole turkey breast

2 tablespoons butter or margarine, melted

8 servings
1 Serving: Calories 370 (Calories from Fat 160); Total Fat 17g (Saturated Fat 6g); Cholesterol 155mg; Sodium 440mg; Total Carbohydrate 0g (Dietary Fiber 0g; Sugars 0g); Protein 54g
% Daily Value: Vitamin A 8%; Vitamin C 4%; Calcium 4%; Iron 10%
Exchanges: 7½ Very Lean Meat, 2½ Fat
Carbohydrate Choices: 0

KITCHEN TIPS

- Garnish the serving platter with sprigs of fresh parsley and twists of fresh lemon.

1. In small bowl, mix garlic, lemon peel, parsley, salt, and pepper. Using fingers, gently loosen skin covering turkey breast. Spread garlic-lemon mixture under the skin. Cover and refrigerate at least 1 hour but no longer than 8 hours.

2. Heat oven to 325°F. On rack in shallow roasting pan, place turkey breast. Insert ovenproof meat thermometer so tip is in thickest part of breast and does not touch bone. Brush turkey with butter.

3. Roast uncovered 2 hours to 2 hours 30 minutes or until thermometer reads 170°F.

Garlic and Lemon Roasted Turkey Breast

Turkey Pasta Primavera

Prep time: 20 min Start to finish: 20 min

1 package (9 oz) refrigerated fettuccine or linguine

2 tablespoons Italian dressing

1 bag (1 lb) Green Giant Select® frozen broccoli, carrots, and cauliflower, thawed, drained

2 cups cut-up cooked turkey or chicken

1 teaspoon salt

2 large tomatoes, seeded, chopped (2 cups)

¼ cup freshly grated Parmesan cheese

2 tablespoons chopped fresh parsley

1. Cook and drain fettuccine as directed on package.

2. Meanwhile, in 10-inch skillet, heat dressing over medium-high heat. Cook vegetable mixture in dressing, stirring occasionally, until crisp-tender.

3. Stir turkey, salt, and tomatoes into vegetables. Cook about 3 minutes or just until turkey is hot. Spoon turkey mixture over fettuccine. Sprinkle with cheese and parsley.

4 servings
1 serving: Calories 400 (Calories from Fat 110); Total Fat 12g (Saturated Fat 3g); Cholesterol 65mg; Sodium 980mg; Total Carbohydrate 44g (Dietary Fiber 6g; Sugars 5g); Protein 33g
% Daily Value: Vitamin A 80%; Vitamin C 45%; Calcium 15%; Iron 20%
Exchanges: 2 Starch, 2 Vegetable, 3½ Lean Meat
Carbohydrate Choices: 2½

KITCHEN TIPS

- To quickly thaw the frozen vegetables, place them in a colander and run cool water over them.
- Complete this easy meal with crusty breadsticks brushed with olive oil, a large leafy green salad, and, for dessert, a bowl of fresh berries.

Turkey Pasta Primavera

Impossibly Easy Turkey Ranch Pie

Prep time: 10 min Start to finish: 55 min

1½ cups cut-up cooked turkey

1½ cups Green Giant frozen mixed vegetables (from 1-pound bag)

½ cup shredded Monterey Jack cheese (2 ounces)

½ cup Original Bisquick mix

1 envelope (1 ounce) ranch dressing mix

1 cup milk

2 eggs

1. Heat oven to 400°F. Spray 9-inch glass pie plate with cooking spray. Place turkey and vegetables in pie plate. Sprinkle with cheese.

2. In medium bowl, stir remaining ingredients until blended. Pour over turkey mixture.

3. Bake 33 to 38 minutes or until knife inserted in center comes out clean. Let stand 5 minutes before serving.

6 servings
1 Serving: Calories 220 (Calories from Fat 80); Total Fat 9g (Saturated Fat 4g); Cholesterol 115mg; Sodium 620mg; Total Carbohydrate 17g (Dietary Fiber 2g; Sugars 6g); Protein 18g
% Daily Value: Vitamin A 45%; Vitamin C 0%; Calcium 20%; Iron 8%
Exchanges: 1 Starch, 2 Lean Meat, ½ Fat
Carbohydrate Choices: 1

KITCHEN TIPS

- Ask at the deli counter to have a thick slice of roast turkey cut for you to take home and cut up. Or check the salad bar for cut-up cooked turkey.

- Use your own leftover cooked vegetables in place of the frozen mix.

Impossibly Easy Turkey Ranch Pie

Onion-Topped Turkey Divan

Prep time: 15 min Start to finish: 1 hr 10 min

1 bag (14 ounces) Green Giant Select frozen broccoli florets, thawed

2 cups diced cooked turkey

1 can (10 3/4 ounces) condensed cream of chicken soup

1/2 cup mayonnaise or salad dressing

1/2 cup milk

1 cup shredded Cheddar cheese (4 ounces)

1 cup French-fried onions (from 2.8-ounce can), coarsely crushed

1. Heat oven to 350°F. Spray 8-inch square (2-quart) glass baking dish with cooking spray.

2. Layer broccoli and turkey in baking dish. In medium bowl, mix soup, mayonnaise and milk; stir in cheese. Spread over turkey and broccoli. Cover baking dish with foil.

3. Bake 30 minutes. Sprinkle with onions. Bake uncovered 20 to 25 minutes longer or until bubbly and broccoli is tender.

4 servings (1 cup each)
1 Serving: Calories 650 (Calories from Fat 440); Total Fat 49g (Saturated Fat 14g); Cholesterol 115mg; Sodium 1080mg; Total Carbohydrate 20g (Dietary Fiber 3g; Sugars 5g); Protein 34g
% Daily Value: Vitamin A 50%; Vitamin C 35%; Calcium 25%; Iron 15%
Exchanges: 1 Starch, 1 Vegetable, 4 Lean Meat, 7 Fat
Carbohydrate Choices: 1

KITCHEN TIPS

● Diced chicken would be a good substitute for the turkey, and cream of celery or mushroom soup could be used instead of the cream of chicken soup.

Onion-Topped Turkey Divan

Green Chili–Turkey Enchiladas

Prep time: 15 min Start to finish: 55 min

1 cup sour cream ranch dip

2 tablespoons Gold Medal all-purpose flour

2 cups diced cooked turkey

2 cups finely shredded Colby-Monterey Jack cheese blend (8 ounces)

1 can (4.5 ounces) Old El Paso chopped green chilies, undrained

1 can (10 ounces) Old El Paso mild enchilada sauce

1 package (11.5 ounces) Old El Paso flour tortillas for burritos (8 inch)

Chopped tomatoes, chopped avocado and shredded lettuce, if desired

1. Heat oven to 350°F. Spray 13 × 9-inch (3-quart) glass baking dish with cooking spray. In large bowl, mix dip and flour. Stir in turkey, 1 cup of the cheese and the chilies.

2. Spread about 2 tablespoons enchilada sauce over bottom of baking dish. Spread 1 to 2 teaspoons enchilada sauce over each tortilla; top each with about $1/3$ cup turkey mixture. Roll up each tortilla and place seam side down in baking dish. Top with remaining enchilada sauce.

3. Cover with foil; bake 25 minutes. Sprinkle with remaining 1 cup cheese. Bake uncovered about 15 minutes longer or until thoroughly heated and cheese is melted. Garnish with tomatoes, avocado and lettuce.

8 servings
1 Serving: Calories 380 (Calories from Fat 190); Total Fat 21g (Saturated Fat 10g); Cholesterol 65mg; Sodium 930mg; Total Carbohydrate 27g (Dietary Fiber 0g; Sugars 2g); Protein 21g
% Daily Value: Vitamin A 10%; Vitamin C 2%; Calcium 30%; Iron 10%
Exchanges: 2 Starch, 2 Lean Meat, $2\frac{1}{2}$ Fat
Carbohydrate Choices: 2

KITCHEN TIPS

● You can use regular sour cream instead of the sour cream ranch dip if you like.

Green Chili–Turkey Enchiladas

Pork Main Dishes

New Family Favorites

Smoky Apple-Butter Ribs (page 156)

Seven-Layer Rigatoni (page 171)

Crown Roast of Pork

Prep time: 35 min Start to finish: 4 hr 15 min

8- to 10- pound pork crown roast (about 16 to 18 ribs)
  2 teaspoons salt
  1 teaspoon pepper
    Mushroom Stuffing (page 220)

1. Heat oven to 325°F. Sprinkle pork with salt and pepper. Place pork with bone ends up on rack in shallow roasting pan. Wrap bone ends in foil to prevent excessive browning. Insert ovenproof meat thermometer so tip is in thickest part of pork and does not touch bone or rest in fat. Place small heat-proof bowl or crumpled foil in crown to hold shape of roast evenly. Do not add water.

2. Roast uncovered 2 hours 40 minutes to 3 hours 20 minutes.

3. Meanwhile, make Mushroom Stuffing. About 1 hour before pork is done, remove bowl and fill center of crown with stuffing. Cover stuffing with foil for first 30 minutes.

4. Remove pork from oven when thermometer reads 150°F; cover with tent of foil and let stand 15 to 20 minutes or until thermometer reads 160°F. (Temperature will continue to rise about 10°F, and pork will be easier to carve.) Remove foil wrapping from bone ends. To serve, spoon stuffing into bowl and cut pork between ribs.

16 servings
1 Serving: Calories 360 (Calories from Fat 180); Total Fat 20g (Saturated Fat 8g); Cholesterol 110mg; Sodium 660mg; Total Carbohydrate 13g (Dietary Fiber 1g; Sugars 2g); Protein 34g
% Daily Value: Vitamin A 6%; Vitamin C 0%; Calcium 2%; Iron 10%
Exchanges: 1 Starch, 4½ Lean Meat, 1 Fat
Carbohydrate Choices: 1

KITCHEN TIPS

- After removing the foil from the bone ends, place paper frills on the ends.
- Show off your beautiful stuffed roast to your guests before removing the stuffing and carving it for the table.

HOW TO MAKE PAPER FRILLS

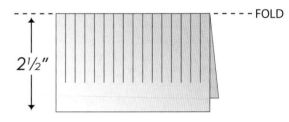

1. For each paper frill, cut paper into 5 × 4-inch rectangle.
2. Fold crosswise in half so paper is 2½ inches × 4 inches.
3. Along folded 4-inch edge, make cuts 1¾ inches deep and ¼ inch apart.
4. Open paper, then fold back the opposite way, being careful not to make a crease where original fold was.
5. Twist uncut end around finger and secure with tape to create frill.

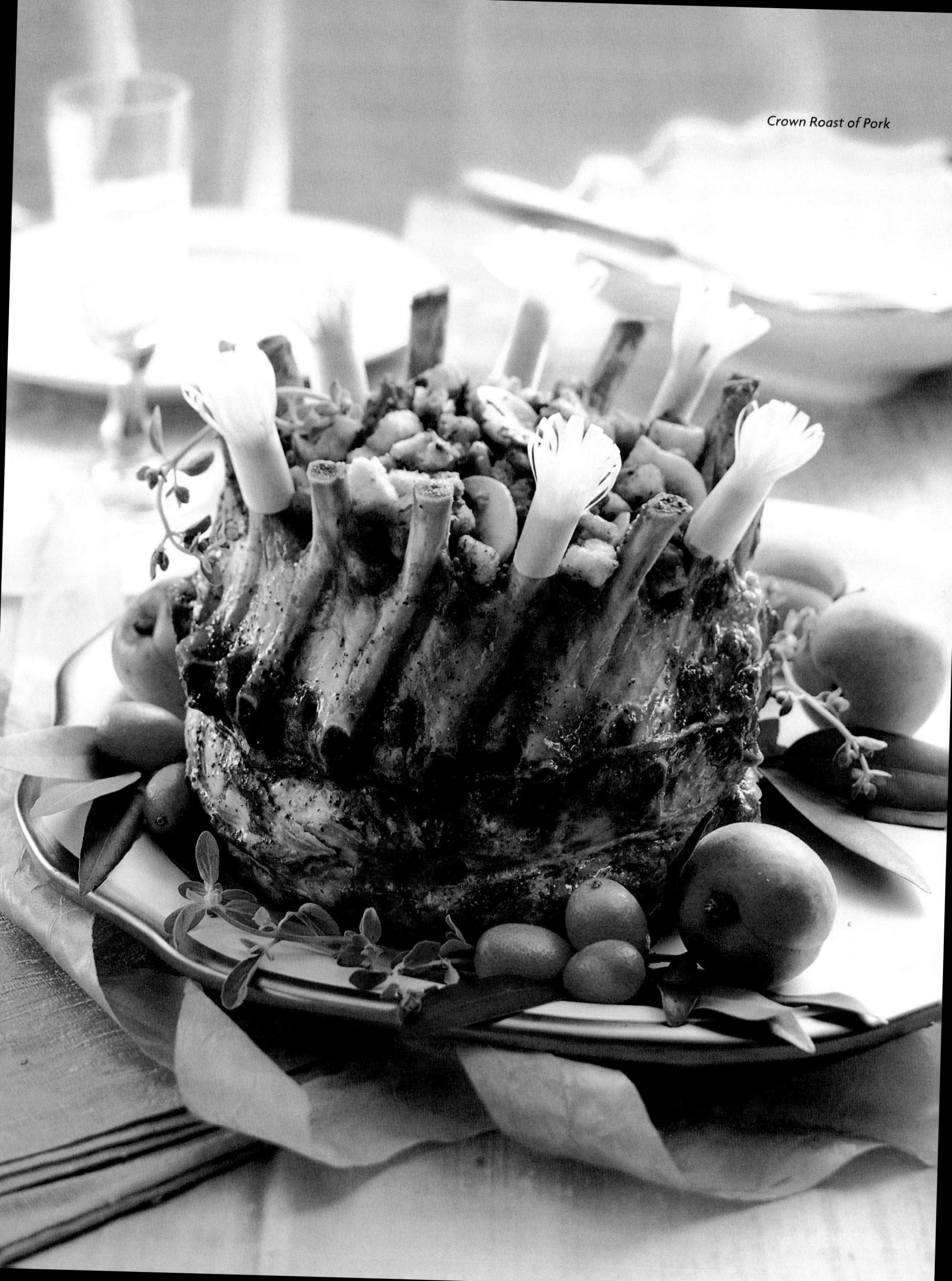

Crown Roast of Pork

Ribs with Cherry Cola Barbecue Sauce

Prep time: 30 min Start to finish: 2 hr

5 to 6   pounds pork baby back ribs
1   teaspoon seasoned salt
1   teaspoon garlic-pepper blend
$\frac{1}{2}$ teaspoon ground ginger
1   cup barbecue sauce
1   can (12 ounces) cherry cola
$\frac{1}{4}$ cup cherry preserves
$\frac{1}{2}$ teaspoon ground mustard
1 to 2   teaspoons buffalo wing hot sauce or other hot sauce

1. Heat oven to 350°F. Cut ribs into serving-size sections. Rub ribs with seasoned salt, garlic pepper and ginger. Place ribs in 15 × 10 × 1-inch pan, overlapping slightly. Bake uncovered about 1 hour 30 minutes or until tender.

2. Meanwhile, in 2-quart saucepan, mix barbecue sauce, cola, preserves, mustard and buffalo wing sauce. Heat to boiling; reduce heat to medium-low. Simmer uncovered 30 to 40 minutes, stirring occasionally, until flavors are blended and sauce is slightly thickened.

3. Heat coals or gas grill for direct heat. Cover and grill ribs over medium heat 10 to 15 minutes, turning and brushing occasionally with barbecue sauce mixture to glaze.

4. Heat remaining barbecue sauce mixture to boiling; boil and stir 1 minute. Serve sauce with ribs.

6 servings
1 Serving: Calories 830 (Calories from Fat 500); Total Fat 55g (Saturated Fat 20g); Cholesterol 220mg; Sodium 840mg; Total Carbohydrate 31g (Dietary Fiber 0g); Protein 53g
% Daily Value: Vitamin A 2%; Vitamin C 4%; Calcium 10%; Iron 20%
Exchanges: 2 Other Carbohydrate, $7\frac{1}{2}$ Medium-Fat Meat, $3\frac{1}{2}$ Fat
Carbohydrate Choices: 2

KITCHEN TIPS

- Precooking the ribs in the oven or microwave shortens the grilling time, helps tenderize the meat and removes some of the fat.
- You can use regular cola instead of the cherry cola if you like.

Ribs with Cherry Cola Barbecue Sauce

Zesty Lemon Spareribs

Prep time: 50 min Start to finish: 6 hr 50 min

6 pounds pork spareribs, cut into serving
  pieces

½ can (12-ounce size) frozen lemonade
  concentrate, thawed

¾ cup barbecue sauce

1. Heat oven to 350°F. Place ribs in 13 × 9-inch pan. Add ¼ cup water to pan. Cover with foil and bake about 2 hours or until tender.

2. Remove ribs from pan; place in 13 × 9-inch (3-quart) glass baking dish or resealable plastic food-storage bag. In small bowl, mix lemonade concentrate and barbecue sauce. Pour over ribs; turn ribs to coat with marinade. Cover dish or seal bag and refrigerate, turning ribs occasionally, at least 4 hours but no longer than 24 hours.

3. Heat coals or gas grill for direct heat. Remove ribs from marinade; reserve marinade. Cover and grill ribs, meaty sides up, over medium heat 20 to 30 minutes, turning and brushing frequently with marinade, until glazed, heated through and browned. Discard any remaining marinade.

8 servings
1 Serving: Calories 540 (Calories from Fat 360); Total Fat 40g (Saturated Fat 15g); Cholesterol 160mg; Sodium 180mg; Total Carbohydrate 5g (Dietary Fiber 0g); Protein 39g
% Daily Value: Vitamin A 0%; Vitamin C 0%; Calcium 6%; Iron 15%
Exchanges: 5½ Medium-Fat Meat, 2½ Fat
Carbohydrate Choices: 0

KITCHEN TIPS

● For a perfect picnic, just add potato salad from the deli and corn on the cob. Bring along some juicy watermelon wedges to complete the meal.

Zesty Lemon Spareribs

Smoky Apple-Butter Ribs

Prep time: 10 min Start to finish: 8 hr 15 min

- 3 pounds boneless country-style pork ribs
- ¾ teaspoon salt
- ½ teaspoon pepper
- 1 medium onion, sliced
- ½ cup apple butter
- 2 tablespoons packed brown sugar
- 1 tablespoon liquid smoke
- 2 cloves garlic, finely chopped

1. Sprinkle ribs with salt and pepper. Place ribs in 3½- to 4-quart slow cooker. Cover with onion slices. In small bowl, mix remaining ingredients; pour over ribs and onion.

2. Cover; cook on Low heat setting 8 to 10 hours.

3. Remove ribs from cooker; place on serving platter. Cover to keep warm.

4. Pour juices from cooker through strainer into 1-quart saucepan. Heat to boiling over medium-high heat; reduce heat to medium. Cook about 5 minutes or until sauce has slightly thickened. Serve sauce with ribs.

4 servings
1 Serving: Calories 750 (Calories from Fat 350); Total Fat 39g (Saturated Fat 14g; Trans Fat 0g); Cholesterol 210mg; Sodium 570mg; Total Carbohydrate 28g (Dietary Fiber 2g; Sugars 24g); Protein 70g
% Daily Value: Vitamin A 0%; Vitamin C 4%; Calcium 4%; Iron 15%
Exchanges: 2 Other Carbohydrate, 10 Lean Meat, 2 Fat
Carbohydrate Choices: 2

KITCHEN TIPS

- Liquid smoke is made by burning hickory chips and condensing the smoke into liquid form. Look for it in the condiment section of the grocery store.

Low-Fat
Apricot-Bourbon Glazed Ham

Prep time: 10 min Start to finish: 1 hr 55 min

- ½ cup apricot preserves
- 2 teaspoons ground ginger
- ¼ cup bourbon or pineapple juice
- 6- to 8- pound fully cooked smoked bone-in ham

1. Heat oven to 325°F. In small bowl, mix preserves, ginger and bourbon until smooth.

2. Place ham on rack in shallow roasting pan. Make cuts about ½ inch apart and ¼ inch deep in diamond pattern around top and sides of ham. Brush with 3 tablespoons of the preserves mixture. Insert oven-proof meat thermometer in thickest part of ham.

3. Bake uncovered 45 minutes. Brush remaining preserves mixture over ham. Bake about 45 minutes longer or until thermometer reads 140°F. Remove ham from oven, cover with tent of foil and let stand 10 to 15 minutes for easier carving.

10 servings
1 Serving: Calories 250 (Calories from Fat 70); Total Fat 8g (Saturated Fat 2.5g); Cholesterol 80mg; Sodium 1770mg; Total Carbohydrate 13g (Dietary Fiber 0g; Sugars 10g); Protein 31g
% Daily Value: Vitamin A 0%; Vitamin C 0%; Calcium 0%; Iron 15%
Exchanges: 1 Other Carbohydrate, 4½ Very Lean Meat, 1 Fat
Carbohydrate Choices: 1

KITCHEN TIPS

- Scoring the ham allows the flavors of the glaze to seep into the meat.

Apricot-Bourbon Glazed Ham

Smoky Apple-Butter Ribs

Sage and Maple Roasted Pork and Squash

Prep time: 15 min Start to finish: 1 hr 10 min

- 4 bone-in pork loin chops, ½ inch thick (about 1¾ pounds)
- 1 medium unpeeled buttercup squash, cut into 4 wedges
- ½ teaspoon seasoned salt
- ½ teaspoon dried sage leaves
- ¼ teaspoon garlic powder
- ¼ cup real maple or maple-flavored syrup
- 2 tablespoons butter or margarine, melted

1. Heat oven to 425°F. Spray 15 × 10 × 1-inch pan with cooking spray. Place pork chops and squash in pan. Sprinkle squash and both sides of pork chops with seasoned salt, sage and garlic powder; rub with fingers to distribute evenly.

2. In small bowl, mix maple syrup and butter. Brush about half of mixture over pork and squash. Cover pan with foil.

3. Bake 40 minutes. Turn pork chops over. Brush pork and squash with maple mixture. Bake uncovered 10 to 15 minutes longer or until pork is no longer pink and squash is tender.

4 servings

1 Serving: Calories 380 (Calories from Fat 160); Total Fat 17g (Saturated Fat 7g); Cholesterol 105mg; Sodium 270mg; Total Carbohydrate 25g (Dietary Fiber 4g; Sugars 17g); Protein 32g
% Daily Value: Vitamin A 80%; Vitamin C 10%; Calcium 4%; Iron 10%
Exchanges: ½ Starch, 1 Other Carbohydrate, 4½ Lean Meat, ½ Fat
Carbohydrate Choices: 1½

KITCHEN TIPS

- In place of the buttercup squash, you could use butternut or acorn squash. Buttercup squash is green and shaped like a turban. Butternut squash is yellow and shaped like a peanut. Both are sweet and mild with firm yellow flesh.

Sage and Maple Roasted Pork and Squash

Quick
Pork Chops with Green Chili Corn

Prep time: 20 min   Start to finish: 20 min

1	tablespoon vegetable oil
4	bone-in pork loin chops, ³⁄₄ inch thick (about 1¹⁄₂ pounds)
¹⁄₂	teaspoon seasoned salt
¹⁄₂	cup chopped red onion
1¹⁄₂	cups Green Giant Niblets frozen whole kernel corn (from 1-pound bag)
1	can (4.5 ounces) Old El Paso chopped green chilies, undrained
¹⁄₄	cup water
1	tablespoon Worcestershire sauce
¹⁄₂	teaspoon dried thyme leaves
1	medium tomato, seeded, chopped (³⁄₄ cup)

Pork Chops with Green Chili Corn

1. In 12-inch nonstick skillet, heat oil over medium-high heat. Sprinkle pork chops with seasoned salt. Cook pork in oil 3 to 4 minutes or until brown on both sides. Remove pork from skillet.

2. Add onion, corn and green chilies to skillet. Cook 2 to 3 minutes over medium heat, stirring occasionally, just until mixture is thoroughly heated.

3. Stir in water, Worcestershire sauce and thyme. Place pork in skillet, pressing into vegetable mixture. Cover and cook 10 to 15 minutes, turning pork and stirring vegetables occasionally, until pork is no longer pink when cut near bone and meat thermometer reads 160°F.

4. Remove pork from skillet. Stir tomato into corn mixture; cook and stir 1 minute. Serve corn mixture with pork.

KITCHEN TIPS

- Boneless pork chops can be used instead of the bone-in type.
- Like spicy food? Add a dash of ground red pepper (cayenne) to the dish.

4 servings
1 Serving: Calories 290 (Calories from Fat 120); Total Fat 13g (Saturated Fat 4g); Cholesterol 75mg; Sodium 380mg; Total Carbohydrate 17g (Dietary Fiber 2g; Sugars 3g); Protein 29g
% Daily Value: Vitamin A 8%; Vitamin C 15%; Calcium 4%; Iron 10%
Exchanges: 1 Starch, 3¹⁄₂ Lean Meat, ¹⁄₂ Fat
Carbohydrate Choices: 1

Pork Tenderloin with Pineapple Salsa

Lemon-Pepper Pork Tenderloin

Quick & Low Fat
Pork Tenderloin with Pineapple Salsa

Prep time: 25 min Start to finish: 25 min

- $^1/_2$ teaspoon finely chopped gingerroot or $^1/_4$ teaspoon ground ginger
- $^1/_2$ teaspoon salt
- $^1/_4$ teaspoon ground cumin
- $^1/_2$ pound pork tenderloin
- 1 kiwifruit, peeled, chopped
- 1 slice ($^1/_2$ inch thick) pineapple, rind removed, cut into $^1/_2$-inch pieces
- 1 tablespoon orange marmalade
- 1 teaspoon finely chopped jalapeño chili

1. Heat gas or charcoal grill. In small bowl, mix gingerroot, salt and cumin. Rub pork with ginger mixture.

2. Cover and grill pork over medium heat 15 to 20 minutes, turning occasionally, until pork has slight blush of pink in center and meat thermometer inserted in center reads 160°F.

3. Meanwhile, in small bowl, stir remaining ingredients until marmalade is completely mixed in.

4. Cut pork into thin slices. Serve pineapple salsa with pork.

2 servings
1 Serving: Calories 210 (Calories from Fat 45); Total Fat 4.5g (Saturated Fat 1.5g); Cholesterol 70mg; Sodium 650mg; Total Carbohydrate 16g (Dietary Fiber 2g; Sugars 12g); Protein 26g
% Daily Value: Vitamin A 0%; Vitamin C 35%; Calcium 2%; Iron 10%
Exchanges: $^1/_2$ Fruit, $^1/_2$ Other Carbohydrate, $3^1/_2$ Very Lean Meat, $^1/_2$ Fat
Carbohydrate Choices: 1

KITCHEN TIPS

- You may have to ask the butcher to cut a $^1/_2$-pound piece from a larger tenderloin for this recipe.
- Serve papaya slices on the side to enhance the flavors of the pineapple salsa.

Quick & Low Fat
Lemon-Pepper Pork Tenderloin

Prep time: 30 min Start to finish: 30 min

- 1 teaspoon grated lemon peel
- $^1/_2$ teaspoon seasoned salt
- $^1/_2$ teaspoon coarse ground pepper
- $^1/_2$ teaspoon paprika
- $^1/_4$ teaspoon dried thyme or marjoram leaves
- 2 pork tenderloins (about $^3/_4$ pound each)
- 2 teaspoons olive or vegetable oil

1. Heat coals or gas grill for direct heat. In small bowl, mix all ingredients except pork and oil. Brush oil over all sides of pork. Rub lemon peel mixture over pork.

2. Cover and grill pork over medium-low heat 15 to 20 minutes, turning occasionally, until pork has slight blush of pink in center and meat thermometer inserted in center reads 160°F.

3. Remove pork from grill; cover with foil. Let stand 5 to 10 minutes before slicing.

6 servings
1 Serving: Calories 160 (Calories from Fat 50); Total Fat 6g (Saturated Fat 1.5g); Cholesterol 70mg; Sodium 160mg; Total Carbohydrate 0g (Dietary Fiber 0g); Protein 26g
% Daily Value: Vitamin A 2%; Vitamin C 0%; Calcium 0%; Iron 8%
Exchanges: $3^1/_2$ Very Lean Meat, 1 Fat
Carbohydrate Choices: 0

KITCHEN TIPS

- The Italian Veggie Grill (page 210) pairs perfectly with this tenderloin because the vegetables can cook alongside the pork.

Slow-Cooked Green Chili Pork Tacos

Prep time: 25 min Start to finish: 8 hr 25 min

1   tablespoon olive or vegetable oil

3- to 4-   pound boneless pork sirloin roast, netting or strings removed

1/4   cup water

1   package (1.25 ounces) Old El Paso taco seasoning mix

1   can (4.5 ounces) Old El Paso chopped green chilies, undrained

2   cups shredded Mexican cheese blend (8 ounces)

1   cup Old El Paso Thick 'n Chunky salsa

1   large tomato, chopped (1 cup)

1   cup fresh cilantro leaves

1   lime, cut into 16 pieces

16   flour tortillas (6 inch)

1. In 12-inch skillet, heat oil over medium-high heat. Add pork roast pieces. Cook 6 to 8 minutes, turning occasionally, until well browned on all sides.

2. Place pork in 3 1/2- to 4-quart slow cooker. Add water to skillet; cook over medium heat 2 to 3 minutes, scraping up browned bits. Pour over pork. Top pork with taco seasoning mix and chilies.

3. Cover and cook on Low heat setting 7 to 8 hours.

4. Remove pork from cooker to cutting board. Pull pork into bite-size chunks, using 2 forks. Return pork to juices in cooker.

5. Place cheese and salsa in separate serving bowls. On serving platter, arrange cheese, salsa, tomato, cilantro and lime pieces. Warm tortillas as directed on package. Spoon pork onto tortillas, using slotted spoon; top with cheese, tomato, cilantro and salsa. Squeeze lime juice over fillings. Fold tortillas in half over filling.

Slow-Cooked Green Chili Pork Tacos

8 servings (2 tacos each)
1 Serving: Calories 580 (Calories from Fat 260); Total Fat 28g (Saturated Fat 12g); Cholesterol 135mg; Sodium 1310mg; Total Carbohydrate 35g (Dietary Fiber 0g; Sugars 2g); Protein 47g
% Daily Value: Vitamin A 15%; Vitamin C 10%; Calcium 25%; Iron 20%
Exchanges: 2 1/2 Starch, 5 1/2 Lean Meat, 2 Fat
Carbohydrate Choices: 2

KITCHEN TIPS

● For spicier tacos, chop 1 or 2 jalapeño chilies and add to the pork with the taco seasoning and green chilies.
● Serve with Spanish rice and hot cheese-topped refried beans.

Low Fat

Ginger Pork in Orange Sauce

Prep time: 20 min Start to finish: 35 min

1	teaspoon ground ginger
1/2	teaspoon garlic powder
1/4	teaspoon pepper
1/2	pound lean boneless pork loin, cut into 1/2-inch cubes
3/4	cup orange juice
1	tablespoon packed brown sugar
1/2	teaspoon grated orange peel
1 1/2	cups sliced fresh mushrooms (4 ounces)
3/4	cup uncooked couscous or rice
1	medium orange, peeled, sectioned

1. In plastic food-storage bag, mix ginger, garlic powder and pepper. Add pork to bag; shake bag to coat pork with seasonings.

2. Heat 10-inch nonstick skillet over medium-high heat. Cook pork in skillet 2 to 3 minutes, stirring frequently, until brown. Stir in orange juice, brown sugar, orange peel and mushrooms. Reduce heat to low. Cover and cook about 15 minutes or until pork is tender.

3. Meanwhile, cook couscous as directed on package. Stir orange sections into pork mixture. Serve over couscous.

2 servings
1 Serving: Calories 530 (Calories from Fat 90); Total Fat 10g (Saturated Fat 2.5g); Cholesterol 70mg; Sodium 65mg; Total Carbohydrate 78g (Dietary Fiber 6g; Sugars 24g); Protein 37g
% Daily Value: Vitamin A 4%; Vitamin C 60%; Calcium 6%; Iron 15%
Exchanges: 3 Starch, 1 Other Carbohydrate, 4 Very Lean Meat, 1 Fat
Carbohydrate Choices: 5

KITCHEN TIPS

● Experiment with a specialty rice like jasmine or basmati, which are both very aromatic and flavorful. Follow package directions for preparation.

Ginger Pork in Orange Sauce

Quick
Sweet-and-Sour Noodles 'n Pork

Prep time: 30 min Start to finish: 30 min

1	tablespoon vegetable oil
1	pound boneless pork loin chops, cut into thin strips
½	teaspoon garlic-pepper blend
1	can (14 ounces) chicken broth
½	cup sweet-and-sour sauce
2	tablespoons chili sauce
1½	cups uncooked medium egg noodles (3 ounces)
1	package (8 ounces) fresh snap pea pods
1	small red bell pepper, cut into thin strips
¼	cup cashew pieces

1. In 12-inch nonstick skillet, heat oil over medium-high heat. Add pork to skillet; sprinkle with garlic pepper. Cook 3 to 5 minutes, stirring frequently, until brown.

2. Stir in broth, sweet-and-sour sauce and chili sauce. Heat to boiling. Stir in noodles. Cover and cook over medium heat 5 minutes.

3. Stir in pea pods and bell pepper. Cover and cook 5 to 8 minutes, stirring occasionally, until vegetables and noodles are tender. Sprinkle with cashews.

4 servings (1 cup each)
1 Serving: Calories 410 (Calories from Fat 160); Total Fat 18g (Saturated Fat 4.5g); Cholesterol 90mg; Sodium 700mg; Total Carbohydrate 32g (Dietary Fiber 4g; Sugars 11g); Protein 33g
% Daily Value: Vitamin A 25%; Vitamin C 50%; Calcium 6%; Iron 20%
Exchanges: 1 Starch, 1 Other Carbohydrate, 1 Vegetable, 4 Lean Meat, 1 Fat
Carbohydrate Choices: 2

KITCHEN TIPS

- Pork tenderloin can be substituted for the pork chops.
- Pop some frozen egg rolls into the oven to serve with this easy dish.

Sweet-and-Sour Noodles 'n Pork

Quick
Sweet-and-Sour Pork

Prep time: 20 min Start to finish: 20 min

1 pound boneless pork loin chops, cut into 1-inch cubes

1 egg, beaten

³⁄₄ cup Original Bisquick mix

¹⁄₂ teaspoon salt

¹⁄₈ teaspoon pepper

¹⁄₂ cup vegetable oil

1¹⁄₂ cups frozen bell pepper and onion stir-fry (from 1-pound bag)

1 can (8 ounces) pineapple chunks, drained

1 jar (11¹⁄₂ ounces) sweet-and-sour sauce

1. In medium bowl, toss pork with egg. In 1-gallon resealable plastic food-storage bag, place Bisquick mix, salt and pepper; seal bag and shake to mix. Drain excess egg from pork. Place pork cubes in plastic bag; seal bag and shake to coat.

2. In 12-inch nonstick skillet, heat oil over medium heat. Cook pork in oil in a single layer 6 to 8 minutes, turning occasionally, until brown and crispy on outside and no longer pink in center. Drain on paper towels. Cover to keep warm.

3. Reserve 1 tablespoon oil in skillet; discard any remaining oil. Cook bell pepper mix and pineapple in oil over medium-high heat 2 to 3 minutes, stirring frequently, until vegetables are crisp-tender. Stir in sweet-and-sour sauce and pork; heat to boiling.

4 servings

1 Serving: Calories 670 (Calories from Fat 380); Total Fat 42g (Saturated Fat 8g); Cholesterol 125mg; Sodium 960mg; Total Carbohydrate 343g (Dietary Fiber 2g; Sugars 22g); Protein 29g % Daily Value: Vitamin A 6%; Vitamin C 25%; Calcium 8%; Iron 15% Exchanges: 1¹⁄₂ Starch, 1¹⁄₂ Other Carbohydrate, 3¹⁄₂ Lean Meat, 6 Fat Carbohydrate Choices: 3

KITCHEN TIPS

● If you can't find the frozen stir-fry mix, use ³⁄₄ cup bell pepper strips and ³⁄₄ cup thin onion wedges.

Sweet-and-Sour Pork

Betty Crocker
ON WHAT'S NEW

Indoor Grills

The Great American Cook-In

Neither rain nor sleet nor snow can discourage grill lovers from seeking the delicious taste they get from grilling. With indoor grilling, however, weather woes are washed away. It's so easy to enjoy foods hot off the grill anytime!

LITTLE GRILL, BIG POWER

Contact grills are indoor-use grills that cook the food between two grids. One grid is on the bottom where the food is placed. The other grid is on the cover that rests on top of the food when the grill is closed. Both grids are heated so the food is cooked from both sides. The result? Foods cook in a fraction of the time of conventional grilling. The dual cooking surfaces also eliminate the need to flip food, but you can if you like.

Contact grills have ridged plates to give the food grill marks. Depending on the type of grill you purchase, these plates may be stationary or removable. If they are stationary, be sure to thoroughly wash them with hot, soapy water after using. Removable plates can be put in the dishwasher or washed by hand.

Grill Successories

When purchasing a grill, you'll want to shop with your cooking style and needs in mind. Grills may have some or all of these features.

WHAT'S THE WATT? Similar to microwave ovens, contact grills can vary in wattage. Higher-wattage grills, over 1,200 watts, shorten cook time.

COOKING GOOD! Contact grills come in lots of shape, size and style options, so whether you're a single cook or feeding a family, you can find a grill that will accommodate your culinary needs.

DIAL IT UP. Some grills offer a thermostat-type dial to help regulate heat, and others have a fixed temperature. The latter are more temperamental, so foods must be watched more closely. Some grills have an automatic shutoff to prevent overcooking.

EXTRA, EXTRA! As the demand for contact grills increases, manufacturers are challenged to provide extras for cooks. Grills may include a bun warmer or grill plates that flip over to become a griddle. Look for special extras if these appeal to you.

Top Indoor Grilling Tips

Just like outdoor grills, **contact grills need to be preheated.** Follow the manufacturer's recommended preheating time for your grill.

Vent! Even though you're cooking indoors, you often have the same type of smoke smell you get when you're grilling outside (but to a lesser extent). **Use your grill under or near an exhaust fan when grilling.** If there's too much buildup, open a window.

Boneless cuts of meat work best with indoor grills because cooking meat to the proper doneness near the bone is more difficult.

Try not to use glazes or sauces while cooking on a contact grill, because they burn easily. Instead, **serve the sauce on the side.**

The closed lid allows the appliance to build up steam. Be sure to **vent or the grill open periodically** to prevent your food from being more steamed than grilled.

Contact grills cook at high temperatures and get very hot. **Use pot holders or oven mitts** when opening or closing the cover to prevent burns.

Keep an eye on the timer and your food. Because these grills cook from both sides, and you don't have to deal with weather variables (wind, temperature and rain), it's easier to overcook foods.

For easy cleanup, unplug the grill and place a couple of wet paper towels between the cover and the base, then close for 10 minutes.

If you want to **try a recipe that uses outdoor grilling times** on your contact grill, start by cutting the time in half and then checking every few minutes.

Pork and Sweet Potato Kabobs

Quick & Low-Fat

Pork and Sweet Potato Kabobs

Prep time: 15 min Start to finish: 15 min

1/3 cup orange marmalade

1 teaspoon finely chopped fresh rosemary leaves

1/4 teaspoon salt

1/2 pound dark orange sweet potatoes, peeled, cut into 8 pieces

2 tablespoons water

1/2 pound pork tenderloin, cut into 1-inch pieces

1 small zucchini, cut into 8 slices

1. Heat gas or charcoal grill. In 1-quart saucepan, heat marmalade, rosemary and salt to boiling, stirring frequently. Remove from heat; set aside.

2. Place sweet potato pieces and water in 1-quart microwavable bowl. Cover loosely with microwavable paper towel. Microwave on High 2 to 3 minutes, stirring once, just until potatoes are tender (do not overcook). Drain sweet potatoes; rinse with cold water.

3. On each of four 10- to 12-inch metal skewers, carefully thread pork, sweet potatoes and zucchini (with cut side facing out) alternately, leaving 1/4-inch space between pieces.

4. Cover and grill kabobs over medium heat 8 to 10 minutes, turning once and brushing with marmalade glaze during last 3 minutes, until pork is no longer pink in center.

2 servings (2 kabobs each)
1 Serving: Calories 360 (Calories from Fat 40); Total Fat 4.5g (Saturated Fat 1.5g); Cholesterol 70mg; Sodium 370mg; Total Carbohydrate 55g (Dietary Fiber 3g; Sugars 37g); Protein 28g
% Daily Value: Vitamin A 210%; Vitamin C 25%; Calcium 4%; Iron 10%
Exchanges: 1 1/2 Starch, 2 Other Carbohydrate, 3 Very Lean Meat, 1/2 Fat
Carbohydrate Choices: 3 1/2

KITCHEN TIPS

● For the best flavor in this recipe, purchase dark orange sweet potatoes, often called yams at the grocery store.

Low Fat

Pork Tenderloin with Vegetables

Prep time: 15 min Start to finish: 1 hr 5 min

1 pound pork tenderloin

2 medium baking or Yukon gold potatoes, peeled

4 small zucchini (1 pound)

1½ cups frozen small whole onions (from 1-pound bag), thawed

2 tablespoons butter or margarine, melted

½ teaspoon dried thyme leaves

½ teaspoon lemon-pepper seasoning

1. Heat oven to 425°F. Place pork in ungreased 15 × 10 × 1-inch pan. Insert meat thermometer horizontally into center of thickest part of pork.

2. Cut potatoes and zucchini lengthwise in half. Arrange potatoes, zucchini and onions around pork. Drizzle butter over vegetables; sprinkle with thyme and lemon-pepper seasoning.

3. Bake uncovered about 35 minutes or until thermometer reads 155°F. Loosely cover pan with foil and bake 10 to 15 minutes longer or until thermometer reads 160°F and vegetables are tender. Cut pork into thin slices. Serve with vegetables.

4 servings

1 Serving: Calories 290 (Calories from Fat 90); Total Fat 10g (Saturated Fat 4.5g); Cholesterol 85mg; Sodium 140mg; Total Carbohydrate 21g (Dietary Fiber 3g; Sugars 3g); Protein 29g
% Daily Value: Vitamin A 20%; Vitamin C 15%; Calcium 4%; Iron 15%
Exchanges: 1 Starch, 1 Vegetable, 3½ Lean Meat
Carbohydrate Choices: 1½

KITCHEN TIPS

● Creamy coleslaw and soft, tender dinner rolls are the perfect sides for this main dish. Add slices of apple pie for dessert.

Pork Tenderloin with Vegetables

Seven-Layer Rigatoni

Prep time: 25 min Start to finish: 1 hr 5 min

3   cups uncooked rigatoni pasta (9 ounces)

1   pound bulk Italian sausage

1   can (28 ounces) crushed tomatoes, undrained

3   cloves garlic, finely chopped

3   tablespoons chopped fresh or 1 tablespoon dried basil leaves

1   package (8 ounces) sliced fresh mushrooms (3 cups)

1   jar (7 ounces) roasted bell peppers, drained, chopped

1   cup shredded Parmesan cheese

2½ cups shredded mozzarella cheese (10 ounces)

1. Heat oven to 375°F. Spray 13 × 9-inch glass baking dish with cooking spray. Cook and drain pasta as directed on package.

2. Meanwhile, in 10-inch skillet, cook sausage over medium heat, stirring occasionally, until no longer pink; drain. In medium bowl, mix tomatoes, garlic and basil.

3. Layer half each of the pasta, sausage, mushrooms, bell peppers, Parmesan cheese, tomato mixture and mozzarella cheese in baking dish. Repeat layers.

4. Bake uncovered 35 to 40 minutes or until hot and cheese is golden brown.

8 servings
1 Serving: Calories 480 (Calories from Fat 200); Total Fat 22g (Saturated Fat 11g); Cholesterol 60mg; Sodium 1110mg; Total Carbohydrate 43g (Dietary Fiber 4g); Protein 30g
% Daily Value: Vitamin A 40%; Vitamin C 50%; Calcium 50%; Iron 20%
Exchanges: 3 Starch, 2½ High-Fat Meat
Carbohydrate Choices: 3

KITCHEN TIPS

● Slash the fat in this family-favorite casserole to 16 grams per serving by using ¾ pound of Italian-seasoned ground turkey.

Seven-Layer Rigatoni

Quick

Cajun Sausage and Rice

Prep time: 30 min Start to finish: 30 min

¾ cup uncooked regular long-grain white rice

2 cups water

1 cup Old El Paso Thick 'n Chunky salsa

8 ounces smoked kielbasa or Polish sausage, thinly sliced

1 can (15 to 16 ounces) black-eyed peas, drained, rinsed

1 cup Green Giant Niblets frozen whole kernel corn (from 1-pound bag)

1. In 4-quart saucepan, mix rice and water. Heat to boiling; reduce heat. Cover and simmer 10 to 12 minutes, stirring occasionally.

2. Stir in salsa, sausage, peas and corn. Cook uncovered 10 to 12 minutes, stirring frequently, until corn is tender and mixture is thoroughly heated.

4 servings (1¼ cups each)
1 Serving: Calories 470 (Calories from Fat 150); Total Fat 17g (Saturated Fat 6g); Cholesterol 35mg; Sodium 1200mg; Total Carbohydrate 66g (Dietary Fiber 6g; Sugars 5g); Protein 18g
% Daily Value: Vitamin A 6%; Vitamin C 0%; Calcium 4%; Iron 25%
Exchanges: 2 Starch, 2½ Other Carbohydrate, 1½ Medium-Fat Meat, 1½ Fat
Carbohydrate Choices: 4

KITCHEN TIPS

● The salsa is added after the rice is cooked because the acid from the tomatoes can prevent the rice from becoming tender.

● A mixed fresh-fruit salad and corn muffins from the bakery are the perfect accompaniments for this meal.

Cajun Sausage and Rice

Sausage Calzone

Prep time: 15 min Start to finish: 55 min

8 ounces bulk Italian sausage

1 medium onion, chopped ($\frac{1}{2}$ cup)

1 jar (4.5 ounces) Green Giant sliced mushrooms, drained

1 can (16 ounces) pizza sauce

3 cups Original Bisquick mix

$\frac{1}{2}$ cup boiling water

2 tablespoons olive or vegetable oil

1 cup shredded mozzarella cheese (4 ounces)

2 tablespoons shredded Parmesan cheese

1. Heat oven to 450°F. In 10-inch skillet, cook sausage and onion over medium-high heat 5 to 7 minutes, stirring occasionally, until sausage is no longer pink; drain. Stir in mushrooms and $\frac{1}{2}$ cup of the pizza sauce; heat through.

2. In medium bowl, stir Bisquick mix, boiling water and oil until dough forms (add additional tablespoon of water if needed). Place dough on surface sprinkled with Bisquick mix; roll in Bisquick mix to coat. Shape dough into a ball; knead about 10 times or until smooth. Roll dough into 12-inch circle.

3. Place dough circle on ungreased cookie sheet. Top half of circle with sausage mixture to within 1 inch of edge. Sprinkle mozzarella cheese over sausage mixture. Fold dough over filling; press edge with fork to seal. Sprinkle with Parmesan cheese.

4. Bake 14 to 18 minutes or until golden brown. Remove from cookie sheet to cutting board. Cool 5 minutes before cutting into 6 wedges. Heat remaining pizza sauce; spoon over each serving.

6 servings

1 Serving: Calories 470 (Calories from Fat 220); Total Fat 24g (Saturated Fat 8g); Cholesterol 35mg; Sodium 1670mg; Total Carbohydrate 46g (Dietary Fiber 3g; Sugars 10g); Protein 17g
% Daily Value: Vitamin A 6%; Vitamin C 4%; Calcium 30%; Iron 20%
Exchanges: 2$\frac{1}{2}$ Starch, $\frac{1}{2}$ Other Carbohydrate, 1$\frac{1}{2}$ High-Fat Meat, 2 Fat
Carbohydrate Choices: 3

Sausage Calzone

KITCHEN TIPS

- To personalize your calzone, add your family's favorite pizza toppings. Try green bell pepper, olives or onions.

- You can use a package of sliced pepperoni in place of the sausage. Just stir the pepperoni together with the pizza sauce and mushrooms and fill the calzone.

Chunky Pork and Mushroom Spaghetti Sauce

Prep time: 15 min Start to finish: 8 hr 35 min

1½ pounds boneless country-style pork ribs

1 cup frozen onions, celery, bell pepper and parsley seasoning blend (from 12-ounce bag), thawed

1 can (29 ounces) tomato puree

1 can (14.5 ounces) diced tomatoes with basil, garlic and oregano, undrained

1 tablespoon Worcestershire sauce

1 teaspoon sugar

1 teaspoon fennel seed

1 package (8 ounces) sliced fresh mushrooms (3 cups)

1 package (16 ounces) spaghetti

1 tablespoon olive or vegetable oil

Grated Parmesan cheese, if desired

1. In 3½- to 4-quart slow cooker, mix all ingredients except mushrooms, spaghetti, oil and cheese.

2. Cover; cook on Low heat setting 8 to 10 hours.

3. Using 2 forks, break pork into bite-size pieces in cooker. Stir in mushrooms. Increase heat setting to High. Cover; cook 15 to 20 minutes. Meanwhile, cook and drain spaghetti as directed on package.

4. Stir oil into sauce. Serve over hot spaghetti. Sprinkle with cheese.

8 servings (1 cup each)
1 Serving: Calories 480 (Calories from Fat 120); Total Fat 13g (Saturated Fat 4g; Trans Fat 0g); Cholesterol 50mg; Sodium 890mg; Total Carbohydrate 62g (Dietary Fiber 6g; Sugars 12g); Protein 28g
% Daily Value: Vitamin A 15%; Vitamin C 15%; Calcium 6%; Iron 25%
Exchanges: 3 Starch, 1 Other Carbohydrate, 1 Vegetable, 2½ Lean Meat, ½ Fat
Carbohydrate Choices: 4

Chunky Pork and Mushroom Spaghetti Sauce

KITCHEN TIPS

● The frozen seasoning blend is found near the bags of chopped onions in the frozen vegetable section.

● Stirring olive oil into the spaghetti sauce at the end of the cooking time smooths out the sharp flavor of the tomatoes.

Beef Main Dishes

Meaty and Delicious Meals

Greek-Style Steak (page 196)

Beef and Creamy Potato Casserole (page 186)

Quick

Saucy Ground Beef and Noodles

Prep time: 25 min Start to finish: 25 min

1 pound lean (at least 80%) ground beef

1 medium onion, chopped (¹⁄₂ cup)

1 medium bell pepper, chopped (1 cup)

3 cups uncooked extra-wide egg noodles (5 ounces)

2¹⁄₂ cups water

¹⁄₂ teaspoon Italian seasoning

1 jar (1 pound 10 ounces) tomato pasta sauce (any variety) or marinara sauce

1 jar (4.5 ounces) Green Giant sliced mushrooms, drained

4 servings (1¹⁄₂ cups each)
1 Serving: Calories 530 (Calories from Fat 190); Total Fat 21g (Saturated Fat 6g); Cholesterol 100mg; Sodium 1110mg; Total Carbohydrate 63g (Dietary Fiber 5g; Sugars 16g); Protein 28g
% Daily Value: Vitamin A 30%; Vitamin C 50%; Calcium 8%; Iron 30%
Exchanges: 3 Starch, 1 Other Carbohydrate, 2¹⁄₂ Medium-Fat Meat, 1 Fat
Carbohydrate Choices: 4

KITCHEN TIPS

- For a more pizza-flavored dish, use two 15-ounce cans of pizza sauce instead of the pasta sauce and add ¹⁄₂ cup pepperoni.
- For super-speedy cooking, keep bags of purchased frozen chopped onions and bell peppers available in your freezer.

1. In 4-quart Dutch oven, cook beef, onion and bell pepper over medium heat 8 to 10 minutes, stirring occasionally, until beef is brown; drain.

2. Stir in remaining ingredients. Heat to boiling, stirring occasionally; reduce heat. Simmer uncovered 10 to 12 minutes or until noodles are tender.

Saucy Ground Beef and Noodles

Taco Beef Bake with Cheddar Biscuit Topping

Prep time: 15 min Start to finish: 50 min

1 pound lean (at least 80%) ground beef

1 package (1.25 ounces) Old El Paso® 40%-less-sodium taco seasoning mix

1 cup Old El Paso® Thick 'n Chunky salsa

2 cups Green Giant Niblets frozen whole kernel corn (from 1-pound bag)

2 cups Original Bisquick mix

1 cup shredded Cheddar cheese (4 ounces)

²⁄₃ cup milk

1. Heat oven to 425°F. In 10-inch skillet, cook beef over medium-high heat 5 to 7 minutes, stirring occasionally, until brown; drain.

2. Stir taco seasoning mix, salsa and corn into beef. Heat to boiling, stirring occasionally. Pour into ungreased 8-inch square pan or 2-quart glass baking dish.

3. Meanwhile, in medium bowl, stir Bisquick mix, cheese and milk until soft dough forms. Drop dough by 12 spoonfuls onto beef mixture.

4. Bake uncovered 20 to 25 minutes or until topping is golden brown.

6 servings (1 cup each)
1 Serving: Calories 450 (Calories from Fat 190); Total Fat 21g (Saturated Fat 9g); Cholesterol 70mg; Sodium 1370mg; Total Carbohydrate 44g (Dietary Fiber 2g; Sugars 7g); Protein 23g
% Daily Value: Vitamin A 15%; Vitamin C 2%; Calcium 20%; Iron 20%
Exchanges: 2½ Starch, ½ Other Carbohydrate, 2 Medium-Fat Meat, 2 Fat
Carbohydrate Choices: 3

KITCHEN TIPS

● Serve with a salad of shredded lettuce and chopped tomatoes drizzled with ranch dressing, along with tall glasses of limeade.

Taco Beef Bake with Cheddar Biscuit Topping

Quick Tomato Pasta Sauce

Prep time: 25 min Start to finish: 25 min

1 pound lean (at least 80%) ground beef

1 medium onion, chopped ($\frac{1}{2}$ cup)

1 can (15 ounces) Italian-style tomato sauce

1 can (14.5 ounces) Italian-style stewed tomatoes, undrained

$\frac{1}{2}$ teaspoon salt

$\frac{1}{2}$ teaspoon garlic-pepper blend

1 tablespoon olive or vegetable oil

2 tablespoons chopped fresh basil leaves or parsley

1. In 12-inch nonstick skillet, cook beef and onion over medium-high heat 5 to 7 minutes, stirring frequently, until beef is brown; drain.

2. Stir remaining ingredients except basil into beef mixture. Heat to boiling. Simmer uncovered 5 to 10 minutes, stirring occasionally and breaking up tomatoes with spoon, until flavors are blended. Stir in basil.

4 servings (1 cup each)
1 Serving: Calories 290 (Calories from Fat 150); Total Fat 16g (Saturated Fat 5g); Cholesterol 70mg; Sodium 1140mg; Total Carbohydrate 15g (Dietary Fiber 3g; Sugars 8g); Protein 23g
% Daily Value: Vitamin A 25%; Vitamin C 25%; Calcium 8%; Iron 20%
Exchanges: $\frac{1}{2}$ Other Carbohydrate, 1 Vegetable, 3 Medium-Fat Meat
Carbohydrate Choices: 1

Macaroni Goulash

Prep time: 15 min Start to finish: 15 min

Quick Tomato Pasta Sauce (left) or 1 jar
(1 pound 10 ounces) tomato pasta sauce
with meat

1 cup water

1 cup uncooked elbow macaroni (4 ounces)

1 cup sliced fresh mushrooms (3 ounces)

1 medium green bell pepper, chopped (1 cup),
if desired

1/4 cup shredded Parmesan cheese, if desired

1. In 12-inch nonstick skillet, mix Quick Tomato Pasta
Sauce and water. Heat to boiling. Stir in macaroni,
mushrooms and bell pepper.

2. Cover and cook over medium-low heat 10 to 12
minutes, stirring frequently to keep macaroni from
sticking, until macaroni is tender. Sprinkle with
cheese.

4 servings (1 cup each)
1 Serving: Calories 430 (Calories from Fat 170); Total Fat 19g
(Saturated Fat 7g); Cholesterol 75mg; Sodium 1260mg; Total
Carbohydrate 38g (Dietary Fiber 5g; Sugars 8g); Protein 29g
% Daily Value: Vitamin A 25%; Vitamin C 25%; Calcium 15%; Iron 30%
Exchanges: 2 Starch, 1/2 Other Carbohydrate, 3 Medium-Fat Meat, 1/2 Fat
Carbohydrate Choices: 2

KITCHEN TIPS

● You can use all mushrooms or all bell peppers instead
of some of each, or omit one or both and add cooked
corn or sliced celery instead.

Macaroni Goulash

Macaroni and Cheese Casserole with Meatballs

Prep time: 20 min Start to finish: 55 min

8 ounces frozen cooked Italian-style meatballs (from 16-ounce bag), thawed

3 cups uncooked rotini pasta (8 ounces)

2¼ cups milk

1 package (1.8 ounces) white sauce mix

1 cup shredded Cheddar cheese (4 ounces)

1 cup shredded mozzarella cheese (4 ounces)

1 tablespoon butter or margarine, melted

3 tablespoons Progresso Italian-style bread crumbs

2 medium green onions, chopped (2 tablespoons)

1. Heat oven to 350°F. Spray 8-inch square (2-quart) glass baking dish with cooking spray. Cut any large meatballs in half. Cook and drain pasta as directed on package.

2. Meanwhile, in 2-quart saucepan, mix milk and sauce with wire whisk. Heat to boiling over medium heat, stirring constantly. Boil 1 minute, stirring constantly.

Stir in cheeses until melted. Stir in pasta and meatballs. Spoon into baking dish. In small bowl, mix butter, bread crumbs and onions; sprinkle over top.

3. Bake uncovered 30 to 35 minutes or until bubbly and top is golden brown.

4 servings (1½ cups each)
1 Serving: Calories 710 (Calories from Fat 280); Total Fat 31g (Saturated Fat 16g); Cholesterol 125mg; Sodium 1690mg; Total Carbohydrate 70g (Dietary Fiber 4g; Sugars 10g); Protein 40g
% Daily Value: Vitamin A 20%; Vitamin C 0%; Calcium 60%; Iron 30%
Exchanges: 4 Starch, ½ Other Carbohydrate, 4 Medium-Fat Meat, 2 Fat
Carbohydrate Choices: 4½

KITCHEN TIPS

● For a great go-with for this family-favorite casserole, pick up a bag of mixed greens, cut a tomato into wedges and toss with Italian dressing.

Macaroni and Cheese Casserole with Meatballs

Cowboy Casserole

Prep time: 15 min Start to finish: 45 min

1 pound lean (at least 80%) ground beef
1 can (16 ounces) baked beans
1/2 cup barbecue sauce
2 cups Original Bisquick mix
2/3 cup milk
1 tablespoon butter or margarine, softened
1/2 cup shredded Cheddar cheese (2 ounces)

1. Heat oven to 425°F. In 10-inch skillet, cook beef over medium-high heat 5 to 7 minutes, stirring occasionally, until brown; drain.

2. Stir baked beans and barbecue sauce into beef. Heat to boiling, stirring occasionally. Pour into ungreased 2-quart casserole.

3. Meanwhile, in medium bowl, stir Bisquick mix, milk and butter until soft dough forms. Drop dough by 12 spoonfuls onto beef mixture.

4. Bake uncovered 18 to 22 minutes or until topping is golden brown. Sprinkle with cheese. Bake about 3 minutes longer or until cheese is melted.

6 servings (1¼ cups each)
1 Serving: Calories 470 (Calories from Fat 180); Total Fat 20g (Saturated Fat 8g); Cholesterol 70mg; Sodium 1230mg; Total Carbohydrate 48g (Dietary Fiber 5g; Sugars 14g); Protein 23g
% Daily Value: Vitamin A 20%; Vitamin C 2%; Calcium 20%; Iron 30%
Exchanges: 2 Starch, 1 Other Carbohydrate, 2½ Medium-Fat Meat, 1 Fat
Carbohydrate Choices: 3

KITCHEN TIPS

- Swing by the deli to pick up coleslaw to serve with this hearty casserole, and add mugs of apple cider.
- Vanilla ice cream with gingersnaps is an easy dessert.

Cowboy Casserole

Creamy Beef Fold-Over Pie

Prep time: 15 min Start to finish: 55 min

1 pound lean (at least 80%) ground beef

1 small onion, chopped (¼ cup)

1 can (10¾ ounces) condensed cream of mushroom soup

1½ cups Green Giant frozen mixed vegetables (from 1-pound bag), thawed

1 tablespoon ketchup

2 cups Original Bisquick mix

½ cup boiling water

¼ cup shredded Cheddar cheese (1 ounce)

1. Move oven rack to lowest position. Heat oven to 375°F. Spray 12-inch pizza pan with cooking spray.

2. In 10-inch skillet, cook beef and onion over medium-high heat 5 to 7 minutes, stirring occasionally, until brown; drain. Stir in soup, vegetables and ketchup. Cook 3 to 4 minutes, stirring occasionally, until heated through.

3. In medium bowl, stir Bisquick mix and boiling water until soft dough forms. Place dough on surface sprinkled with Bisquick mix; gently roll in Bisquick mix to coat. Shape into a ball; knead about 5 minutes or until smooth. Roll dough into 14-inch circle; place on pizza pan.

4. Spoon beef mixture over dough to within 2 inches of edge. Fold edge of dough over beef mixture. Bake 24 to 27 minutes or until crust is golden brown. Top with cheese. Bake 3 to 4 minutes longer or until cheese is melted. Let stand 5 minutes before cutting.

6 servings
1 Serving: Calories 390 (Calories from Fat 170); Total Fat 19g (Saturated Fat 6g); Cholesterol 55mg; Sodium 1030mg; Total Carbohydrate 35g (Dietary Fiber 3g; Sugars 7g); Protein 19g
% Daily Value: Vitamin A 45%; Vitamin C 0%; Calcium 15%; Iron 20%
Exchanges: 2 Starch, ½ Other Carbohydrate, 2 Medium-Fat Meat, 1½ Fat
Carbohydrate Choices: 2

KITCHEN TIPS

- Serve wedges of this beefy pie with a fresh spinach salad and milk.
- Dessert is as simple as apple slices with caramel topping for dipping.

Philly Beef Squares

Prep time: 15 min Start to finish: 1 hr 5 min

1½ teaspoons dried minced onion
1 pound lean (at least 80%) ground beef
¾ cup cheese dip (from 15-ounce jar)
2 cups Original Bisquick mix
1 cup milk
1 egg
2 cups frozen bell pepper and onion stir-fry (from 1-pound bag), thawed, drained

1. Heat oven to 375°F. Spray 8-inch square pan or 2-quart glass baking dish with cooking spray. In small bowl, cover onion with hot water.

2. In 10-inch skillet, cook beef over medium-high heat 5 to 7 minutes, stirring occasionally, until brown; drain. Stir in cheese dip. Cook 2 to 3 minutes or until hot.

3. In medium bowl, mix Bisquick mix, milk and egg until blended. Pour half of the batter into pan. Top with beef mixture and bell pepper mixture. Pour remaining batter evenly over top. Drain onion; sprinkle over batter.

4. Bake 40 to 45 minutes or until golden brown and center is set. Let stand 5 minutes before cutting into squares. If desired, heat leftover cheese dip as directed on jar and spoon over each serving.

6 servings
1 Serving: Calories 390 (Calories from Fat 180); Total Fat 20g (Saturated Fat 8g); Cholesterol 95mg; Sodium 810mg; Total Carbohydrate 32g (Dietary Fiber 1g; Sugars 7g); Protein 21g
% Daily Value: Vitamin A 10%; Vitamin C 20%; Calcium 20%; Iron 15%
Exchanges: 1½ Starch, ½ Other Carbohydrate, 2½ Medium-Fat Meat, 1½ Fat
Carbohydrate Choices: 2

KITCHEN TIPS

- The rehydrated dried minced onion adds a toasty onion flavor to these sandwiches.

Philly Beef Squares

Spinach and Beef Enchiladas

Prep time: 25 min Start to finish: 1 hr 10 min

1 pound lean (at least 80%) ground beef

1 medium onion, chopped ($\frac{1}{2}$ cup)

1 box (9 ounces) Green Giant frozen spinach

1 can (4.5 ounces) Old El Paso chopped green chilies, undrained

$\frac{1}{2}$ teaspoon ground cumin

$\frac{1}{2}$ teaspoon garlic-pepper blend

$\frac{1}{2}$ cup sour cream

2 cups shredded Colby-Monterey Jack cheese blend (8 ounces)

1 can (10 ounces) Old El Paso enchilada sauce

1 package (11.5 ounces) Old El Paso flour tortillas (8 tortillas)

$\frac{1}{2}$ cup Old El Paso Thick 'n Chunky salsa

1. Heat oven to 350°F. Spray 13 × 9-inch (3-quart) glass baking dish with cooking spray. In 12-inch nonstick skillet, cook beef and onion over medium-high heat 5 to 7 minutes; stirring occasionally, until beef is brown.

2. Stir in spinach; cook, stirring frequently, until thawed. Stir in green chilies, cumin, garlic pepper, sour cream and 1 cup of the cheese.

3. Spread about 1 teaspoon enchilada sauce on each tortilla. Top each with about $\frac{1}{2}$ cup beef mixture. Roll up tortillas; place seam side down in baking dish. In small bowl, mix remaining enchilada sauce and the salsa; spoon over enchiladas. Sprinkle with remaining 1 cup cheese.

4. Spray sheet of foil with cooking spray; cover baking dish with foil. Bake 40 to 45 minutes or until thoroughly heated.

8 enchiladas

1 Enchilada: Calories 400 (Calories from Fat 200); Total Fat 23g (Saturated Fat 11g); Cholesterol 70mg; Sodium 860mg; Total Carbohydrate 28g (Dietary Fiber 0g; Sugars 3g); Protein 21g
% Daily Value: Vitamin A 45%; Vitamin C 6%; Calcium 35%; Iron 15%
Exchanges: 2 Starch, 2 High-Fat Meat, 1 Fat
Carbohydrate Choices: 2

Spinach and Beef Enchiladas

KITCHEN TIPS

● Serve these easy enchiladas with colorful toppings, such as chopped tomato, shredded lettuce, chopped green onions and sliced ripe olives.

● Don't care for spinach? Use 1 cup frozen corn or drained and rinsed canned pinto beans instead.

Beef and Creamy Potato Casserole

Prep time: 15 min Start to finish: 6 hr 15 min

1 pound lean (at least 80%) ground beef

1 can (10¾ ounces) condensed cream of mushroom soup

½ cup milk

¼ teaspoon pepper

1 can (2.8 ounces) French-fried onions

4 cups frozen country-style shredded hash brown potatoes (from 30-ounce bag)

2 cups Green Giant frozen cut green beans (from 1-pound bag)

1. In 10-inch skillet, cook beef over medium-high heat 5 to 7 minutes, stirring occasionally, until brown; drain. Stir in soup, milk, pepper and half of the onions.

2. Spray 3½- to 4-quart slow cooker with cooking spray. Layer potatoes and green beans in cooker. Top with beef mixture; spread evenly.

3. Cover; cook on Low heat setting 6 to 7 hours. Top with remaining onions before serving.

4 servings
1 Serving: Calories 600 (Calories from Fat 250); Total Fat 28g (Saturated Fat 9g; Trans Fat 3.5g); Cholesterol 75mg; Sodium 820mg; Total Carbohydrate 60g (Dietary Fiber 6g; Sugars 6g); Protein 27g % Daily Value: Vitamin A 10%; Vitamin C 15%; Calcium 15%; Iron 20% Exchanges: 3½ Starch, 1 Vegetable, 2 Medium-Fat Meat, 3 Fat Carbohydrate Choices: 4

KITCHEN TIPS

• If you prefer, use cream of chicken or cream of celery soup instead of the cream of mushroom.

Beef and Creamy Potato Casserole

Herb-Rubbed Rib Roast

Prep time: 15 min Start to finish: 3 hr 20 min

Roast

4-	pound beef rib roast
1	clove garlic, cut in half
¼	cup country-style Dijon mustard
¾	cup chopped fresh parsley
1½	tablespoons chopped fresh or 1½ teaspoons dried thyme leaves
1½	tablespoons chopped fresh or 1½ teaspoons dried rosemary leaves
2	cloves garlic, finely chopped
1	tablespoon olive or vegetable oil

Sauce

1	cup reduced-fat or regular sour cream
1	tablespoon plus 1 teaspoon horseradish sauce
1	tablespoon plus 1 teaspoon country-style Dijon mustard
¼	teaspoon coarse ground black pepper

Herb-Rubbed Rib Roast

1. Heat oven to 350°F. On rack in shallow roasting pan, place beef, fat side up. Rub garlic halves over beef. Spread mustard over top and sides of beef. In small bowl, mix parsley, thyme, rosemary and chopped garlic; stir in oil. Spread herb mixture over top and sides of beef. Insert ovenproof meat thermometer so tip is in center of thickest part of beef and does not touch bone.

2. Roast uncovered 2 hours 15 minutes to 2 hours 45 minutes. Meanwhile, in small bowl, mix all sauce ingredients. Cover and refrigerate at least 1 hour to blend flavors.

3. Remove beef from oven when thermometer reads 150°F. Cover beef loosely with foil and let stand 15 to 20 minutes or until thermometer reads 160°F. (Temperature will continue to rise about 10°F, and beef will be easier to carve.) Serve beef with sauce.

8 servings (with 2 tablespoons sauce each)
1 Serving: Calories 320 (Calories from Fat 190); Total Fat 21g (Saturated Fat 8g); Cholesterol 95mg; Sodium 340mg; Total Carbohydrate 3g (Dietary Fiber 0g; Sugars 1g); Protein 29g
% Daily Value: Vitamin A 15%; Vitamin C 8%; Calcium 6%; Iron 20%
Exchanges: 4 Lean Meat, 2 Fat
Carbohydrate Choices: 0

KITCHEN TIPS

- For the best flavor, be sure to use plain prepared horseradish sauce, not the creamy style.
- Tender, rich rib roasts are best when cut into ½-inch-thick slices.

Peppered Beef Tenderloin with Mushroom Sauce

Prep time: 25 min Start to finish: 1 hr 30 min

4- to 4½- pound beef tenderloin roast
2 tablespoons olive or vegetable oil
2 teaspoons coarse ground black pepper
¼ cup butter or margarine
1 medium onion, finely chopped (½ cup)
1 clove garlic, finely chopped
1 package (8 ounces) sliced fresh mushrooms (3 cups)
2 tablespoons dry sherry, if desired
1 tablespoon cornstarch
¼ cup cold water
2 teaspoons chopped fresh or ½ teaspoon dried thyme leaves
⅛ teaspoon pepper
1 can (10½ ounces) condensed beef consommé
1 teaspoon Dijon mustard
1 teaspoon tomato paste (from 6-ounce can)

Peppered Beef Tenderloin with Mushroom Sauce

1. Heat oven to 425°F. Rub beef with oil; sprinkle with pepper. Place beef on rack in shallow roasting pan or place diagonally in 15 × 10 × 1-inch pan. Insert ovenproof meat thermometer so tip is in center of thickest part of beef.

2. Bake uncovered 30 to 45 minutes or until thermometer reads 135°F. Cover beef loosely with tent of foil and let stand 15 to 20 minutes until thermometer reads 145°F (medium-rare doneness). (Temperature will continue to rise about 10°F and beef will be easier to carve.)

3. Meanwhile, in 12-inch nonstick skillet, melt butter over medium heat. Cook onion, garlic and mushrooms in butter 8 to 10 minutes, stirring occasionally, until mushrooms are completely tender and beginning to brown. Stir in sherry. In small bowl, mix cornstarch and water; stir cornstarch mixture into mushroom mixture. Stir in thyme, pepper and beef consommé; cook and stir about 2 minutes or until slightly thickened and bubbly. Stir in mustard and tomato paste until well blended. Heat just until hot. Spoon sauce over sliced beef.

12 servings (with ¼ cup sauce each)
1 Serving: Calories 270 (Calories from Fat 140); Total Fat 15g (Saturated Fat 6g); Cholesterol 85mg; Sodium 240mg; Total Carbohydrate 3g (Dietary Fiber 0g; Sugars 0g); Protein 30g
% Daily Value: Vitamin A 6%; Vitamin C 0%; Calcium 0%; Iron 15%
Exchanges: 4½ Lean Meat, ½ Fat
Carbohydrate Choices: 0

KITCHEN TIPS

- Make the sauce up to a day ahead, then cover and refrigerate. Stir sauce; cover and microwave on High 1 minute or until hot. Stir again.
- Drop leftover tomato paste by tablespoonfuls onto a cookie sheet lined with plastic wrap, then freeze. Store in a freezer bag for future use.

Low Fat
Beef Roast with Onions and Potatoes

Prep time: 15 min Start to finish: 9 hr 30 min

1 large sweet onion, cut in half, then cut into thin slices

3- pound boneless beef bottom round roast

3 baking potatoes, cut into 1½- to 2-inch cubes

2 cloves garlic, finely chopped

1 can (14 ounces) beef broth

1 package (1 ounce) onion soup mix (from 2-ounce box)

¼ cup Gold Medal all-purpose flour

1. Place onion in 5- to 6-quart slow cooker. If beef roast comes in netting or is tied, remove netting or strings. Place beef on onion. Place potatoes and garlic around beef. In small bowl, mix 1¼ cups of the broth and the dry soup mix; pour over beef. (Refrigerate remaining broth.)

2. Cover; cook on Low heat setting 9 to 10 hours.

3. Remove beef and vegetables from cooker; place on serving platter. Cover to keep warm.

4. In small bowl, mix remaining ½ cup broth and the flour; gradually stir into juices in cooker. Increase heat setting to High. Cover; cook about 15 minutes, stirring occasionally, until sauce has thickened. Serve sauce over beef and vegetables.

6 servings
1 Serving: Calories 350 (Calories from Fat 70); Total Fat 7g (Saturated Fat 2.5g; Trans Fat 0g); Cholesterol 120mg; Sodium 800mg; Total Carbohydrate 23g (Dietary Fiber 2g; Sugars 4g); Protein 49g
% Daily Value: Vitamin A 4%; Vitamin C 8%; Calcium 4%; Iron 30%
Exchanges: 1½ Starch, 6½ Very Lean Meat, ½ Fat
Carbohydrate Choices: 1½

KITCHEN TIPS

- Warm frozen dinner rolls while the juices are thickening in the slow cooker. Cook frozen broccoli in the microwave, and the meal is ready in minutes.

- To save precious time in the morning, cut the onion and chop the garlic the night before and refrigerate.

Beef Roast with Onions and Potatoes

Strip Steaks with Balsamic Onions

Simple Teriyaki Steak Dinner

Quick
Strip Steaks
with Balsamic Onions

Prep time: 30 min Start to finish: 30 min

 1   medium red onion, thinly sliced
 1/4 cup balsamic vinaigrette dressing
 1   cup sliced fresh mushrooms
 4   boneless beef top loin (New York strip) steaks, about 1/2 inch thick (6 ounces each)
 1/2 teaspoon salt
 1/2 teaspoon chili powder
 1/2 teaspoon garlic-pepper blend
 1/4 teaspoon ground cumin

1. Heat closed medium-size contact grill for 5 minutes. In medium bowl, toss onion with dressing. Remove onion from dressing with tongs; place on grill. Reserve dressing in bowl. Close grill. Grill 4 minutes.

2. Meanwhile, toss mushrooms with dressing in bowl. Add mushrooms to grill with onions. Close grill. Grill 2 to 4 minutes or until vegetables are tender. Remove vegetables from grill; cover to keep warm.

3. Brush beef steaks with remaining dressing in bowl. Sprinkle both sides of steaks with salt, chili powder, garlic pepper and cumin. Place on grill. Close grill; grill 3 to 5 minutes or until desired doneness. Serve onions and mushrooms with steaks.

4 servings
1 Serving: Calories 330 (Calories from Fat 170); Total Fat 19g (Saturated Fat 6g); Cholesterol 95mg; Sodium 540mg; Total Carbohydrate 4g (Dietary Fiber 0g); Protein 37g
% Daily Value: Vitamin A 6%; Vitamin C 2%; Calcium 2%; Iron 20%
Exchanges: 1 Vegetable, 5 Lean Meat, 1 Fat
Carbohydrate Choices: 0

KITCHEN TIPS

- You can substitute Italian dressing for the balsamic vinaigrette if you like.
- All this juicy steak with its savory topping needs is a Caesar salad and twice-baked potatoes from the deli.

Quick & Low Fat
Simple Teriyaki
Steak Dinner

Prep time: 20 min Start to finish: 20 min

 1   tablespoon butter or margarine
 1   medium bell pepper (any color), coarsely chopped (1 cup)
 1 1/2 cups sliced fresh mushrooms (about 5 ounces)
 4   boneless beef strip steaks, about 3/4 inch thick (6 ounces each)
 1/2 teaspoon garlic salt
 1/4 teaspoon coarse ground pepper
 1/4 cup teriyaki baste and glaze (from 12-ounce bottle)
 2   tablespoons water

1. In 12-inch nonstick skillet, melt butter over medium-high heat. Cook bell pepper in butter 2 minutes, stirring frequently. Stir in mushrooms. Cook 2 to 3 minutes, stirring frequently, until vegetables are tender. Remove vegetable mixture from skillet; cover to keep warm.

2. Sprinkle beef steaks with garlic salt and pepper. In same skillet, cook steaks over medium heat 6 to 8 minutes, turning once or twice, until desired doneness.

3. Return vegetables to skillet. Stir teriyaki glaze and water into vegetables and spoon over steaks. Cook about 1 minute, stirring vegetables occasionally, until thoroughly heated.

4 servings
1 Serving: Calories 250 (Calories from Fat 70); Total Fat 8g (Saturated Fat 3.5g); Cholesterol 100mg; Sodium 610mg; Total Carbohydrate 9g (Dietary Fiber 0g; Sugars 6g); Protein 36g
% Daily Value: Vitamin A 6%; Vitamin C 30%; Calcium 4%; Iron 25%
Exchanges: 1/2 Other Carbohydrate, 5 Very Lean Meat, 1 Fat
Carbohydrate Choices: 1/2

KITCHEN TIPS

- Mix up some Betty Crocker roasted garlic mashed potatoes to serve with the steaks.

Low-Fat

Balsamic and Roasted Garlic–Marinated Steak

Prep time: 30 min Start to finish: 8 hr 30 min

$\frac{1}{2}$ cup balsamic vinegar

$\frac{1}{4}$ cup chili sauce

2 tablespoons packed brown sugar

2 tablespoons olive or vegetable oil

2 teaspoons chopped roasted garlic (from 4-ounce jar)

$\frac{1}{2}$ teaspoon Italian seasoning

$\frac{1}{4}$ teaspoon salt

$\frac{1}{4}$ teaspoon coarse ground pepper

1$\frac{1}{2}$ pounds boneless beef top round steak, 1 to 1$\frac{1}{2}$ inches thick

1. In shallow glass dish or resealable plastic food-storage bag, mix all ingredients except beef. Add beef; turn to coat. Cover dish or seal bag. Refrigerate at least 8 hours or overnight, turning beef occasionally.

2. Heat coals or gas grill for direct heat. Remove beef from marinade; reserve marinade.

3. Cover and grill beef over medium heat 12 to 18 minutes, turning and brushing with marinade once or twice, until desired doneness. Discard any remaining marinade. To serve, cut beef across grain into slices.

6 servings
1 Serving: Calories 140 (Calories from Fat 40); Total Fat 4.5g (Saturated Fat 1.5g); Cholesterol 60mg; Sodium 105mg; Total Carbohydrate 2g (Dietary Fiber 0g); Protein 23g
% Daily Value: Vitamin A 0%; Vitamin C 0%; Calcium 0%; Iron 10%
Exchanges: 3 Very Lean Meat, $\frac{1}{2}$ Fat
Carbohydrate Choices: 0

Balsamic and Roasted Garlic–Marinated Steak

KITCHEN TIPS

● Make sure the grill is hot before adding the steak. A hot grill quickly sears the outside of the steak, sealing it so the meat stays juicy and tender.

● Two great grilled side dishes round out this steak dinner: Parmesan Broccoli (page 202) and Roasted Red Potatoes (page 213).

Quick & Low-Fat
Peppered Beef with Pasta

Prep time: 30 min Start to finish: 30 min

1²⁄₃ cups uncooked farfalle (bow-tie) pasta or 2 ounces uncooked soba (buckwheat) noodles

½ pound boneless beef sirloin steak, about ½ inch thick, cut into 2 pieces

½ teaspoon coarse ground pepper

3 tablespoons tomato sauce

1 tablespoon red wine vinegar

1 teaspoon chopped fresh or ½ teaspoon dried thyme leaves

¼ teaspoon sugar

1 small onion, chopped (¼ cup)

1 medium bell pepper, chopped (¾ cup)

1. Cook and drain pasta as directed on package, omitting salt.

2. Meanwhile, rub both sides of beef pieces with ground pepper. Heat 10-inch nonstick skillet over medium heat. Cook beef in skillet 8 to 12 minutes, turning once, until almost done.

3. Add remaining ingredients except pasta to skillet. Reduce heat to medium-low. Cook uncovered about 5 minutes or until beef is medium doneness (160°F). Mix vegetables with pasta; top with beef.

2 servings
1 Serving: Calories 550 (Calories from Fat 50); Total Fat 6g (Saturated Fat 1.5g); Cholesterol 60mg; Sodium 190mg; Total Carbohydrate 92g (Dietary Fiber 8g; Sugars 5g); Protein 38g
% Daily Value: Vitamin A 10%; Vitamin C 45%; Calcium 4%; Iron 40%
Exchanges: 5½ Starch, 1 Vegetable, 2½ Very Lean Meat
Carbohydrate Choices: 5½

KITCHEN TIPS

● Add a sprinkle of sliced green onion for a finishing touch.

Peppered Beef with Pasta

Beef Main Dishes   193

Quick

Cheesy Steak and Potato Skillet

Prep time: 30 min Start to finish: 30 min

1 pound boneless beef sirloin steak, cut into 4 serving pieces

¾ teaspoon seasoned salt

½ teaspoon garlic-pepper blend

2 tablespoons butter or margarine

1½ cups frozen bell pepper and onion stir-fry (from 1-pound bag)

1 bag (1 pound 4 ounces) refrigerated home-style potato slices

1 cup shredded American-Cheddar cheese blend (4 ounces)

1. Sprinkle beef pieces with ¼ teaspoon of the seasoned salt and ¼ teaspoon of the garlic pepper. In 12-inch nonstick skillet, cook beef over medium-high heat 3 to 4 minutes, turning once or twice, until brown and desired doneness. Remove from skillet; keep warm.

2. In same skillet, melt butter over medium heat. Cook stir-fry vegetables in butter 2 minutes, stirring frequently. Add potatoes; sprinkle with remaining ½ teaspoon seasoned salt and ¼ teaspoon garlic pepper. Cook uncovered 8 to 10 minutes, stirring frequently, until tender.

3. Place beef in skillet with potatoes, pushing potatoes around beef. Cook 1 to 2 minutes, turning beef once, until thoroughly heated. Sprinkle with cheese; cover and heat until cheese is melted.

4 servings
1 Serving: Calories 420 (Calories from Fat 170); Total Fat 19g (Saturated Fat 10g); Cholesterol 105mg; Sodium 980mg; Total Carbohydrate 30g (Dietary Fiber 4g;Sugars 3g); Protein 32g
% Daily Value: Vitamin A 15%; Vitamin C 30%; Calcium 20%; Iron 25%
Exchanges: 2 Starch, 3½ Lean Meat, 1½ Fat
Carbohydrate Choices: 2

KITCHEN TIPS

● To substitute for the frozen bell pepper mixture, use about ¾ cup each coarsely chopped bell pepper and onion.

Cheesy Steak and Potato Skillet

Quick & Low-Fat
Greek-Style Steak

Prep time: 15 min Start to finish: 15 min

- ½ pound boneless beef top sirloin steak, cut into 2 pieces
- 1 teaspoon finely chopped garlic
- ¼ teaspoon lemon-pepper seasoning
- ¼ cup lightly packed chopped fresh spinach leaves
- ¼ cup crumbled feta cheese (1 ounce)
- 1 tablespoon chopped ripe olives

1. Heat gas or charcoal grill. Rub both sides of each piece of beef with garlic; sprinkle with lemon-pepper seasoning.

2. Cover and grill beef over medium heat 9 to 11 minutes, turning once, until beef is desired doneness.

3. In small bowl, mix remaining ingredients. Spoon over beef.

2 servings
1 Serving: Calories 180 (Calories from Fat 70); Total Fat 8g (Saturated Fat 4g); Cholesterol 75mg; Sodium 340mg; Total Carbohydrate 2g (Dietary Fiber 0g; Sugars 0g); Protein 26g
% Daily Value: Vitamin A 10%; Vitamin C 0%; Calcium 10%; Iron 15%
Exchanges: 3½ Lean Meat
Carbohydrate Choices: 0

KITCHEN TIPS

- For a more authentic Greek topping, use pitted and chopped Kalamata olives in place of the ripe olives.
- Serve with sliced fresh tomatoes, ripe from the farmers' market or your garden.

Greek-Style Steak

Quick & Low-Fat
Quick Beef Tips and Vegetables
Prep time: 15 min Start to finish: 15 min

¼ pound boneless beef sirloin tip steak, cut into ½-inch cubes

½ bag (1-pound size) frozen stir-fry vegetables with snap pea pods

2 teaspoons water

1 tablespoon stir-fry sauce with garlic and ginger

½ cup uncooked instant white rice

½ cup water

1. Heat 10-inch nonstick skillet over medium-high heat. Cook beef in skillet about 2 minutes, stirring frequently, until brown. Stir in vegetables and 2 teaspoons water. Cook 1 minute, stirring frequently.

2. Stir in stir-fry sauce until well mixed; reduce heat to medium. Cover and cook 2 to 3 minutes, stirring frequently, until vegetables are crisp-tender.

3. Meanwhile, cook rice in water as directed on package. Serve beef mixture over rice.

2 servings
1 Serving: Calories 210 (Calories from Fat 20); Total Fat 2g (Saturated Fat 0.5g); Cholesterol 30mg; Sodium 640mg; Total Carbohydrate 34g (Dietary Fiber 3g; Sugars 2g); Protein 15g
% Daily Value: Vitamin A 35%; Vitamin C 34%; Calcium 4%; Iron 15%
Exchanges: 2 Starch, 1 Vegetable, 2 Very Lean Meat
Carbohydrate Choices: 2

KITCHEN TIPS

● Buy a variety of fresh produce at your local farmers' market to use instead of frozen vegetables. Use a total of 8 ounces for this recipe.

Quick Beef Tips and Vegetables

Bourbon-Glazed Beef Kabobs

Prep time: 25 min Start to finish: 25 min

Glaze

- 2 tablespoons bourbon or water
- 1 tablespoon teriyaki baste and glaze (from 12-ounce bottle)
- 1 tablespoon frozen (thawed) orange juice concentrate
- ¼ cup packed brown sugar
  Dash of crushed red pepper flakes

Kabobs

- ½ pound boneless beef top sirloin steak, cut into 1½-inch cubes
- 8 pieces (1½ inch) red onion
- 8 fresh whole mushrooms
- 8 pieces (1½ inch) red bell pepper
- 1 teaspoon olive or vegetable oil
- ¼ teaspoon salt

1. Heat gas or charcoal grill. In 1-quart saucepan, mix 1 tablespoon of the bourbon, the teriyaki glaze, orange juice concentrate, brown sugar and crushed red pepper. Heat to boiling over medium heat; reduce heat to low. Simmer 5 minutes, stirring occasionally; remove from heat. Stir in remaining 1 tablespoon bourbon. Reserve 2 tablespoons glaze.

2. In medium bowl, place beef, onion, mushrooms and bell pepper. Drizzle with oil; toss to coat. Sprinkle with salt; toss to coat. On each of two 10- to 12-inch metal skewers, thread beef, onion, mushrooms and bell pepper alternately, leaving ¼-inch space between pieces.

3. Cover and grill kabobs over medium heat 9 to 11 minutes, turning once and brushing with glaze during last 3 minutes, until beef is desired doneness and vegetables are tender.

4. Just before serving, generously brush kabobs with reserved 2 tablespoons glaze.

Bourbon-Glazed Beef Kabobs

2 servings
1 Serving: Calories 350 (Calories from Fat 60); Total Fat 6g (Saturated Fat 1.5g); Cholesterol 60mg; Sodium 560mg; Total Carbohydrate 50g (Dietary Fiber 4g; Sugars 43g); Protein 27g
% Daily Value: Vitamin A 70%; Vitamin C 110%; Calcium 8%; Iron 25%
Exchanges: 2½ Other Carbohydrate, 2 Vegetable, 3½ Very Lean Meat, ½ Fat
Carbohydrate Choices: 3

KITCHEN TIPS

- Add more color to these kabobs by using a variety of colored bell peppers, including red, green, yellow and orange.
- The perfect accompaniment for these kabobs is hot cooked rice.

Side Items

Delicious Additions to Any Menu

Warm Caramelized Vegetables (page 209)

Make-Ahead Sour Cream 'n Chive Mashed Potatoes (page 216)

Maple- and Pecan-Topped Butternut Squash

Prep time: 1 hr 5 min Start to finish: 1 hr 5 min

  2   small butternut squash (1½ pounds each)
 ¼   teaspoon salt
  2   tablespoons butter or margarine, melted
  2   teaspoons grated orange peel
  4   tablespoons pure maple syrup
 ¼   cup chopped pecans

1. Heat coals or gas grill for direct heat. Cut four 18 × 12-inch pieces of heavy-duty foil. Cut each squash lengthwise in half; remove seeds. Place squash half, cut side up, on each piece of foil. Sprinkle with salt.

2. In small bowl, mix butter, orange peel and 2 tablespoons of the maple syrup. Brush over squash halves. Fold foil over squash so edges meet. Seal edges, making tight ½-inch fold; fold again. Allow space on sides for circulation and expansion.

3. Cover and grill packets over medium-low heat 50 to 60 minutes, rotating packets ½ turn after 25 minutes, until squash is tender. Place packets on plates. Cut large X across top of each packet; fold back foil. Sprinkle pecans over squash; drizzle with remaining 2 tablespoons maple syrup.

4 servings
1 Serving: Calories 260 (Calories from Fat 100); Total Fat 11g (Saturated Fat 3.5g); Cholesterol 15mg; Sodium 200mg; Total Carbohydrate 41g (Dietary Fiber 4g); Protein 3g
% Daily Value: Vitamin A 440%; Vitamin C 30%; Calcium 10%; Iron 10%
Exchanges: 1 Starch, 1½ Other Carbohydrate, 2 Fat
Carbohydrate Choices: 3

KITCHEN TIPS

● Winter squash, such as butternut, are excellent sources of beta-carotene and potassium.

Maple- and Pecan-Topped Butternut Squash

Roasted Butternut Squash Combo

Prep time: 15 min Start to finish: 45 min

1 medium butternut squash, peeled, seeded and cut into 1-inch chunks (about 4 cups)

1 medium red or green bell pepper, cut into 16 pieces

2 tablespoons olive or vegetable oil

1/2 teaspoon seasoned salt

1/2 teaspoon dried basil leaves

1/4 teaspoon coarse ground pepper

1/4 teaspoon garlic powder

1. Heat oven to 425°F. Spray 13 × 9-inch pan with cooking spray. In large bowl, mix all ingredients until squash and bell pepper are coated. Spread in pan.

2. Roast uncovered 25 to 30 minutes, stirring once, until squash is tender.

8 servings (1/2 cup each)
1 Serving: Calories 60 (Calories from Fat 30); Total Fat 3.5g (Saturated Fat 0g); Cholesterol 0mg; Sodium 90mg; Total Carbohydrate 7g (Dietary Fiber 1g; Sugars 3g); Protein 0g
% Daily Value: Vitamin A 120%; Vitamin C 30%; Calcium 2%; Iron 2%
Exchanges: 1/2 Starch, 1/2 Fat
Carbohydrate Choices: 1/2

KITCHEN TIPS

● Butternut squash is shaped like a peanut. It's a great source of vitamins A and C.

Roasted Butternut Squash Combo

Quick
Asparagus with Maple-Mustard Sauce

Prep time: 10 min Start to finish: 10 min

- 2 pounds asparagus
- 2 tablespoons real maple or maple-flavored syrup
- 2 tablespoons Dijon mustard
- 2 tablespoons olive or vegetable oil

1. Snap off tough ends of asparagus spears. In 12-inch skillet or 4-quart Dutch oven, heat 1 inch water to boiling. Add asparagus. Heat to boiling; reduce heat to medium. Cover and cook 4 to 5 minutes or until asparagus is crisp-tender; drain.

2. In small bowl, mix maple syrup, mustard and oil. Drizzle over asparagus.

8 servings
1 Serving: Calories 70 (Calories from Fat 35); Total Fat 4g (Saturated Fat 0.5g); Cholesterol 0mg; Sodium 95mg; Total Carbohydrate 6g (Dietary Fiber 0g); Protein 2g
% Daily Value: Vitamin A 10%; Vitamin C 10%; Calcium 0%; Iron 2%
Exchanges: $^1/_2$ Vegetable, 1 Fat
Carbohydrate Choices: $^1/_2$

KITCHEN TIPS

- Honey can be used instead of the maple syrup.

Quick
Parmesan Broccoli

Prep time: 25 min Start to finish: 25 min

- 2 tablespoons butter or margarine
- $^1/_2$ cup thinly sliced red onion
- 4 cups fresh broccoli florets
- 2 tablespoons water
- $^1/_2$ teaspoon peppered seasoned salt
- $^1/_4$ teaspoon Italian seasoning
- $^1/_4$ cup shredded Parmesan cheese

1. In 12-inch nonstick skillet, melt butter over medium heat. Cook onion in butter 2 minutes, stirring occasionally.

2. Add broccoli and water. Cover; cook 6 to 8 minutes, stirring occasionally, until broccoli is crisp-tender and water has evaporated.

3. Sprinkle with peppered seasoned salt and Italian seasoning; toss to mix. Sprinkle with cheese.

6 servings ($^1/_2$ cup each)
1 Serving: Calories 70 (Calories from Fat 45); Total Fat 5g (Saturated Fat 2.5g); Cholesterol 15mg; Sodium 230mg; Total Carbohydrate 4g (Dietary Fiber 2g; Sugars 1g); Protein 3g
% Daily Value: Vitamin A 15%; Vitamin C 35%; Calcium 8%; Iron 2%
Exchanges: 1 Vegetable, $^1/_2$ Fat
Carbohydrate Choices: 0

KITCHEN TIPS

- Choose broccoli that is firm and looks fresh. Keep it tightly wrapped in the refrigerator for up to 3 days after purchasing.
- Green Giant Select frozen broccoli florets, thawed, can be substituted for fresh florets.

Asparagus with Maple-Mustard Sauce

Parmesan Broccoli

Classic Baked Corn Pudding

Prep time: 20 min Start to finish: 1 hr 35 min

1/2 cup butter or margarine

1 small onion, chopped (1/4 cup)

1/2 cup Gold Medal all-purpose flour

1/2 teaspoon salt

1/2 teaspoon pepper

4 cups milk (1 quart)

6 eggs, slightly beaten

2 cups shredded Cheddar cheese (8 ounces)

2 bags (1 pound each) Green Giant Niblets frozen whole kernel corn, thawed

1/2 cup chopped fresh parsley or 2 tablespoons parsley flakes

3/4 cup Progresso plain dry bread crumbs

3 tablespoons butter or margarine, melted

1. Heat oven to 350°F. Spray 13 x 9-inch glass baking dish or 3-quart casserole with cooking spray.

2. In 4-quart Dutch oven, melt 1/2 cup butter over medium heat. Cook onion in butter 3 to 4 minutes, stirring frequently, until tender. Stir in flour, salt and pepper until well blended. Stir in milk. Cook 4 to 5 minutes, stirring constantly, until thickened. Gradually stir in eggs and cheese. Stir in corn and parsley. Pour into baking dish.

3. In small bowl, mix bread crumbs and 3 tablespoons melted butter; sprinkle over corn mixture. Bake uncovered 55 to 65 minutes or until mixture is set and knife inserted in center comes out clean. Let stand 5 to 10 minutes before serving.

16 servings (1/2 cup each)
1 Serving: Calories 270 (Calories from Fat 150); Total Fat 16g (Saturated Fat 8g); Cholesterol 120mg; Sodium 310mg; Total Carbohydrate 21g (Dietary Fiber 2g; Sugars 5g); Protein 11g
% Daily Value: Vitamin A 20%; Vitamin C 4%; Calcium 15%; Iron 6%
Exchanges: 1 1/2 Starch, 1 High-Fat Meat, 1 1/2 Fat
Carbohydrate Choices: 1 1/2

KITCHEN TIPS

- You can use three 15.25-ounce cans of Green Giant whole kernel corn, drained, instead of the frozen corn.
- For a change of flavor, add 1/2 teaspoon dried basil leaves with the parsley.

Classic Baked Corn Pudding

Cilantro Grilled Corn

Prep time: 15 min Start to finish: 15 min

1 teaspoon finely chopped garlic

2 teaspoons finely chopped fresh cilantro

¼ teaspoon salt

Butter-flavored cooking spray

2 ears corn, husked

2 servings
1 Serving: Calories 120 (Calories from Fat 20); Total Fat 2g (Saturated Fat 0g); Cholesterol 0mg; Sodium 310mg; Total Carbohydrate 26g (Dietary Fiber 4g; Sugars 3g); Protein 3g
% Daily Value: Vitamin A 4%; Vitamin C 6%; Calcium 0%; Iron 4%
Exchanges: 1½ Starch
Carbohydrate Choices: 2

1. Heat gas or charcoal grill. In small bowl, mix garlic, cilantro and salt.

2. Cut two 12-inch square pieces of heavy-duty foil. Spray each ear of corn generously with cooking spray. Spread garlic mixture over each ear of corn. Wrap each ear of corn in foil piece, sealing edges. Allow space for circulation and expansion.

3. Cover and grill corn over medium heat 10 to 12 minutes, turning occasionally, until tender.

KITCHEN TIPS

- Use your fingers to spread the garlic mixture on the corn. It may be a little messy, but it's an easy way to evenly spread the mixture over the corn.

Cilantro Grilled Corn

Roasted Vegetables with Basil

Roasted Vegetables with Basil

Prep time: 20 min Start to finish: 1 hr 20 min

3 cups ready-to-eat baby-cut carrots, cut in half lengthwise

2 medium red bell peppers, coarsely chopped (2 cups)

1 cup Green Giant Niblets frozen whole kernel corn (from 1-pound bag)

$1/2$ cup zesty Italian dressing

1 bag (14 ounces) Green Giant Select frozen whole green beans

2 medium green onions, sliced (2 tablespoons)

$1/4$ cup shredded fresh basil leaves

1. Heat oven to 450°F. Spray 15 × 10 × 1-inch pan with cooking spray. In large bowl, mix carrots, bell peppers, corn and dressing. Spread in pan. Roast uncovered 30 minutes.

2. Add frozen green beans to vegetable mixture in pan; stir to mix.

3. Roast uncovered 25 to 30 minutes longer or until vegetables are crisp-tender. Sprinkle with onions and basil; stir gently to mix.

12 servings ($1/2$ cup each)
1 Serving: Calories 90 (Calories from Fat 40); Total Fat 4.5g (Saturated Fat 0g); Cholesterol 0mg; Sodium 105mg; Total Carbohydrate 10g (Dietary Fiber 3g; Sugars 5g); Protein 2g
% Daily Value: Vitamin A 150%; Vitamin C 45%; Calcium 4%; Iron 4%
Exchanges: 1 Vegetable, 1 Fat
Carbohydrate Choices: $1/2$

KITCHEN TIPS

- Serve the vegetables on a pretty platter and garnish with fresh basil sprigs.
- To reduce fat and calories a bit, use reduced-fat Italian dressing.

Quick
Peas and Corn with Thyme Butter

Prep time: 20 min Start to finish: 20 min

3   slices bacon, cut into ¹/₂-inch pieces

2   cups Green Giant Select LeSueur frozen baby sweet peas (from 1-pound bag)

2   cups Green Giant Niblets frozen extra-sweet whole kernel corn (from 1-pound bag)

2   tablespoons water

¹/₄   teaspoon salt

¹/₄ to ¹/₂   teaspoon dried thyme leaves

2   tablespoons butter or margarine

1. In 12-inch nonstick skillet, cook bacon over medium heat, stirring frequently, until crisp. Remove bacon from skillet; drain on paper towel. Reserve 1 tablespoon drippings in skillet; discard any remaining drippings.

2. Add peas, corn and water to skillet. Cover and cook over medium heat 6 to 8 minutes, stirring occasionally, until vegetables are tender and water has evaporated.

3. Stir in salt, thyme and butter until vegetables are coated. Spoon into serving bowl. Sprinkle with bacon.

6 servings (¹/₂ cup each)
1 Serving: Calories 160 (Calories from Fat 70); Total Fat 8g (Saturated Fat 3.5g); Cholesterol 15mg; Sodium 220mg; Total Carbohydrate 16g (Dietary Fiber 3g; Sugars 4g); Protein 5g
% Daily Value: Vitamin A 10%; Vitamin C 4%; Calcium 0%; Iron 6%
Exchanges: 1 Starch, 1¹/₂ Fat
Carbohydrate Choices: 1

KITCHEN TIPS

- If you have fresh thyme, use 1 to 2 teaspoons of it instead of dried thyme.
- The vegetable combination in this recipe is great, but you could make it with all peas or all corn.

Peas and Corn with Thyme Butter

Quick

Warm Caramelized Vegetables

Prep time: 30 min Start to finish: 30 min

2 pounds small red potatoes, cut into 1-inch pieces

$\frac{1}{2}$ teaspoon salt

1 pound asparagus, cut into 2-inch pieces

$\frac{1}{3}$ cup butter or margarine

1 large onion, chopped (1 cup)

$\frac{1}{4}$ cup balsamic vinegar

$\frac{1}{4}$ cup packed brown sugar

$\frac{1}{4}$ teaspoon salt

Freshly ground pepper, if desired

1. In 3-quart saucepan, heat 1 inch water to boiling. Add potatoes and $\frac{1}{2}$ teaspoon salt. Heat to boiling; reduce heat to medium. Cover and cook about 12 minutes or until tender; drain and return to saucepan.

2. Meanwhile, in 2-quart saucepan, heat 1 inch water to boiling. Add asparagus. Heat to boiling; reduce heat to medium. Cover and cook about 5 minutes or until crisp-tender; drain and add to potatoes.

3. While vegetables are cooking, in 10-inch skillet, melt butter over medium-high heat. Cook onion in butter about 5 minutes, stirring occasionally, until golden brown. Stir in vinegar, brown sugar and $\frac{1}{4}$ teaspoon salt. Pour onion mixture over potatoes and asparagus; stir until coated. Sprinkle with pepper.

6 servings
1 Serving: Calories 260 (Calories from Fat 100); Total Fat 11g (Saturated Fat 5g); Cholesterol 25mg; Sodium 380mg; Total Carbohydrate 39g (Dietary Fiber 4g); Protein 5g
% Daily Value: Vitamin A 15%; Vitamin C 20%; Calcium 4%; Iron 10%
Exchanges: $1\frac{1}{2}$ Starch, 1 Other Carbohydrate, 2 Fat
Carbohydrate Choices: $2\frac{1}{2}$

KITCHEN TIPS

- Balsamic vinegar is a great flavor booster, but if you don't have any on hand, you can use cider or red wine vinegar.
- Green beans can be used instead of asparagus.

Warm Carmelized Vegetables

Italian Veggie Grill

Prep time: 45 min Start to finish: 45 min

8 ounces fresh green beans

2 fennel bulbs, cut into $\frac{1}{2}$-inch wedges

1 medium yellow or red bell pepper, cut into 1-inch pieces

1 small red onion, cut into thin wedges

$\frac{1}{3}$ cup Italian dressing

$\frac{1}{4}$ teaspoon coarse ground pepper

1. Heat coals or gas grill for direct heat. In 3-quart saucepan, heat 3 cups water to boiling. Add green beans and fennel; cook 5 minutes. Drain well.

2. In large bowl, mix green beans, fennel and remaining ingredients. Place vegetables in grill basket (grill "wok"). Reserve dressing in bowl.

3. Cover and grill vegetables over medium heat 10 to 15 minutes, shaking basket or stirring vegetables occasionally, until crisp-tender. Return vegetables to bowl with dressing; toss to coat.

4 servings
1 Serving: Calories 140 (Calories from Fat 80); Total Fat 9g (Saturated Fat 0.5g); Cholesterol 0mg; Sodium 240mg; Total Carbohydrate 17g (Dietary Fiber 6g); Protein 3g
% Daily Value: Vitamin A 15%; Vitamin C 60%; Calcium 10%; Iron 8%
Exchanges: $\frac{1}{2}$ Other Carbohydrate, 2 Vegetable, $1\frac{1}{2}$ Fat
Carbohydrate Choices: 1

KITCHEN TIPS

● A bulb with celery-like stalks and pale green, feathery foliage, fennel has a wonderful, very light anise or licorice flavor.

Italian Veggie Grill

Quick & Low Fat

Grilled Cheesy Garlic Potato Packet

Prep time: 30 min Start to finish: 30 min

1/2 teaspoon olive or vegetable oil

1 Yukon gold potato (8 ounces), cut into 1/2-inch pieces

2 teaspoons chopped fresh chives

1/2 teaspoon garlic salt

1 tablespoon grated Parmesan cheese

1. Heat gas or charcoal grill. Cut one 14 × 12-inch piece of heavy-duty foil. Spray one side generously with cooking spray.

2. In small bowl, pour oil over potato pieces; toss to coat. Add chives and garlic salt, toss to coat. Sprinkle with cheese; toss to coat.

3. Place potatoes on center of sprayed side of foil piece. Fold foil over potatoes so edges meet. Seal edges, making tight 1/2-inch fold; fold again. Allow space on sides for circulation and expansion.

4. Cover and grill packet over medium-low heat 15 to 20 minutes, turning once, until potatoes are golden brown and tender.

2 servings
1 Serving: Calories 110 (Calories from Fat 20); Total Fat 2g (Saturated Fat 1g); Cholesterol 0mg; Sodium 310mg; Total Carbohydrate 20g (Dietary Fiber 3g; Sugars 1g); Protein 3g
% Daily Value: Vitamin A 0%; Vitamin C 10%; Calcium 6%; Iron 10%
Exchanges: 1 1/2 Starch
Carbohydrate Choices: 1

KITCHEN TIPS

- Sprinkle with coarse ground pepper right before serving.
- These delicious potatoes partner perfectly with grilled steak or chicken.

Grilled Cheesy Garlic Potato Packet

Roasted Red Potatoes

Prep time: 10 min Start to finish: 1 hr 25 min

12   small red potatoes (about 1½ pounds)

2   tablespoons olive or vegetable oil

2   medium green onions, sliced (2 tablespoons)

2   tablespoons chopped fresh or 2 teaspoons dried rosemary leaves, crushed

4 servings
1 Serving: Calories 200 (Calories from Fat 60); Total Fat 1g (Saturated Fat 1g); Cholesterol 0mg; Sodium 15mg; Total Carbohydrate 30g (Dietary Fiber 3g; Sugars 2g); Protein 4g
% Daily Value: Vitamin A 0%; Vitamin C 10%; Calcium 2%; Iron 10%
Exchanges: 2 Starch, 1 Fat
Carbohydrate Choices: 2

1. Heat oven to 350°F. Place potatoes in ungreased 8- or 9-inch square pan or 13 × 9-inch pan. Drizzle oil over potatoes; turn so all sides are coated. Sprinkle onions and rosemary over potatoes; stir.

2. Roast uncovered about 1 hour 15 minutes, stirring occasionally, until potatoes are tender.

KITCHEN TIPS

● Most small red potatoes are about 2 inches in diameter. If you have larger ones, cut each one in half.

Roasted Red Potatoes

Twice-Baked Sweet Potatoes

Prep time: 25 min Start to finish: 1 hr 15 min

6   small dark orange sweet potatoes (5 to 6 ounces each)

2   tablespoons Gold Medal all-purpose flour

2   tablespoons packed brown sugar

2   tablespoons butter or margarine, softened

1/4   cup chopped pecans

2   tablespoons butter or margarine, softened

2   tablespoons half-and-half

1   teaspoon pumpkin pie spice

1/4   teaspoon salt

1. Pierce each potato twice with point of sharp knife to vent steam. Place in single layer in microwave oven. Microwave on High 5 minutes. If potatoes are not cooked through, turn potatoes over and continue microwaving 1 minute at a time until softened. Remove any fully cooked potatoes from microwave while cooking remaining potatoes. Cool 10 minutes.

2. Meanwhile, in small bowl, mix flour, brown sugar, 2 tablespoons butter and the pecans; set aside.

3. Heat oven to 350°F. Cut off top one-third of each potato. Using spoon, scoop flesh into large bowl, being careful not to tear potato skins; discard potato tops. Add 2 tablespoons butter, half-and-half, pumpkin pie spice and salt to potatoes. Mash potato mixture with potato masher or beat with electric mixer on medium speed until creamy. Spoon potato mixture back into skins. Place filled potatoes in 13 x 9-inch pan. (Potatoes can be covered and refrigerated at this point up to 8 hours.)

4. Sprinkle pecan mixture over tops of potatoes. Bake uncovered 30 to 35 minutes or until topping is brown and potatoes are hot. (If filled potatoes are refrigerated, remove from refrigerator 30 minutes before serving; top and bake as directed.)

6 servings

1 Serving: Calories 250 (Calories from Fat 110); Total Fat 12g (Saturated Fat 4.5g); Cholesterol 20mg; Sodium 160mg; Total Carbohydrate 34g (Dietary Fiber 4g; Sugars 21g); Protein 3g
% Daily Value: Vitamin A 340%; Vitamin C 25%; Calcium 4%; Iron 4%
Exchanges: 1 Starch, 1 Other Carbohydrate, 2 1/2 Fat
Carbohydrate Choices: 2

KITCHEN TIPS

- Prepare 2 1/4 pounds large sweet potatoes as directed, but bake mashed mixture topped with pecan mixture in a 2-quart casserole instead of filling the potato skins.
- Make the pecan topping ahead and freeze in a freezer bag for up to 6 months.

Twice-Baked Sweet Potatoes

Make-Ahead Sour Cream 'n Chive Mashed Potatoes

Prep time: 40 min Start to finish: 9 hr 30 min

- 3 pounds small red potatoes
- 1 container (8 ounces) chive-and-onion cream cheese spread
- 1 container (12 ounces) chive-and-onion sour cream
- 1½ teaspoons salt
- ¼ teaspoon pepper
- 3 tablespoons butter or margarine, melted
- ½ cup French-fried onions (from 2.8-ounce can)

1. Spray 13 × 9-inch pan with cooking spray; set aside. Place potatoes in 4-quart Dutch oven; add enough water just to cover potatoes. Cover and heat to boiling; reduce heat. Simmer covered 20 to 25 minutes or until potatoes are tender; drain. Shake potatoes in Dutch oven over low heat to dry.

2. Mash potatoes until no lumps remain. Add cream cheese, sour cream, salt and pepper; mix until well blended. Spoon into pan. Cover tightly with foil and refrigerate at least 8 hours but no longer than 24 hours. (To bake immediately, drizzle with butter and bake 30 minutes, adding onions for last 15 minutes of baking.)

3. Heat oven to 350°F. Drizzle butter over potatoes. Cover and bake 30 minutes. Sprinkle onions over potatoes. Bake uncovered 15 to 20 minutes longer or until potatoes are hot.

16 servings
1 Serving: Calories 170 (Calories from Fat 100); Total Fat 11g (Saturated Fat 6g); Cholesterol 25mg; Sodium 500mg; Total Carbohydrate 17g (Dietary Fiber 2g); Protein 3g
% Daily Value: Vitamin A 8%; Vitamin C 8%; Calcium 6%; Iron 8%
Exchanges: 1 Starch, 2 Fat
Carbohydrate Choices: 1

Make-Ahead Sour Cream 'n Chive Mashed Potatoes

KITCHEN TIPS

● Eight cups of unseasoned cooked Potato Buds® mashed potatoes or refrigerated mashed potatoes can be substituted for the fresh potatoes. Stiff mashed potatoes will be better than soft and creamy mashed potatoes.

Easy Mashed Potato Casserole

Prep time: 15 min Start to finish: 45 min

2 teaspoons butter or margarine

16 medium green onions, sliced (1 cup)

1 medium yellow or orange bell pepper, chopped (1 cup)

3 cups hot water

1 cup half-and-half or whole milk

¼ cup butter or margarine

1 package (7.2 ounces) Betty Crocker roasted garlic mashed potatoes (2 pouches)

1½ cups shredded Cheddar cheese (6 ounces)

1. Heat oven to 350°F. Spray 2-quart casserole with cooking spray. In 10-inch nonstick skillet, melt 2 teaspoons butter over medium-high heat. Cook onions and bell pepper in butter 1 minute, stirring occasionally. Remove from heat; set aside.

2. In 2-quart saucepan, heat water, half-and-half and ¼ cup butter to boiling; remove from heat. Stir in both pouches of potatoes (and seasoning) just until moistened. Let stand about 1 minute or until liquid is absorbed. Beat with fork until smooth.

3. Spoon 1⅓ cups of the potatoes into casserole; top with half of the onion mixture and ¾ cup of the cheese. Spoon another 1⅓ cups potatoes over cheese; carefully spread to cover. Sprinkle evenly with remaining onion mixture. Top with remaining potatoes; carefully spread to cover. Sprinkle with remaining ¾ cup cheese.

4. Bake uncovered about 30 minutes or until hot.

8 servings
1 Serving: Calories 290 (Calories from Fat 170); Total Fat 19g (Saturated Fat 11g); Cholesterol 50mg; Sodium 530mg; Total Carbohydrate 22g (Dietary Fiber 1g; Sugars 4g); Protein 9g
% Daily Value: Vitamin A 15%; Vitamin C 30%; Calcium 15%; Iron 4%
Exchanges: 1½ Starch, ½ High-Fat Meat, 3 Fat
Carbohydrate Choices: 1½

KITCHEN TIPS

- Make this casserole up to 24 hours ahead of time; cover and refrigerate. You'll need to bake it about 45 minutes or until hot.

- Substitute Colby or Colby-Monterey Jack cheese blend for the Cheddar, if you like.

Easy Mashed Potato Casserole

Smoky Stove-Top Beans

Prep time: 10 min Start to finish: 15 min

- 1 slice turkey bacon, cut into small slices
- 2 tablespoons finely chopped green bell pepper
- 1 can (8.3 ounces) baked beans
- ¼ cup chopped tomato
- 1 tablespoon thick-and-spicy hickory-smoked barbecue sauce

1. In 1-quart saucepan, cook bacon over medium heat, stirring occasionally, until crisp. Remove bacon from saucepan, leaving drippings in pan. Cook bell pepper in bacon drippings, stirring occasionally, until tender.

2. Reduce heat to medium-low. Stir in beans, tomato, barbecue sauce and bacon. Cook until thoroughly heated.

2 servings
1 Serving: Calories 140 (Calories from Fat 25); Total Fat 2.5g (Saturated Fat 1g); Cholesterol 10mg; Sodium 690mg; Total Carbohydrate 27g (Dietary Fiber 7g; Sugars 8g); Protein 7g
% Daily Value: Vitamin A 25%; Vitamin C 15%; Calcium 8%; Iron 25%
Exchanges: 1 Starch, 1 Other Carbohydrate, ½ Very Lean Meat
Carbohydrate Choices: 1

KITCHEN TIPS

- Have regular bacon on hand? Use it in place of the turkey bacon.
- These beans are the perfect partners for grilled hamburgers.

Low-Fat
So-Simple Cranberry Gelatin Salad

Prep time: 15 min Start to finish: 6 hr 15 min

- 2 cups boiling water
- 2 boxes (4-serving size each) lemon-flavored gelatin
- 2 tubs (10 ounces each) frozen cranberry-orange sauce, thawed
- 1 cup fresh raspberries

1. Lightly brush 6½-cup ring mold or 1½-quart decorative bowl with vegetable oil.

2. In large bowl, pour boiling water on gelatin; stir until gelatin is dissolved. Stir in cranberry-orange sauce. Fold in raspberries. Pour into mold or bowl. Cover and refrigerate at least 6 hours but no longer than 24 hours.

3. To unmold salad from ring mold, dip mold into hot water for 10 seconds. Place serving plate upside down onto mold; turn plate and mold over, then remove mold. Refrigerate salad until serving. If using decorative bowl, do not unmold; scoop salad from bowl to serve.

10 servings (½ cup each)
1 Serving: Calories 180 (Calories from Fat 0); Total Fat 0g (Saturated Fat 0g); Cholesterol 0mg; Sodium 100mg; Total Carbohydrate 43g (Dietary Fiber 2g; Sugars 41g); Protein 2g
% Daily Value: Vitamin A 0%; Vitamin C 10%; Calcium 0%; Iron 0%
Exchanges: 3 Other Carbohydrate
Carbohydrate Choices: 3

KITCHEN TIPS

- Add flair by garnishing the center of the salad with sprigs of watercress and sugared cranberries.

So-Simple Cranberry Gelatin Salad

Smoky Stove-Top Beans

Mushroom Stuffing

Prep time: 25 min Start to finish: 1 hr 10 min

²/₃ cup butter or margarine

2 medium stalks celery, chopped (1 cup)

1 medium onion, finely chopped (¹/₂ cup)

1 pound fresh mushrooms, sliced (6 cups)

8 cups unseasoned croutons

1 tablespoon chopped fresh or 1 teaspoon dried sage, thyme or marjoram leaves

1 teaspoon poultry seasoning

1 teaspoon salt

¹/₂ teaspoon pepper

1. In 4-quart Dutch oven, melt butter over medium heat. Cook celery, onion and mushrooms in butter about 3 minutes, stirring occasionally, until tender.

2. Stir in half of the croutons. Cook, stirring frequently, until evenly mixed and croutons are softened. Stir in remaining croutons and ingredients. Stuff turkey just before roasting. Or spoon stuffing into greased 3-quart casserole or 13 × 9-inch glass baking dish; cover and bake at 325°F for 30 minutes, then uncover and bake 15 minutes longer.

16 servings (¹/₂ cup each)
1 Serving: Calories 140 (Calories from Fat 80); Total Fat 9g (Saturated Fat 5g); Cholesterol 20mg; Sodium 310mg; Total Carbohydrate 13g (Dietary Fiber 1g; Sugars 1g); Protein 3g
% Daily Value: Vitamin A 6%; Vitamin C 0%; Calcium 0%; Iron 4%
Exchanges: 1 Starch, 1¹/₂ Fat
Carbohydrate Choices: 1

KITCHEN TIPS

● Look for the croutons near the salad dressings or stocked in the produce department.

Mushroom Stuffing

Bacon-Cornbread Stuffing

Prep time: 25 min Start to finish: 55 min

4 slices bacon, cut into ¹/₂-inch pieces

¹/₂ cup chopped green bell pepper

¹/₂ cup chopped onion

¹/₂ cup sweetened dried cranberries

2¹/₄ cups water

4 cups seasoned cornbread stuffing crumbs (from 16-ounce bag)

¹/₂ teaspoon seasoned salt

¹/₄ teaspoon dried marjoram leaves

1. Heat oven to 350°F. Spray 8-inch square (2-quart) glass baking dish with cooking spray. In 12-inch non-stick skillet, cook bacon over medium heat about 6 minutes, stirring occasionally, until browned but not crisp. Stir in bell pepper and onion. Cook 3 to 4 minutes, stirring occasionally, until tender. Stir in cranberries. Add water; heat to boiling. Remove skillet from heat.

2. Stir in stuffing mix, seasoned salt and marjoram until well mixed. Spoon into baking dish.

3. Cover with foil; bake about 30 minutes or until thoroughly heated.

8 servings (¹/₂ cup each)
1 Serving: Calories 190 (Calories from Fat 50); Total Fat 6g (Saturated Fat 1.5g); Cholesterol 5mg; Sodium 470mg; Total Carbohydrate 30g (Dietary Fiber 2g; Sugars 8g); Protein 4g
% Daily Value: Vitamin A 0%; Vitamin C 8%; Calcium 4%; Iron 8%
Exchanges: 1¹/₂ Starch, ¹/₂ Other Carbohydrate, 1 Fat
Carbohydrate Choices: 2

KITCHEN TIPS

● You can make this easy stuffing up to 4 hours ahead. Cover and refrigerate until it's time to bake. Add 5 to 10 minutes to the bake time.

Bacon-Cornbread Stuffing

Quick

Classic Pan Gravy

Prep time: 20 min Start to finish: 20 min

Drippings from roasted turkey
1 cup liquid (turkey juices, broth, water)
2 tablespoons Gold Medal all-purpose flour
Browning sauce, if desired
Salt and pepper to taste

1. After removing turkey from roasting pan, pour drippings (turkey juices and fat) into bowl or glass measuring cup, leaving brown bits in pan. Let drippings stand 5 minutes to allow fat to rise. Skim 2 tablespoons fat from top of drippings and return to pan; discard any remaining fat. Add enough broth or water to remaining drippings to measure 1 cup; set aside.

2. Stir flour into fat in pan. Cook over low heat, stirring constantly and scraping up brown bits, until mixture is smooth and bubbly; remove from heat.

3. Gradually stir in reserved 1 cup drippings. Heat to boiling, stirring constantly. Boil and stir 1 minute. Stir in a few drops of browning sauce if a darker color is desired. Stir in salt and pepper.

EASY-MIXING GRAVY

Substitute Bisquick mix for the all-purpose flour.

THIN GRAVY

Decrease turkey fat from drippings to 1 tablespoon and flour to 1 tablespoon.

WINE-FLAVORED GRAVY

White wine, dry sherry or Madeira wine adds a wonderful flavor to gravy. Replace half of the liquid with your choice of wine.

4 servings ($\frac{1}{4}$ cup each)
1 Serving: Calories 70 (Calories from Fat 60); Total Fat 7g (Saturated Fat 2g); Cholesterol 5mg; Sodium 105mg; Total Carbohydrate 3g (Dietary Fiber 0g; Sugars 0g); Protein 0g
% Daily Value: Vitamin A 0%; Vitamin C 0%; Calcium 0%; Iron 0%
Exchanges: $1\frac{1}{2}$ Fat
Carbohydrate Choices: 0

KITCHEN TIPS

- The trick to smooth, creamy gravy is to use a wire whisk when adding the flour to the drippings, beating rapidly until smooth.
- For added flavor, use vegetable cooking water, tomato juice or vegetable juice as part of the liquid.

Cupcakes, Brownies, Bars and Cookies

The Very Best of the Bake Sale

PB and J Strips (page 238)

White Chocolate Chunk Blonde Brownies (page 227)

Chocolate Chip Cheesecake Swirl Cupcakes

Prep time: 30 min Start to finish: 1 hr 5 min

$\frac{1}{2}$ cup sugar

2 packages (3 ounces each) cream cheese, softened

1 egg

1 bag (6 ounces) semisweet chocolate chips (1 cup)

2$\frac{1}{4}$ cups Gold Medal all-purpose flour

1$\frac{2}{3}$ cups sugar

$\frac{1}{4}$ cup baking cocoa

1$\frac{1}{4}$ cups water

$\frac{1}{2}$ cup vegetable oil

2 tablespoons white vinegar

2 teaspoons baking soda

2 teaspoons vanilla

1 teaspoon salt

1. Heat oven to 350°F. Line 24 regular-size muffin cups with paper baking cups. In medium bowl, beat $\frac{1}{2}$ cup sugar and the cream cheese with electric mixer on medium speed until smooth. Beat in egg. Stir in chocolate chips; set aside.

2. In large bowl, beat remaining ingredients on low speed 30 seconds, scraping bowl occasionally. Beat on high speed 3 minutes, scraping bowl occasionally. Reserve 1$\frac{1}{2}$ cups batter.

3. Fill each muffin cup one-third full (1 round table-spoon) with batter. Spoon 1 tablespoon cream cheese mixture onto batter in each cup. Top each with reserved batter ($\frac{1}{2}$ rounded tablespoon).

4. Bake 30 to 35 minutes or until toothpick inserted in center comes out clean.

24 cupcakes
1 Cupcake: Calories 220 (Calories from Fat 90); Total Fat 10g (Saturated Fat 3.5g); Cholesterol 15mg; Sodium 230mg; Total Carbohydrate 32g (Dietary Fiber 1g); Protein 2g
% Daily Value: Vitamin A 2%; Vitamin C 0%; Calcium 0%; Iron 6%
Exchanges: $\frac{1}{2}$ Starch, 1$\frac{1}{2}$ Other Carbohydrate, 2 Fat
Carbohydrate Choices: 2

Chocolate Chip Cheesecake Swirl Cupcakes

KITCHEN TIPS

● These cupcakes with a cream cheese swirl are great for picnics. They can be made the day before, so you can have them ready to serve to kids of all ages!

Red Velvet Cupcakes
with Marshmallow Buttercream Frosting

Prep time: 40 min Start to finish: 1 hr 30 min

Cupcakes

- 2¼ cups Gold Medal all-purpose flour
- ¼ cup baking cocoa
- 1 teaspoon salt
- ½ cup butter or margarine, softened
- 1½ cups granulated sugar
- 2 eggs
- 1 bottle (1 ounce) red food color (about 2 tablespoons)
- 1½ teaspoons vanilla
- 1 cup buttermilk
- 1 teaspoon baking soda
- 1 tablespoon white vinegar

Frosting

- 1 jar (7 to 7½ ounces) marshmallow creme
- 1 cup butter or margarine, softened
- 2 cups powdered sugar

1. Heat oven to 350°F. Line 24 regular-size muffin cups with paper baking cups. In small bowl, mix flour, cocoa and salt; set aside. In large bowl, beat ½ cup butter and granulated sugar with electric mixer on medium speed until mixed. Add eggs; beat 1 to 2 minutes or until light and fluffy. Stir in food color and vanilla.

2. Beat in flour mixture alternately with buttermilk on low speed just until blended. Beat in baking soda and vinegar until well blended. Fill muffin cups two-thirds full.

3. Bake 20 to 22 minutes or until toothpick inserted in center of cupcake comes out clean. Remove from pan to wire racks. Cool completely, about 30 minutes.

4. Remove lid and foil seal from jar of marshmallow creme. Microwave on High 15 to 20 seconds to soften. In large bowl, beat marshmallow creme and 1 cup butter with electric mixer on medium speed until smooth. Beat in powdered sugar until smooth. Spoon 1 heaping tablespoon frosting onto each cupcake, swirling frosting with back of spoon.

Red Velvet Cupcakes with Marshmallow Buttercream Frosting

24 servings
1 Serving: Calories 280 (Calories from Fat 110); Total Fat 12g (Saturated Fat 6g); Cholesterol 50mg; Sodium 250mg; Total Carbohydrate 39g (Dietary Fiber 0g; Sugars 28g); Protein 2g
% Daily Value: Vitamin A 10%; Vitamin C 0%; Calcium 2%; Iron 4%
Exchanges: 2½ Other Carbohydrate, 2½ Fat
Carbohydrate Choices: 2½

KITCHEN TIPS

- Add a little holiday cheer to each cupcake with a holly sprig. Make two holly leaves by splitting one green spearmint leaf candy in half horizontally and add 3 red cinnamon candies for berries. Or top frosted cupcakes with a snowy drift of flaked coconut.

Orange-Toffee-Almond Truffles

Prep time: 45 min Start to finish: 3 hr 15 min

1⅓ cups semisweet chocolate chips (8 ounces)
½ cup whipping (heavy) cream
½ teaspoon grated orange peel
½ cup toffee bits
1 cup sliced almonds, chopped, toasted*

1. In large microwavable bowl, microwave chocolate chips uncovered on High about 1 minute or until softened; stir until smooth. (If not completely softened, continue microwaving 15 seconds at a time, stirring after each microwave time, until smooth.)

2. Stir whipping cream into chocolate until very smooth and glossy. Stir in orange peel and toffee bits. Cover and refrigerate about 2 hours or until firm.

3. Place almonds in small bowl. Shape chocolate mixture into 1-inch balls. Immediately roll balls in almonds, pressing to coat. Place on ungreased cookie sheet or in paper candy cups. Refrigerate about 30 minutes or until firm. Remove from refrigerator 20 minutes before serving.

* To toast nuts, bake uncovered in ungreased shallow pan in 350°F oven 6 to 10 minutes, stirring occasionally, until golden brown. Or cook in ungreased heavy skillet over medium-low heat 5 to 7 minutes, stirring frequently until browning begins, then stirring constantly until golden brown.

About 2½ dozen truffles
1 Truffle: Calories 90 (Calories from Fat 60); Total Fat 6g (Saturated Fat 3g); Cholesterol 5mg; Sodium 20mg; Total Carbohydrate 8g (Dietary Fiber 0g; Sugars 6g); Protein 1g
% Daily Value: Vitamin A 0%; Vitamin C 0%; Calcium 0%; Iron 2%
Exchanges: ½ Other Carbohydrate, 1 Fat
Carbohydrate Choices: ½

KITCHEN TIPS

● At each place at the table, place a truffle wrapped in tulle and tied with a ribbon. Add a gift tag for a pretty and delicious place card.

Orange-Toffee-Almond Truffles

White Chocolate Chunk Blonde Brownies

Prep Time: 20 min Start to finish: 2 hr 55 min

2 cups packed brown sugar

$1/2$ cup butter or margarine, softened

2 teaspoons vanilla

$1/2$ teaspoon rum extract

2 eggs

2 cups Gold Medal all-purpose flour

1 teaspoon baking powder

$1/4$ teaspoon salt

1 bag (12 ounces) white chocolate chunks

1 cup chopped walnuts

$1/4$ cup semisweet chocolate chunks (from 12-ounce bag)

1 teaspoon vegetable oil

1. Heat oven to 350°F. In large bowl, beat brown sugar, butter, vanilla, rum extract and eggs with electric mixer on medium speed until light and fluffy.

2. Beat in flour, baking powder and salt on low speed until well blended. Stir in white chocolate chunks and walnuts. Spread batter evenly in ungreased 13 × 9-inch pan.

3. Bake 25 to 35 minutes or until top is golden brown and set. Cool completely, about 2 hours.

4. In small microwavable bowl, microwave semisweet chocolate chunks and oil uncovered on High 30 to 60 seconds, stirring every 15 seconds, until melted; stir well. Spread chocolate glaze over brownies. If desired, place glaze in small plastic food-storage bag and cut off small tip from one corner of bag; drizzle glaze in diagonal lines over brownies. Let stand until glaze sets. Cut into 6 rows by 6 rows of brownies.

36 brownies
1 Brownie: Calories 180 (Calories from Fat 80); Total Fat 9g (Saturated Fat 3.5g); Cholesterol 20mg; Sodium 65mg; Total Carbohydrate 24g (Dietary Fiber 0g; Sugars 18g); Protein 2g
% Daily Value: Vitamin A 26%; Vitamin C 0%; Calcium 4%; Iron 4%
Exchanges: $1/2$ Other Carbohydrate, 2 Fat
Carbohydrate Choices: $1/2$

White Chocolate Chunk Blonde Brownies

KITCHEN TIPS

● You could use pecans instead of walnuts, or you can make the brownies without nuts if you like.

● For easy cutting, line the pan with foil. When the brownies are cool, use the foil to lift them from the pan and place on a flat surface for cutting.

Double-Chocolate Chunk Brownies

Prep time: 25 min Start to finish: 2 hr

Brownies

1	cup	butter or margarine
1	cup	granulated sugar
1	cup	packed brown sugar
2	teaspoons	vanilla
4	eggs	
1¼	cups	Gold Medal all-purpose flour
¾	cup	baking cocoa
¼	teaspoon	salt
1	cup	semisweet chocolate chunks
1	cup	white chocolate chunks

Frosting

1½	cups	powdered sugar
¼	cup	baking cocoa
¼	cup	butter or margarine, softened
2 to 3	tablespoons	milk
½	cup	white chocolate chunks
1	teaspoon	vegetable oil

1. Heat oven to 350°F (325°F for dark or nonstick pan). Grease bottom and sides of 13 x 9-inch pan with shortening or spray with cooking spray. In 4-quart saucepan, melt 1 cup butter over medium heat; remove from heat. Mix in granulated and brown sugars, vanilla and eggs until well blended. Stir in flour, ¾ cup cocoa and salt until well blended. Stir in 1 cup each semisweet and white chocolate chunks. Spread in pan.

2. Bake 30 to 35 minutes or until set. Cool completely, about 1 hour.

3. In large bowl, beat powdered sugar, ¼ cup cocoa, ¼ cup butter and enough of the milk with electric mixer on low speed until frosting is smooth and spreadable. Spread over brownies.

4. In microwavable bowl, microwave ½ cup white chocolate chunks and the oil uncovered on High 30 to 60 seconds, stirring once or twice, until thin enough to drizzle. Place in small plastic food-storage bag; cut off small tip from one corner of bag. Drizzle over frosting. Cut into 6 rows by 4 rows of brownies.

24 brownies
1 Brownie: Calories 360 (Calories from Fat 170); Total Fat 19g (Saturated Fat 10g); Cholesterol 60mg; Sodium 120mg; Total Carbohydrate 46g (Dietary Fiber 2g; Sugars 39g); Protein 4g
% Daily Value: Vitamin A 8%; Vitamin C 0%; Calcium 6%; Iron 8%
Exchanges: ½ Starch, 2½ Other Carbohydrate, 3½ Fat
Carbohydrate Choices: 3

KITCHEN TIPS

- For the best results, use chocolate chunks, not chocolate chips. The chunks contribute to the fudgy texture and richness of the brownies.

Double-Chocolate Chunk Brownies

Salted Nut Bars

Prep time: 30 min Start to finish: 50 min

1½ cups Gold Medal all-purpose flour
¾ cup packed brown sugar
¼ teaspoon salt
½ cup butter or margarine, softened
2 cups salted mixed nuts or peanuts
1 cup butterscotch-flavored chips
½ cup light corn syrup
2 tablespoons butter or margarine

1. Heat oven to 350°F. In medium bowl, mix flour, brown sugar and salt. Cut in ½ cup butter, using pastry blender (or pulling 2 table knives through ingredients in opposite directions), until evenly mixed. Press evenly in bottom of ungreased 13 × 9-inch pan. Bake 15 minutes.

2. Cut up any large nuts. Sprinkle nuts evenly over crust. In 1-quart saucepan, heat remaining ingredients over low heat, stirring occasionally, just until chips are melted.

3. Drizzle butterscotch mixture evenly over nuts. Bake 5 minutes. Cut into 8 rows by 4 rows of bars while warm for easiest cutting.

32 bars
1 Bar: Calories 170 (Calories from Fat 90); Total Fat 10g (Saturated Fat 4g); Cholesterol 10mg; Sodium 115mg; Total Carbohydrate 19g (Dietary Fiber 0g; Sugars 11g); Protein 2g
% Daily Value: Vitamin A 2%; Vitamin C 0%; Calcium 0%; Iron 4%
Exchanges: ½ Starch, 1 Other Carbohydrate, 2 Fat
Carbohydrate Choices: 1

KITCHEN TIPS

● These bars are perfect to wrap individually and pack in lunch boxes.

Confetti Caramel Bars

Prep time: 30 min Start to finish: 3 hr 30 min

1 cup packed brown sugar
1 cup butter or margarine, softened
1½ teaspoons vanilla
1 egg
2 cups Gold Medal all-purpose flour
½ cup light corn syrup
2 tablespoons butter or margarine
1 cup butterscotch-flavored chips
1½ to 2 cups assorted candies and nuts (such as candy corn, candy-coated chocolate candies and salted peanuts)

1. Heat oven to 350°F. In large bowl, beat brown sugar, 1 cup butter, the vanilla and egg with electric mixer on medium speed or mix with spoon. Stir in flour. Press evenly in bottom of ungreased 13 × 9-inch pan. Bake 20 to 22 minutes or until light brown. Cool 20 minutes.

2. In 1-quart saucepan, heat corn syrup, 2 tablespoons butter and the butterscotch chips over medium heat, stirring occasionally, until chips are melted; remove from heat. Cool 10 minutes.

3. Spread butterscotch mixture over crust. Sprinkle with candies and nuts; gently press into butterscotch mixture. Cover and refrigerate at least 2 hours until butterscotch mixture is firm. Cut into 8 rows by 4 rows of bars or cut into triangle shapes.

32 bars
1 Bar: Calories 210 (Calories from Fat 90); Total Fat 10g (Saturated Fat 5g); Cholesterol 25mg; Sodium 80mg; Total Carbohydrate 27g (Dietary Fiber 0g; Sugars 18g); Protein 2g
% Daily Value: Vitamin A 6%; Vitamin C 0%; Calcium 0%; Iron 4%
Exchanges: 1 Starch, 1 Other Carbohydrate, 1½ Fat
Carbohydrate Choices: 2

KITCHEN TIPS

● If you line the pan with foil, you can lift out the bars for easy cutting and cleanup.

Confetti Caramel Bars

Salted Nut Bars

Saucepan Granola Bars

Prep time: 10 min Start to finish: 1 hr 35 min

$\frac{1}{2}$ cup butter or margarine

$2\frac{1}{2}$ cups Original Bisquick mix

2 cups granola with fruit

1 cup packed brown sugar

$\frac{1}{2}$ cup chopped nuts

1 teaspoon vanilla

2 eggs

48 bars
1 Bar: Calories 90 (Calories from Fat 40); Total Fat 4.5g (Saturated Fat 1.5g); Cholesterol 15mg; Sodium 110mg; Total Carbohydrate 11g (Dietary Fiber 0g; Sugars 6g); Protein 1g
% Daily Value: Vitamin A 0%; Vitamin C 0%; Calcium 2%; Iron 2%
Exchanges: $\frac{1}{2}$ Starch, 1 Fat
Carbohydrate Choices: 1

KITCHEN TIPS

● Drizzle cooled bars with melted chocolate chips for a pretty and tasty finish.

1. Heat oven to 375°F. In 3-quart saucepan, melt butter over low heat. Stir in remaining ingredients until blended. Spoon into ungreased 13 × 9-inch pan; spread evenly.

2. Bake 20 to 25 minutes or until deep golden brown. Cool completely, about 1 hour. Cut into 8 rows by 6 rows of bars.

Saucepan Granola Bars

Chocolate Chip Dream Bars

Prep time: 25 min Start to finish: 2 hr 15 min

1/2 cup packed brown sugar

1/3 cup butter or margarine, softened

1 cup Gold Medal all-purpose flour

2 eggs

1 cup packed brown sugar

1 teaspoon vanilla

2 tablespoons Gold Medal all-purpose flour

1 teaspoon baking powder

1/2 teaspoon salt

1 bag (6 ounces) semisweet chocolate chips (1 cup)

1 3/4 cups milk chocolate chips

2 teaspoons vegetable oil

1. Heat oven to 350°F. In medium bowl, mix 1/2 cup brown sugar and the butter. Stir in 1 cup flour. Press in ungreased 13 × 9-inch pan. Bake 10 minutes.

2. Meanwhile, in medium bowl, mix eggs, 1 cup brown sugar and the vanilla. Stir in 2 tablespoons flour, the baking powder and salt. Stir in semisweet chocolate chips and 1 cup of the milk chocolate chips. Spread over hot crust.

3. Bake 15 to 20 minutes or until golden brown. Cool completely in pan on wire rack, about 30 minutes.

4. In 1-quart saucepan, heat remaining 3/4 cup milk chocolate chips and the oil over low heat, stirring constantly, until chocolate is melted; drizzle glaze over bars. Refrigerate at least 1 hour until firm. Cut into 8 rows by 4 rows of bars. Store at room temperature.

32 bars
1 Bar: Calories 160 (Calories from Fat 60); Total Fat 7g (Saturated Fat 4g); Cholesterol 20mg; Sodium 80mg; Total Carbohydrate 22g (Dietary Fiber 0g); Protein 2g
% Daily Value: Vitamin A 2%; Vitamin C 0%; Calcium 4%; Iron 4%
Exchanges: 1/2 Starch, 1 Other Carbohydrate, 1 1/2 Fat
Carbohydrate Choices: 1 1/2

KITCHEN TIPS

● You could use 3/4 cup semisweet chocolate chips or even white baking chips for the glaze on these delectable bars.

Chocolate Chip Dream Bars

Ultimate Triple-Chocolate Bars

Prep time: 15 min Start to finish: 2 hr 50 min

1 bag (12 ounces) semisweet chocolate chips (2 cups)

2 packages (3 ounces each) cream cheese

²⁄₃ cup evaporated milk

2 cups Original Bisquick mix

¾ cup sugar

½ cup baking cocoa

¾ cup butter or margarine, softened

1 cup white baking chips

1 bag (6 ounces) semisweet chocolate chips (1 cup)

1. Heat oven to 375°F. In 2-quart saucepan, heat 2 cups chocolate chips, the cream cheese and milk over low heat, stirring constantly, until chips are melted and mixture is smooth. Cool while making crust.

2. In medium bowl, mix Bisquick mix, sugar and cocoa. Cut in butter, using pastry blender (or pulling 2 table knives through ingredients in opposite directions), until mixture is crumbly. Press half of the crumbly mixture (2 cups) on bottom of ungreased 13 × 9-inch pan. Sprinkle with white baking chips. Spoon chocolate mixture over crumbly mixture and chips; spread evenly. Sprinkle with remaining crumbly mixture and 1 cup chocolate chips. Press lightly with fork.

3. Bake 30 to 35 minutes until center is set. Cool completely, about 1 hour. Refrigerate 1 hour or until chilled. Cut into 8 rows by 6 rows of bars. Store covered in refrigerator.

48 bars
1 Bar: Calories 160 (Calories from Fat 90); Total Fat 10g (Saturated Fat 5g); Cholesterol 15mg; Sodium 110mg; Total Carbohydrate 16g (Dietary Fiber 0g; Sugars 12g); Protein 2g
% Daily Value: Vitamin A 4%; Vitamin C 0%; Calcium 4%; Iron 4%
Exchanges: 1 Other Carbohydrate, 2 Fat
Carbohydrate Choices: 1

KITCHEN TIPS

● Coconut lovers can add ½ cup flaked coconut to the chocolate–cream cheese mixture.

Ultimate Triple-Chocolate Bars

Cinnamon Espresso Bars

Prep time: 15 min Start to finish: 35 min

Bars

1	cup packed brown sugar
⅓	cup butter or margarine, softened
1	egg
1½	cups Gold Medal all-purpose flour
1	tablespoon instant espresso coffee (dry)
1	teaspoon baking powder
½	teaspoon ground cinnamon
¼	teaspoon salt
¼	teaspoon baking soda
½	cup water

Glaze

1	cup powdered sugar
¼	teaspoon vanilla
⅛	teaspoon ground cinnamon
4 to 5	teaspoons cold espresso coffee or strong coffee

Cinnamon Espresso Bars

1. Heat oven to 350°F. Grease bottom and sides of 13 × 9-inch pan with shortening or spray with cooking spray; coat with flour. In large bowl, beat brown sugar, butter and egg with electric mixer on medium speed until blended or mix with spoon. Stir in remaining bar ingredients. Spread in pan.

2. Bake 20 to 22 minutes or until top springs back when touched in center.

3. Meanwhile, in small bowl, mix all glaze ingredients with spoon until smooth and thin enough to drizzle. Drizzle over bars while warm. Cool completely, about 1 hour. Cut into 8 rows by 6 rows of bars.

48 bars
1 Bar: Calories 50 (Calories from Fat 15); Total Fat 1.5g (Saturated Fat 0.5g); Cholesterol 10mg; Sodium 40mg; Total Carbohydrate 10g (Dietary Fiber 0g; Sugars 7g); Protein 0g
% Daily Value: Vitamin A 0%; Vitamin C 0%; Calcium 0%; Iron 0%
Exchanges: ½ Other Carbohydrate, ½ Fat
Carbohydrate Choices: ½

KITCHEN TIPS

● Espresso gives these bars a rich coffee flavor, but if you don't have it on hand, you could use regular instant coffee granules for a milder flavor.

Red, White and Blue Cookies

Rainbow Sprinklers

Red, White and Blue Cookies

Prep time: 1 hr 15 min Start to finish: 2 hr 15 min

1	cup granulated sugar
1	cup butter or margarine, softened
1/2	teaspoon almond extract
1	egg
2 1/4	cups Gold Medal all-purpose flour
2	tablespoons red colored sugar
2	tablespoons blue colored sugar

1. In large bowl, beat granulated sugar, butter, almond extract and egg with electric mixer on medium speed 2 minutes. Stir in flour.

2. Divide dough in half; cover half and set aside. Place remaining half on plastic wrap; press into 8-inch square. Sprinkle with 1 tablespoon each of the red and blue sugars. Using plastic wrap to lift, roll up dough. Repeat with remaining dough and colored sugars. Refrigerate about 1 hour or until firm.

3. Heat oven to 375°F. Cut rolls into 1/4-inch slices. Place slices about 2 inches apart on ungreased cookie sheet.

4. Bake 6 to 8 minutes or until edges begin to brown. Cool 1 minute; remove from cookie sheet to wire rack.

About 6 dozen cookies

1 Cookie: Calories 50 (Calories from Fat 25); Total Fat 2.5g (Saturated Fat 1.5g); Cholesterol 10mg; Sodium 20mg; Total Carbohydrate 6g (Dietary Fiber 0g); Protein 0g
% Daily Value: Vitamin A 2%; Vitamin C 0%; Calcium 0%; Iron 0%
Exchanges: 1/2 Other Carbohydrate, 1/2 Fat
Carbohydrate Choices: 1/2

Low Fat
Rainbow Sprinklers

Prep time: 1 hr 15 min Start to finish: 1 hr 15 min

1 1/2	cups sugar
1/2	cup butter or margarine, softened
1/2	cup shortening
2	eggs
2 3/4	cups Gold Medal all-purpose flour
2	teaspoons cream of tartar
1	teaspoon baking soda
1/4	teaspoon salt
	About 1/2 cup assorted Betty Crocker® colored sugars or candy decors

1. Heat oven to 400°F. In large bowl, stir sugar, butter, shortening and eggs with spoon until mixed. Stir in flour, cream of tartar, baking soda and salt.

2. Shape dough by rounded teaspoonfuls into balls. Roll balls in colored sugar until coated. Place balls about 2 inches apart on ungreased cookie sheet.

3. Bake 8 to 10 minutes or until centers are almost set. Cool 1 minute; remove from cookie sheet to wire rack.

About 6 dozen cookies

1 Cookie: Calories 80 (Calories from Fat 25); Total Fat 3g (Saturated Fat 1g); Cholesterol 10mg; Sodium 35mg; Total Carbohydrate 12g (Dietary Fiber 0g; Sugars 8g); Protein 0g
% Daily Value: Vitamin A 0%; Vitamin C 0%; Calcium 0%; Iron 0%
Exchanges: 1/2 Starch, 1/2 Other Carbohydrate, 1/2 Fat
Carbohydrate Choices: 1

KITCHEN TIPS

● Be sure to use butter or margarine. Whipped products and low-fat spreads contain more water and air, making them unpredictable for baking.

Rich Peanut Butter Cookies

Prep time: 40 min Start to finish: 40 min

  1   cup packed brown sugar
  1/2   cup peanut butter
  1/2   cup butter or margarine, softened
  1   egg
  1 1/4 cups Gold Medal all-purpose flour
  3/4   teaspoon baking soda
  1/2   teaspoon baking powder
  1/4   teaspoon salt
  1   cup peanut butter chips
        Granulated sugar

1. Heat oven to 375°F. In large bowl, beat brown sugar, peanut butter, butter and egg with electric mixer on medium speed until creamy or mix with spoon. Stir in flour, baking soda, baking powder and salt. Stir in peanut butter chips.

2. Shape dough into 1 1/2-inch balls. Dip tops of balls into granulated sugar. Place balls, sugared sides up, about 3 inches apart on ungreased cookie sheet (do not flatten).

3. Bake 9 to 10 minutes or until light brown. Cool 5 minutes; remove from cookie sheet to wire rack.

About 2 dozen cookies
1 Cookie: Calories 170 (Calories from Fat 80); Total Fat 9g (Saturated Fat 3g); Cholesterol 20mg; Sodium 150mg; Total Carbohydrate 19g (Dietary Fiber 0g; Sugars 13g); Protein 3g
% Daily Value: Vitamin A 4%; Vitamin C 0%; Calcium 2%; Iron 4%
Exchanges: 1 Starch, 1/2 Other Carbohydrate, 1 1/2 Fat
Carbohydrate Choices: 1

KITCHEN TIPS

- Why not try semisweet or milk chocolate chips instead of the peanut butter chips?
- For the best results, always place cookie dough on a cooled cookie sheet. This will help prevent spreading during baking.

Quick & Low-Fat
PB and J Strips

Prep time: 20 min Start to finish: 35 min

  1/2   cup granulated sugar
  1/2   cup packed brown sugar
  1/2   cup peanut butter
  1/4   cup shortening
  1   egg
  1 1/2 cups Original Bisquick mix
  1/3   cup strawberry jam or preserves

1. Heat oven to 375°F. In large bowl, beat sugars, peanut butter, shortening and egg with electric mixer on low speed 30 seconds, scraping bowl constantly. Beat on medium speed 1 minute, scraping bowl occasionally. Stir in Bisquick mix until blended.

2. Place dough on surface sprinkled with Bisquick mix; gently roll in Bisquick mix to coat. Divide dough into 4 parts. Shape each part into roll 3/4 inch in diameter and about 13 inches long. Place rolls about 2 inches apart on large ungreased cookie sheet.

3. Make indentation lengthwise in center of each roll with handle of wooden spoon. Spoon jam into resealable plastic food-storage bag; cut very small (1/4-inch) tip from corner of bag. Squeeze preserves evenly into indentations.

4. Bake 9 to 11 minutes until light golden brown and set. Cool on cookie sheet 5 minutes. Cut each roll into 12 slices. Remove from cookie sheet to wire rack.

About 4 dozen cookies
1 Serving: Calories 70 (Calories from Fat 30); Total Fat 3g (Saturated Fat 0.5g); Cholesterol 0mg; Sodium 80mg; Total Carbohydrate 9g (Dietary Fiber 0g; Sugars 6g); Protein 1g
% Daily Value: Vitamin A 0%; Vitamin C 0%; Calcium 0%; Iron 0%
Exchanges: 1/2 Starch, 1/2 Fat
Carbohydrate Choices: 1/2

KITCHEN TIPS

- Bake the strips without the jam. When strips have cooled, top with chocolate frosting in place of the jam.

PB and J Strips

Rich Peanut Butter Cookies

Apricot Spice Cookies

Prep time: 1 hr 20 min Start to finish: 1 hr 20 min

²/₃ cup granulated sugar

²/₃ cup packed brown sugar

½ cup butter or margarine, softened

½ cup shortening

1 teaspoon baking soda

1 teaspoon ground cinnamon or cardamom

1 teaspoon vanilla

½ teaspoon baking powder

½ teaspoon salt

2 eggs

3 cups quick-cooking oats

1 cup Gold Medal all-purpose flour

¾ cup chopped dried apricots

½ cup finely chopped pecans

1. Heat oven to 375°F. In large bowl, beat all ingredients except oats, flour, apricots and pecans with electric mixer on medium speed until creamy or mix with spoon. Stir in remaining ingredients.

2. Drop dough by rounded teaspoonfuls about 2 inches apart on ungreased cookie sheet.

3. Bake 8 to 10 minutes or until edges are brown and centers are soft. Cool 1 to 2 minutes; remove from cookie sheet to wire rack.

About 6 dozen cookies

1 Cookie: Calories 70 (Calories from Fat 35); Total Fat 3.5g (Saturated Fat 1g); Cholesterol 10mg; Sodium 50mg; Total Carbohydrate 8g (Dietary Fiber 0g; Sugars 5g); Protein 1g
% Daily Value: Vitamin A 2%; Vitamin C 0%; Calcium 0%; Iron 0%
Exchanges: ½ Starch, ½ Fat
Carbohydrate Choices: ½

KITCHEN TIPS

● To make drop cookies uniform in size, use a spring-handled cookie scoop available in a variety of sizes at most grocery and discount stores.

Apricot Spice Cookies

Trail Mix Cookies

Prep time: 1 hr 20 min Start to finish: 1 hr 20 min

- 1 cup granulated sugar
- 1 cup packed brown sugar
- 1 cup peanut butter
- $\frac{1}{2}$ cup butter or margarine, softened
- $\frac{1}{2}$ cup shortening
- 2 teaspoons vanilla
- 2 eggs
- 2 cups Gold Medal all-purpose flour
- $1\frac{1}{2}$ cups quick-cooking or old-fashioned oats
- 1 teaspoon baking powder
- 1 teaspoon baking soda
- 2 cups candy-coated chocolate candies
- 1 cup peanuts
- $\frac{3}{4}$ cup raisins

1. Heat oven to 375°F. In large bowl, beat sugars, peanut butter, butter, shortening, vanilla and eggs with electric mixer on medium speed until creamy or mix with spoon. Stir in flour, oats, baking powder and baking soda; combine thoroughly. Stir in candies, peanuts and raisins.

2. Drop dough by rounded tablespoons about 2 inches apart on ungreased cookie sheet; flatten slightly with fork.

3. Bake 9 to 10 minutes or until light brown. Cool 1 minute; remove from cookie sheet to wire rack.

Trail Mix Cookies

About 5 dozen cookies
1 Cookie: Calories 160 (Calories from Fat 80); Total Fat 8g (Saturated Fat 3g); Cholesterol 10mg; Sodium 85mg; Total Carbohydrate 19g (Dietary Fiber 1g); Protein 3g
% Daily Value: Vitamin A 0%; Vitamin C 0%; Calcium 2%; Iron 4%
Exchanges: $\frac{1}{2}$ Starch, 1 Other Carbohydrate, $1\frac{1}{2}$ Fat
Carbohydrate Choices: 1

Monster Cookies

Prep time: 50 min Start to finish: 50 min

1¼ cups packed brown sugar

½ cup shortening

2 eggs

2½ cups Original Bisquick mix

1 cup old-fashioned or quick-cooking oats

1 cup candy-coated chocolate candies

½ cup raisins

½ cup chopped nuts, if desired

1. Heat oven to 375°F. In large bowl, beat brown sugar, shortening and eggs with electric mixer on medium speed or mix with spoon. Stir in remaining ingredients.

2. Drop dough by ¼ cupfuls about 2 inches apart on ungreased cookie sheet. Flatten to about ½-inch thickness with bottom of glass that has been greased and dipped into granulated sugar.

3. Bake 12 to 16 minutes or until golden brown. Cool 3 minutes; carefully remove from cookie sheet to wire rack.

About 1½ dozen 3½-inch cookies
1 Cookie: Calories 270 (Calories from Fat 100); Total Fat 11g (Saturated Fat 3.5g); Cholesterol 25mg; Sodium 260mg; Total Carbohydrate 39g (Dietary Fiber 1g; Sugars 25g); Protein 3g
% Daily Value: Vitamin A 0%; Vitamin C 0%; Calcium 6%; Iron 8%
Exchanges: 1 Starch, 1½ Other Carbohydrate, 2 Fat
Carbohydrate Choices: 2½

KITCHEN TIPS

● Don't have a lot of free time? Make the dough a day earlier and refrigerate, then bake the cookies when you get a few spare minutes.

Monster Cookies

Quick
Crunchy Muncher Cookies
Prep time: 2 hr 10 min Start to finish: 2 hr 10 min

1 cup granulated sugar
1 cup packed brown sugar
1 cup butter or margarine, softened
²/₃ cup vegetable oil
1 teaspoon vanilla
3 eggs
3¹/₂ cups Gold Medal all-purpose flour
1 teaspoon baking soda
1 teaspoon cream of tartar
¹/₄ teaspoon salt
2²/₃ cups small pretzel twists, coarsely crushed
1 cup old-fashioned or quick-cooking oats
1 cup Wheaties® cereal or Country® Corn Flakes cereal, slightly crushed
1 cup miniature semisweet chocolate chips
1 cup butterscotch-flavored chips

1. Heat oven to 350°F. In large bowl, beat sugars, butter, oil, vanilla and eggs with electric mixer on medium speed until light and fluffy or mix with spoon. Stir in flour, baking soda, cream of tartar and salt. Stir in remaining ingredients.

2. Drop dough by heaping teaspoonfuls about 2 inches apart on ungreased cookie sheet.

3. Bake 9 to 11 minutes or until light brown. Cool 1 minute; remove from cookie sheet to wire rack.

About 9 dozen cookies
1 Cookie: Calories 80 (Calories from Fat 40); Total Fat 4.5g (Saturated Fat 2g); Cholesterol 10mg; Sodium 60mg; Total Carbohydrate 11g (Dietary Fiber 0g; Sugars 6g); Protein 0g
% Daily Value: Vitamin A 0%; Vitamin C 0%; Calcium 0%; Iron 2%
Exchanges: ¹/₂ Other Carbohydrate, 1 Fat
Carbohydrate Choices: 1

Crunchy Muncher Cookies

KITCHEN TIPS

● You could vary the flavor of chips used in these cookies. Use all chocolate or all butterscotch or add some peanut butter or white baking chips.

Low Fat

Chocolate Malt–Cherry Mix

Prep time: 15 min Start to finish: 20 min

2 cups Corn Chex cereal
2 cups Rice Chex cereal
2 cups Wheat Chex cereal
1 cup dry-roasted peanuts
¼ cup butter or margarine
1 cup semisweet chocolate chips
1 cup natural-flavor malted milk powder
2 cups miniature marshmallows
1½ cups coarsely chopped malted milk balls
½ cup dried cherries, chopped

Chocolate Malt–Cherry Mix

1. In large bowl, mix cereals and peanuts; set aside.

2. In 1-quart saucepan, heat butter and chocolate chips over low heat, stirring occasionally, until melted and blended. Pour over cereal mixture, stirring until evenly coated.

3. Gradually stir in malted milk powder until evenly coated. Stir in remaining ingredients. Stir in airtight container.

25 servings (½ cup each)
1 Serving: Calories 180 (Calories from Fat 70); Total Fat 8g (Saturated Fat 3.5g); Cholesterol 5mg; Sodium 160mg; Total Carbohydrate 24g (Dietary Fiber 2g); Protein 3g
% Daily Value: Vitamin A 10%; Vitamin C 4%; Calcium 6%; Iron 20%
Exchanges: 1 Starch, ½ Other Carbohydrate, 1½ Fat
Carbohydrate Choices: 1½

Cakes, Pies and Other Desserts

Amazing Endings for Every Meal

Impossibly Easy French Apple Pie (page 261)

Cranberry Mousse (page 254)

Roasted Almond-Cranberry-Pear Crisp

Prep time: 25 min Start to finish: 1 hr 30 min

5 to 6   pears, peeled, sliced (5 cups)

2   cups fresh or frozen cranberries

1   cup granulated sugar

3   tablespoons Gold Medal all-purpose flour

6   Nature Valley® roasted almond crunchy granola bars (3 pouches from 8.9-ounce box), finely crushed

½   cup Gold Medal all-purpose flour

¼   cup packed brown sugar

¼   cup butter or margarine, melted

Whipped cream or vanilla ice cream, if desired

1. Heat oven to 350°F. Spray 8-inch square (2-quart) glass baking dish with cooking spray. In large bowl, mix pears, cranberries, granulated sugar and 3 table-spoons flour. Spoon evenly into baking dish.

2. In medium bowl, mix crushed granola bars, ½ cup flour, the brown sugar and butter until crumbly. Sprinkle over pear mixture.

3. Bake 55 to 65 minutes or until top is golden brown and fruit is tender (mixture will be bubbly). Cool slightly. Serve warm or cool with whipped cream or ice cream.

8 servings

1 Serving: Calories 370 (Calories from Fat 80); Total Fat 9g (Saturated Fat 3g); Cholesterol 15mg; Sodium 100mg; Total Carbohydrate 69g (Dietary Fiber 5g; Sugars 49g); Protein 3g
% Daily Value: Vitamin A 6%; Vitamin C 6%; Calcium 2%; Iron 8%
Exchanges: 1 Starch, 3½ Other Carbohydrate, 2 Fat
Carbohydrate Choices: 4½

KITCHEN TIPS

- You can crush the granola bars right in their pouches or put them in a food processor for crushing.
- If your pears are not quite ripe, let them stand at room temperature for 1 to 2 days.

Roasted Almond-Cranberry-Pear Crisp

Pear and Raspberry Crisp

Prep time: 15 min Start to finish: 1 hr 20 min

4 pears, peeled, sliced (about 4 cups)

1 cup fresh raspberries

$^1\!/_2$ cup sugar

3 tablespoons cornstarch

$^1\!/_4$ teaspoon ground cinnamon

1 teaspoon vanilla

1 cup finely crushed vanilla wafer cookies (about 25 cookies)

$^1\!/_2$ cup sliced almonds

3 tablespoons butter or margarine, melted

Vanilla ice cream, if desired

Fresh raspberries, if desired

Mint leaves, if desired

1. Heat oven to 350°F. In large bowl, toss pears, raspberries, sugar, cornstarch, cinnamon and vanilla. Spread fruit mixture in 8- or 9-inch square (2-quart) glass baking dish.

2. In medium bowl, mix remaining ingredients except ice cream, raspberries and mint until crumbly. Sprinkle over fruit.

3. Bake 45 to 50 minutes or until pears are tender. Cool 15 minutes. Serve warm with ice cream. Garnish with raspberries and mint leaves.

Pear and Raspberry Crisp

6 servings
1 Serving: Calories 330 (Calories from Fat 120); Total Fat 13g (Saturated Fat 4g; Trans Fat 1g); Cholesterol 15mg; Sodium 100mg; Potassium, 250mg; Total Carbohydrate 51g (Dietary Fiber 6g; Sugars 35g); Protein 3g
% Daily Value: Vitamin A 6%; Vitamin C 8%; Calcium 4%; Iron 6%
Exchanges: 1 Starch, 2$^1\!/_2$ Other Carbohydrate, 2$^1\!/_2$ Fat
Carbohydrate Choices: 3

Chocolate-Cherry Crisp

Prep time: 10 min Start to finish: 45 min

  1   can (21 ounces) cherry pie filling
  1/2 cup Original Bisquick mix
  1/2 cup packed brown sugar
  1/2 cup quick-cooking oats
  1/4 cup firm butter or margarine
  1/2 cup semisweet chocolate chips

1. Heat oven to 350°F. Spread pie filling in ungreased 8-inch square pan or 2-quart glass baking dish.

2. In medium bowl, mix Bisquick mix, brown sugar and oats. Cut in butter, using pastry blender (or pulling 2 table knives through ingredients in opposite directions), until crumbly. Stir in chocolate chips. Spoon evenly over pie filling.

3. Bake 30 to 35 minutes or until very bubbly around edges. Serve warm.

9 servings
1 Serving: Calories 260 (Calories from Fat 90); Total Fat 10g (Saturated Fat 4.5g); Cholesterol 15mg; Sodium 135mg; Total Carbohydrate 41g (Dietary Fiber 2g; Sugars 32g); Protein 2g
% Daily Value: Vitamin A 4%; Vitamin C 2%; Calcium 4%; Iron 6%
Exchanges: 1/2 Starch, 2 Other Carbohydrate, 2 Fat
Carbohydrate Choices: 3

KITCHEN TIPS

● Mix the topping and keep in the refrigerator up to a week or in the freezer up to 6 months. When ready to bake, just finish the recipe as directed.

Apple-Raspberry Cobbler

Prep time: 10 min Start to finish: 1 hr 20 min

  1   can (21 ounces) apple pie filling with more fruit
  1   can (21 ounces) raspberry pie filling with more fruit
  1   tablespoon finely chopped crystallized ginger
  1   Pillsbury refrigerated pie crust (from 15-ounce box), softened as directed on box
  2   teaspoons milk
  1   tablespoon sugar

1. Heat oven to 400°F. Spoon both pie fillings and ginger into ungreased 8- or 9-inch square (2-quart) glass baking dish; stir gently to mix well.

2. Remove pie crust from pouch; place flat on cutting board. Cut crust into 1/2-inch-wide strips. Place half of the strips about 1/2 inch apart on filling mixture. Weave a cross-strip through center by first folding back every other strip of the first layer of strips. Continue weaving cross-strips with second half of strips, folding back alternate strips before adding each cross-strip, until lattice is complete. Trim ends as needed. Brush crust with milk; sprinkle with sugar.

3. Bake 40 to 50 minutes or until filling is bubbly and crust is golden brown. Cool at least 20 minutes before serving.

8 servings
1 Serving: Calories 250 (Calories from Fat 50); Total Fat 6g (Saturated Fat 2g); Cholesterol 0mg; Sodium 95mg; Total Carbohydrate 49g (Dietary Fiber 2g; Sugars 33g); Protein 0g
% Daily Value: Vitamin A 0%; Vitamin C 0%; Calcium 0%; Iron 0%
Exchanges: 3 Other Carbohydrate, 1 1/2 Fat
Carbohydrate Choices: 3

Apple-Raspberry Cobbler

Chocolate-Cherry Crisp

Raspberry-Peach Cobbler

Lemon Bread Pudding

Raspberry-Peach Cobbler

Prep time: 15 min Start to finish: 1 hr

2½ cups sliced fresh peaches
2 cups fresh raspberries
½ cup granulated sugar
1 tablespoon cornstarch
1 teaspoon ground nutmeg
2 cups Original Bisquick mix
½ cup milk
3 tablespoons butter or margarine, melted
2 tablespoons packed brown sugar

1. Heat oven to 375°F. Lightly butter bottom and sides of 9 × 1½-inch deep-dish pie plate.

2. In large bowl, mix peaches, raspberries, granulated sugar, cornstarch and nutmeg. Let stand 10 minutes. Spoon into pie plate.

3. In same bowl, stir remaining ingredients until dough forms. Drop dough by spoonfuls onto fruit mixture. Bake 37 to 45 minutes or until fruit is bubbly and topping is deep golden brown and baked through.

9 servings
1 Serving: Calories 250 (Calories from Fat 70); Total Fat 8g (Saturated Fat 3g); Cholesterol 10mg; Sodium 410mg; Total Carbohydrate 40g (Dietary Fiber 4g; Sugars 24g); Protein 3g
% Daily Value: Vitamin A 6%; Vitamin C 8%; Calcium 8%; Iron 6%
Exchanges: 1 Starch, 1½ Other Carbohydrate, 1½ Fat
Carbohydrate Choices: 2½

KITCHEN TIPS

● Just before baking, sprinkle cobbler with 2 tablespoons additional granulated sugar for a crunchy top.

Lemon Bread Pudding

Prep time: 20 min Start to finish: 1 hr 10 min

½ cup sugar
½ teaspoon vanilla
6 eggs
½ cup Original Bisquick mix
2 cups milk
10 cups cubed French bread (about ten 1-inch slices)
1 can (15.75 ounces) lemon pie filling
1 cup frozen (thawed) whipped topping

1. Heat oven to 350°F. Generously grease bottom and sides of 3-quart casserole with shortening or spray with cooking spray. In large bowl, beat sugar, vanilla and eggs with wire whisk until blended. Stir in Bisquick mix and milk. Stir in bread cubes until coated.

2. Spoon half of the bread mixture into casserole. Spoon 1 cup of the pie filling randomly over bread mixture. Top with remaining bread mixture.

3. Bake 45 to 50 minutes or until golden brown and knife inserted in center comes out clean. In small bowl, mix remaining pie filling and the whipped topping. Serve warm pudding with whipped topping mixture. Store covered in refrigerator.

9 servings
1 Serving: Calories 320 (Calories from Fat 80); Total Fat 8g (Saturated Fat 3.5g); Cholesterol 145mg; Sodium 390mg; Total Carbohydrate 51g (Dietary Fiber 2g; Sugars 26g); Protein 10g
% Daily Value: Vitamin A 6%; Vitamin C 0%; Calcium 10%; Iron 10%
Exchanges: 3 Starch, ½ Other Carbohydrate, 1 Fat
Carbohydrate Choices: 3½

KITCHEN TIPS

● Serve with fresh fruit for a great brunch dish.
● For a variation, use other flavors of fruit pie fillings.

White Chocolate Bread Pudding

Prep time: 30 min Start to finish: 2 hr 20 min

- 2 cups whipping (heavy) cream
- 2 cups half-and-half
- 8 ounces white baking bars (white chocolate), cut into $\frac{1}{4}$- to $\frac{1}{2}$-inch pieces
- 1$\frac{1}{2}$ cups sugar
- 8 egg yolks
- 1 teaspoon vanilla
- $\frac{1}{4}$ teaspoon salt
- 1 baguette (about 25 inches), thinly sliced
- 1 bag (12 ounces) frozen raspberries, thawed

1. Heat oven to 325°F. Grease shallow 3-quart casserole with shortening or spray with cooking spray. In 3-quart saucepan, heat whipping cream and half-and-half to boiling over medium-high heat, stirring constantly. Stir in baking bar pieces; remove from heat.

2. In large bowl, beat sugar, egg yolks, vanilla and salt with electric mixer on medium speed until creamy. Gradually add cream mixture, beating constantly until smooth.

3. Line bottom and sides of casserole with some of the baguette slices. Pour 2 cups of the cream mixture over bread; let stand a few minutes until bread absorbs mixture. Add remaining baguette slices. Pour remaining cream mixture, 2 cups at a time, over bread; let stand a few minutes until bread absorbs mixture. Place casserole in roasting pan; place in oven. Pour boiling water into roasting pan until 1 inch deep.

4. Bake uncovered 45 minutes. Cover with foil and bake about 1 hour 5 minutes longer or until knife inserted 1 inch from edge comes out clean.

5. Place raspberries in blender. Cover and blend on high speed until smooth; strain out seeds. Serve warm bread pudding with raspberry sauce and, if desired, fresh raspberries.

White Chocolate Bread Pudding

10 servings
1 Serving: Calories 640 (Calories from Fat 300); Total Fat 34g (Saturated Fat 19g); Cholesterol 240mg; Sodium 390mg; Total Carbohydrate 74g (Dietary Fiber 4g; Sugars 51g); Protein 10g
% Daily Value: Vitamin A 20%; Vitamin C 8%; Calcium 20%; Iron 10%
Exchanges: 3 Starch, 2 Other Carbohydrate, 6$\frac{1}{2}$ Fat
Carbohydrate Choices: 5

KITCHEN TIPS

- Serve this cozy pudding spooned into holiday mugs.
- Add a scoop of vanilla ice cream to each serving before drizzling with raspberry sauce.

Fudgy Brownie Trifle

Prep time: 15 min Start to finish: 6 hr 15 min

1 package (1 pound 3.8 ounces) Betty Crocker fudge brownie mix

¼ cup water

½ cup vegetable oil

2 eggs

1 tablespoon instant coffee crystals (dry)

1 package (4-serving size) chocolate fudge instant pudding and pie filling mix

2 cups cold milk

1 bag (10 ounces) toffee bits

1 container (8 ounces) frozen whipped topping, thawed

1. Heat oven to 350°F. Grease bottom only of 13 × 9-inch pan with shortening or spray bottom with cooking spray. In medium bowl, stir brownie mix, water, oil and eggs until well blended. Stir coffee crystals into batter. Spread in pan.

2. Bake 28 to 30 minutes or until toothpick inserted 2 inches from side of pan comes out almost clean. Cool completely, about 1 hour 30 minutes.

3. Cut brownies into 1-inch squares. Place half of the squares in bottom of 3-quart glass bowl. Make pudding mix as directed on package for pudding, using milk. Pour half of the pudding over brownies in bowl. Top with half each of the toffee bits and whipped topping. Repeat with remaining brownies, pudding, toffee bits and whipped topping.

4. Cover and refrigerate at least 4 hours before serving. Store covered in refrigerator.

20 servings
1 Serving: Calories 310 (Calories from Fat 140); Total Fat 15g (Saturated Fat 6g); Cholesterol 35mg; Sodium 260mg; Total Carbohydrate 41g (Dietary Fiber 1g; Sugars 32g); Protein 3g
% Daily Value: Vitamin A 0%; Vitamin C 0%; Calcium 6%; Iron 6%
Exchanges: 1 Starch, 1½ Other Carbohydrate, 3 Fat
Carbohydrate Choices: 3

KITCHEN TIPS

● Top with fresh strawberries and mint sprigs to brighten up a buffet.

Fudgy Brownie Trifle

Cranberry Mousse

Prep time: 15 min Start to finish: 2 hr 45 min

1½ cups cranberry-raspberry juice

¾ cup sugar

3 tablespoons cornstarch

½ cup frozen cranberry-orange sauce (from 10-ounce tub), thawed

1 cup whipping (heavy) cream

1. In 1-quart saucepan, heat cranberry-raspberry juice, sugar and cornstarch to boiling over medium-low heat, stirring frequently. Cook 1 minute. Stir in cranberry-orange sauce. Pour into medium bowl. Place plastic wrap directly on surface of mixture; refrigerate about 2 hours or until chilled.

2. In chilled small bowl, beat whipping cream with electric mixer on high speed until soft peaks form.

3. Stir chilled cranberry-raspberry mixture with wire whisk until smooth. Fold whipped cream into mixture. Spoon into 6 dessert dishes. Refrigerate about 30 minutes or until set.

6 servings
1 Serving: Calories 320 (Calories from Fat 110); Total Fat 12g (Saturated Fat 8g); Cholesterol 45mg; Sodium 20mg; Total Carbohydrate 51g (Dietary Fiber 0g; Sugars 45g); Protein 1g
% Daily Value: Vitamin A 10%; Vitamin C 15%; Calcium 4%; Iron 0%
Exchanges: 3½ Other Carbohydrate, 2½ Fat
Carbohydrate Choices: 3½

KITCHEN TIPS

● Garnish each serving of this festive mousse with raspberries and fresh mint leaves.

Cranberry Mousse

Quick
Caramel-Coffee Fondue

Prep time: 20 min Start to finish: 20 min

1/4 cup water

1 tablespoon instant coffee crystals (dry)

1 can (14 ounces) sweetened condensed milk

1 bag (14 ounces) caramels, unwrapped

1/2 cup coarsely chopped pecans

2 apples (1 Braeburn, 1 Granny Smith), cut into 1/2-inch slices

2 cups fresh pineapple chunks

1/2 package (16-ounce size) pound cake, cut into 1-inch cubes (about 4 cups)

1. In 2-quart nonstick saucepan, heat water over high heat until hot. Dissolve coffee crystals in water.

2. Add milk, caramels and pecans to coffee. Heat over medium-low heat, stirring frequently, until caramels are melted and mixture is hot. Pour mixture into fondue pot and keep warm.

3. Arrange apples, pineapple and cake on serving plate. Use skewers or fondue forks to dip into fondue.

8 servings (1/4 cup dip, 4 apple slices, 3 pineapple chunks and 1/2 cup cake cubes each)
1 Serving: Calories 590 (Calories from Fat 190); Total Fat 21g (Saturated Fat 10g); Cholesterol 55mg; Sodium 210mg; Total Carbohydrate 90g (Dietary Fiber 3g; Sugars 65g); Protein 9g
% Daily Value: Vitamin A 6%; Vitamin C 8%; Calcium 25%; Iron 6%
Exchanges: 3 Starch, 3 Other Carbohydrate, 4 Fat
Carbohydrate Choices: 6

KITCHEN TIPS

● Use a small slow cooker, uncovered, in place of a fondue pot.

Caramel-Coffee Fondue

Quick
Layered Strawberry Shakes

Prep time: 20 min Start to finish: 20 min

1 container (16 ounces) fresh strawberries, coarsely chopped

4 cups vanilla ice cream

¾ cup milk

1. Place strawberries in blender. Cover and blend on high speed about 1 minute, stopping blender occasionally to stir, until smooth. Remove from blender. Rinse blender.

2. Place ice cream and milk in blender. Cover and blend on high speed about 2 minutes, stopping blender occasionally to stir, until smooth and creamy.

3. When ready to serve, in each of six 10- to 12-ounce glasses, layer ¼ cup blended ice cream, ⅓ cup strawberry puree and another ¼ cup blended ice cream.

6 servings (about ¾ cup each)
1 Serving: Calories 230 (Calories from Fat 100); Total Fat 11g (Saturated Fat 7g); Cholesterol 45mg; Sodium 90mg; Total Carbohydrate 29g (Dietary Fiber 2g; Sugars 22g); Protein 5g
% Daily Value: Total Fat 18% (Saturated Fat 34%); Cholesterol 15%; Sodium 4%, Total Carbohydrate 10% (Dietary Fiber 9%); Vitamin A 10%; Vitamin C 70%; Calcium 15%; Iron 2%
Exchanges: 1½ Starch, ½ Fruit, 2 Fat
Carbohydrate Choices: 2

KITCHEN TIPS

● Make these shakes the centerpiece of a kids' party along with peanut butter and jelly sandwiches, grape clusters and sugar wafer cookies.

Layered Strawberry Shakes

Strawberry-Filled Cheesecake

Prep time: 25 min Start to finish: 7 hr 10 min

1 cup graham cracker crumbs

¼ cup sugar

2 tablespoons butter or margarine, melted

3 packages (8 ounces each) cream cheese, softened

1 cup sugar

4 eggs

1 teaspoon vanilla

1 container (8 ounces) sour cream

1 can (21 ounces) strawberry pie filling

1. Heat oven to 325°F. Wrap outside bottom and side of 10-inch springform pan with foil to prevent leaking. In small bowl, mix cracker crumbs and ¼ cup sugar; stir in butter. Press firmly in bottom of pan. Bake 12 to 15 minutes or until set.

2. In large bowl, beat cream cheese, 1 cup sugar, the eggs and vanilla with electric mixer on medium speed until smooth. Beat in sour cream. Spread half of mixture (about 3 cups) over crust. Spoon half of pie filling by tablespoonfuls onto cream cheese mixture. Top with remaining cream cheese mixture. (Refrigerate remaining pie filling.)

3. Bake 1 hour 5 minutes to 1 hour 15 minutes or until center is set. Cool 15 minutes. Run metal spatula carefully along edge of cheesecake to loosen. Cool completely, about 1 hour. Cover and refrigerate at least 4 hours.

4. To serve, run metal spatula carefully along side of cheesecake to loosen again; remove foil and side of pan. Spoon remaining pie filling over cheesecake.

12 servings
1 Serving: Calories 440 (Calories from Fat 250); Total Fat 28g (Saturated Fat 16g); Cholesterol 150mg; Sodium 250mg; Total Carbohydrate 40g (Dietary Fiber 0g; Sugars 36g); Protein 7g
% Daily Value: Vitamin A 20%; Vitamin C 0%; Calcium 8%; Iron 6%
Exchanges: 2 Starch, ½ Other Carbohydrate, 5½ Fat
Carbohydrate Choices: 2½

KITCHEN TIPS

- If taking the cheesecake to a party, leave the side of the pan on to make transporting it easier.
- Garnish each slice with a fresh strawberry—a welcome treat during the winter!

Strawberry-Filled Cheesecake

Raspberry-Topped Eggnog Cheesecake

Raspberry-Topped Eggnog Cheesecake

Prep time: 35 min Start to finish: 8 hr 35 min

Cheesecake

1¼ cups crushed shortbread cookies (21 cookies)

¼ cup butter or margarine, melted

3 packages (8 ounces each) cream cheese, softened

1 cup sugar

3 eggs

½ cup eggnog

½ teaspoon rum extract

¼ teaspoon ground nutmeg

Sauce

1 package (10 ounces) frozen raspberries in syrup, thawed, undrained

2 tablespoons sugar

2 teaspoons cornstarch

1½ cups fresh raspberries

1. Heat oven to 350°F. In small bowl, mix crushed cookies and butter. Press cookie mixture over bottom of ungreased 9-inch springform pan. Wrap foil around outside of pan to prevent drips. Bake crust about 10 minutes or until set.

2. Reduce oven temperature to 325°F. In large bowl, beat cream cheese with electric mixer on medium speed until creamy. Gradually beat in 1 cup sugar until well blended. Beat in eggs, one at a time, on low speed until combined. Beat in eggnog, rum extract and nutmeg just until blended (do not overmix). Pour over crust.

3. Bake 50 to 60 minutes or until set but center still jiggles slightly when moved. Cool 15 minutes; run knife around edge of pan to loosen cheesecake. Cool in pan on wire rack 1 hour. Refrigerate at least 6 hours or overnight.

4. Place raspberries in food processor. Cover; process until smooth. If desired, strain to remove seeds. In 1-quart saucepan, mix pureed raspberries, 2 tablespoons sugar and the cornstarch. Heat to boiling over medium heat, stirring constantly. Refrigerate sauce 30 minutes to cool. Stir fresh raspberries into sauce. Before cutting cheesecake, carefully remove side of pan. Serve sauce over wedges of cheesecake. Store cheesecake covered in refrigerator.

16 servings
1 Serving: Calories 330 (Calories from Fat 190); Total Fat 22g (Saturated Fat 12g); Cholesterol 100mg; Sodium 200mg; Total Carbohydrate 29g (Dietary Fiber 2g; Sugars 24g); Protein 6g
% Daily Value: Vitamin A 15%; Vitamin C 4%; Calcium 6%; Iron 6%
Exchanges: 2 Starch, 4 Fat
Carbohydrate Choices: 2

KITCHEN TIPS

- Use a food processor to crush the shortbread cookies, or place them in a sturdy plastic food-storage bag and crush with a rolling pin.
- Be sure to save a few fresh raspberries so you can garnish each serving plate.

Luscious Orange Cheesecake with Raspberries

Prep time: 35 min Start to finish: 6 hr 25 min

Cheesecake

1½ cups crushed vanilla wafer cookies (about 50 cookies)

¼ cup butter or margarine, melted

3 packages (8 ounces each) cream cheese, softened

1 can (14 ounces) sweetened condensed milk

3 eggs

1 teaspoon vanilla

1 teaspoon grated orange peel

Sauce and Garnish

1 cup whipping (heavy) cream

3 egg yolks

⅔ cup sugar

1 teaspoon grated orange peel

2 tablespoons orange-flavored liqueur or orange juice

2 cups fresh raspberries

Luscious Orange Cheesecake with Raspberries

1. Heat oven to 300°F. In bottom of 9-inch springform pan, stir cookie crumbs and butter until crumbs are well coated. Press firmly on bottom and 1 inch up side of pan.

2. In large bowl, beat cream cheese with electric mixer on medium speed until smooth. Beat in milk, eggs, vanilla and 1 teaspoon orange peel, scraping bowl twice, until well blended. Pour over crust.

3. Bake 1 hour to 1 hour 20 minutes or until edge is light golden brown and center is still slightly jiggly. Cool on wire rack 30 minutes. Refrigerate 4 hours until chilled.

4. In 3-quart saucepan, heat whipping cream just to boiling over low heat. In small bowl, beat egg yolks, sugar and 1 teaspoon orange peel with fork or wire whisk until well blended. Stir small amount of hot cream into yolk mixture, then stir yolk mixture back into cream in saucepan. Cook over low heat 10 to 15 minutes, stirring constantly, until mixture coats a spoon. DO NOT BOIL. Remove from heat. Cool 30 minutes or until room temperature. Stir in liqueur. Refrigerate until serving.

5. To serve, spoon about 2 tablespoons sauce onto individual serving plates. Place wedge of cheesecake on sauce. Top with raspberries.

16 servings
1 Serving: Calories 470 (Calories from Fat 300); Total Fat 33g (Saturated Fat 19g); Cholesterol 175mg; Sodium 250mg; Total Carbohydrate 34g (Dietary Fiber 1g; Sugars 28g); Protein 8g
% Daily Value: Vitamin A 25%; Vitamin C 4%; Calcium 15%; Iron 6%
Exchanges: 2 Starch, 6½ Fat
Carbohydrate Choices: 2

Impossibly Easy French Apple Pie

Prep time: 15 min Start to finish: 1 hr 5 min

Streusel

¹⁄₂	cup Original Bisquick mix
¹⁄₄	cup packed brown sugar
¹⁄₄	cup chopped nuts
2	tablespoons firm butter or margarine

Pie

3	cups sliced peeled tart apples (3 medium)
1	teaspoon ground cinnamon
¹⁄₄	teaspoon ground nutmeg
¹⁄₂	cup Original Bisquick mix
¹⁄₂	cup granulated sugar
¹⁄₂	cup milk
1	tablespoon butter or margarine, softened
2	eggs

1. Heat oven to 325°F. Spray 9-inch glass pie plate with cooking spray. In small bowl, mix ¹⁄₂ cup Bisquick mix, the brown sugar and nuts. Cut in 2 tablespoons butter, using pastry blender (or pulling 2 table knives through ingredients in opposite directions), until crumbly; set aside.

2. In medium bowl, mix apples, cinnamon and nutmeg. Spread in pie plate.

3. In medium bowl, stir remaining ingredients until blended. Pour into pie plate. Sprinkle with streusel.

4. Bake 40 to 45 minutes or until knife inserted in center comes out clean and top is golden brown. Cool 5 minutes. Serve warm or cool. Store covered in refrigerator.

8 servings
1 Serving: Calories 250 (Calories from Fat 100); Total Fat 11g (Saturated Fat 3.5g); Cholesterol 65mg; Sodium 270mg; Total Carbohydrate 36g (Dietary Fiber 1g; Sugars 26g); Protein 4g
% Daily Value: Vitamin A 6%; Vitamin C 0%; Calcium 6%; Iron 6%
Exchanges: 1 Starch, 1¹⁄₂ Other Carbohydrate, 2 Fat
Carbohydrate Choices: 2¹⁄₂

Impossibly Easy French Apple Pie

KITCHEN TIPS

- Each slice cries out for a scoop of cinnamon or vanilla ice cream.
- Substitute 2 cans (16 ounces each) sliced peaches, well drained, or 4 medium peaches, peeled and sliced (3 cups), for the apples.

Making It Easy As Pie

1. Easy-Does-It Mixing

- Use a pastry blender to cut shortening into flour. If you don't have one, pull two table knives through flour and shortening in opposite directions.

- Mix only until flour is worked in. If you overwork pastry dough, it'll become tough.

- For easier rolling, after you've made the pastry dough and shaped it into a flattened round, wrap it tightly and refrigerate for at least 45 minutes or overnight.

2. Nonstick Rolling

- Anchor a pastry cloth or kitchen towel (not terry cloth) around a large cutting board (at least 12 × 12 inches) with masking tape and use a cloth cover (stockinet) for your rolling pin. Rub flour into both cloths (this will prevent sticking and won't work flour into the pastry). If you don't have a rolling pin cover or pastry cloth, rub flour on the rolling pin and the countertop or a large cutting board.

- Place pastry dough on a flat surface and start rolling from the center out, lifting and turning pastry occasionally to keep it from sticking. If the pastry begins to stick, rub more flour, a little at a time, on the surface and rolling pin.

3. Placing the Pastry

- Fold pastry into fourths and place it in the pie plate with the point in the center of the plate. Unfold and ease into the plate, being careful not to stretch pastry, which causes it to shrink when baked.

- Instead of folding pastry, you can roll it loosely around the rolling pin and transfer to the pie plate. Unroll pastry and ease into the plate.

Finishing Touch

Fluting the pastry edge makes your pie picture pretty. Choose from:

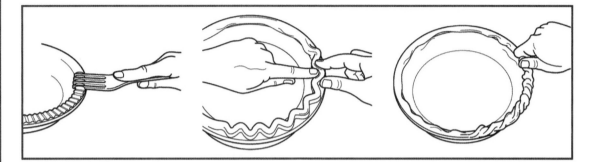

Fork Edge: Flatten pastry evenly on rim of pie plate. Firmly press tines of fork around edge. To prevent sticking, occasionally dip fork into flour.

Pinch Edge: Place index finger on inside of pastry rim and thumb and index finger (or knuckles) on outside. Pinch pastry into V shape along edge. Pinch again to sharpen points.

Rope Edge: Place side of thumb on pastry rim at an angle. Pinch pastry by pressing the knuckle of your index finger down into pastry toward thumb.

WHAT IF MY PASTRY IS	POSSIBLE CAUSE
PALE IN COLOR	• Baked in shiny pan • Underbaked
LOOKS SMOOTH	• Pastry was handled too much
BOTTOM CRUST SOGGY	• Baked in shiny pan • Oven temperature too low
TOUGH	• Too much water • Too much flour • Pastry mixed and handled too much
TOO TENDER; FALLS APART	• Too little water • Too much shortening
DRY AND MEALY, NOT FLAKY	• Shortening cut in too finely • Too little water

Orange Swirl Pumpkin Pie

Prep time: 25 min Start to finish: 3 hr 15 min

1 Pillsbury refrigerated pie crust (from 15-ounce box), softened as directed on box

1 can (14 ounces) sweetened condensed milk

2 eggs

1 package (3 ounces) cream cheese, softened

¼ cup orange marmalade

1 can (15 ounces) pumpkin (not pumpkin pie mix)

1 teaspoon pumpkin pie spice

1 cup whipping (heavy) cream

2 tablespoons orange marmalade

Orange peel curls, if desired

1. Heat oven to 350°F. Place one pie crust in 9-inch glass pie plate as directed on box for One-Crust Filled Pie.

2. In large bowl, beat milk and eggs with electric mixer on medium speed until smooth. In medium bowl, beat cream cheese and ¼ cup marmalade on medium speed until well blended. Add 2 tablespoons milk-egg mixture to cream cheese mixture; beat on medium speed until smooth.

3. Add pumpkin pie spice to remaining milk-egg mixture; beat on medium speed until smooth. Carefully pour into crust-lined pie plate. Drop cream cheese mixture by spoonfuls over pumpkin mixture; carefully swirl into pumpkin mixture. Cover edge of crust with 2- to 3-inch strip of foil to prevent excessive browning; remove foil during last 15 minutes of baking. Bake 50 to 55 minutes or until set and knife inserted in center comes out clean. Cool completely, about 2 hours.

4. In chilled medium bowl, beat whipping cream and 2 tablespoons marmalade on high speed until soft peaks form. Top pie or individual servings with whipped cream and orange peel curls.

Orange Swirl Pumpkin Pie

8 servings
1 Serving: Calories 490 (Calories from Fat 230); Total Fat 26g (Saturated Fat 14g); Cholesterol 120mg; Sodium 240mg; Total Carbohydrate 56g (Dietary Fiber 2g; Sugars 38g); Protein 8g
% Daily Value: Vitamin A 180%; Vitamin C 4%; Calcium 20%; Iron 6%
Exchanges: 2½ Starch, 1 Other Carbohydrate, 5 Fat
Carbohydrate Choices: 4

KITCHEN TIPS

- Make this pretty pie up to 24 hours ahead of time. Keep it refrigerated until serving.
- Beat the whipping cream up to 2 hours ahead of time and store in the refrigerator until serving.

Frosty Pumpkin Squares

Prep time: 15 min Start to finish: 4 hr 45 min

1	quart (4 cups) vanilla ice cream
1¼	cups graham cracker crumbs (about 16 squares)
¼	cup butter or margarine, melted
1	cup canned pumpkin (not pumpkin pie mix)
½	cup packed brown sugar
½	teaspoon salt
½	teaspoon ground cinnamon
½	teaspoon ground ginger
¼	teaspoon ground nutmeg

1. Let ice cream stand at room temperature 30 to 45 minutes to soften.

2. Meanwhile, in small bowl, mix cracker crumbs and butter; reserve 2 to 3 tablespoons crumb mixture. In ungreased 8- or 9-inch square pan, press remaining crumb mixture firmly and evenly over bottom.

3. In large bowl, beat remaining ingredients with wire whisk until well blended. Stir in ice cream with spoon. Spread over crumb mixture in pan. Sprinkle reserved crumb mixture over top.

4. Freeze uncovered at least 4 hours or until top of pumpkin mixture is firm, then cover and return to freezer. Let stand at room temperature 15 to 20 minutes before cutting.

9 servings
1 Serving: Calories 290 (Calories from Fat 120); Total Fat 13g (Saturated Fat 7g); Cholesterol 40mg; Sodium 290mg; Total Carbohydrate 38g (Dietary Fiber 1g; Sugars 29g); Protein 3g
% Daily Value: Vitamin A 90%; Vitamin C 2%; Calcium 10%; Iron 6%
Exchanges: ½ Starch, 2 Other Carbohydrate, 2½ Fat
Carbohydrate Choices: 2½

KITCHEN TIPS

● This is a great make-ahead recipe. Prepare and freeze up to 2 weeks before. For easy cutting, let stand at room temperature for 15 to 20 minutes.

Frosty Pumpkin Squares

Classic Pumpkin Pie

Prep time: 25 min Start to finish: 6 hr 45 min

Pie

One-Crust Flaky Pastry (right)

2 eggs

$^1/_2$ cup granulated sugar

1 teaspoon ground cinnamon

$^1/_2$ teaspoon salt

$^1/_2$ teaspoon ground ginger

$^1/_8$ teaspoon ground cloves

1 can (15 ounces) pumpkin (not pumpkin pie mix)

1 can (12 ounces) evaporated milk

Spiced Cream Clouds

$^1/_2$ cup whipping (heavy) cream

1 tablespoon packed brown sugar

$^1/_4$ teaspoon pumpkin pie spice or ground cinnamon

1. Heat oven to 425°F. Make One-Crust Flaky Pastry.

2. In medium bowl, beat eggs slightly with wire whisk or hand beater. Beat in remaining pie ingredients.

3. Place pastry-lined pie plate on oven rack to prevent spilling the filling. Pour filling into pie plate. Cover edge of crust with 2- to 3-inch strip of foil to prevent excessive browning; remove foil during last 15 minutes of baking. Bake 15 minutes.

4. Reduce oven temperature to 350°F. Bake about 45 minutes longer or until knife inserted in center comes out clean. Cool 30 minutes. Refrigerate about 4 hours or until chilled.

5. In chilled small bowl, beat whipping cream, brown sugar and pumpkin pie spice with electric mixer on high speed until stiff. Place waxed paper on cookie sheet. Drop whipped cream by 8 spoonfuls onto waxed paper. Freeze uncovered at least 2 hours.

6. Top slices of pie with frozen spiced cream clouds; let stand 5 minutes before serving. Store pie covered in refrigerator.

Classic Pumpkin Pie

8 servings
1 Serving: Calories 350 (Calories from Fat 180); Total Fat 20g (Saturated Fat 8g); Cholesterol 85mg; Sodium 370mg; Total Carbohydrate 36g (Dietary Fiber 2g; Sugars 21g); Protein 7g
% Daily Value: Vitamin A 170%; Vitamin C 2%; Calcium 15%; Iron 10%
Exchanges: $2^1/_2$ Starch, $3^1/_2$ Fat
Carbohydrate Choices: $2^1/_2$

KITCHEN TIPS

- Sprinkle the spiced cream clouds with pumpkin pie spice just before serving.

One-Crust Flaky Pastry

Prep time: 20 min Start to finish: 1 hr 5 min

1 cup Gold Medal all-purpose flour
1/2 teaspoon salt
1/3 cup plus 1 tablespoon shortening
2 to 3 tablespoons cold water

1. In medium bowl, mix flour and salt. Cut in shortening, using pastry blender (or pulling 2 table knives through ingredients in opposite directions), until particles are size of small peas. Sprinkle with cold water, 1 tablespoon at a time, tossing with fork until all flour is moistened and pastry almost leaves side of bowl (1 to 2 teaspoons more water can be added if necessary).

2. Gather pastry into a ball. Shape into flattened round on lightly floured surface. Wrap flattened round of pastry in plastic wrap and refrigerate about 45 minutes or until dough is firm and cold yet pliable. This allows the shortening to become slightly firm, which helps make the baked pastry more flaky. If refrigerated longer, let pastry soften slightly before rolling.

3. Roll pastry on lightly floured surface, using floured rolling pin, into circle 2 inches larger than upside-down 9-inch glass pie plate. Fold pastry into fourths; place in pie plate. Unfold and ease into plate, pressing firmly against bottom and side. Trim overhanging edge of pastry 1 inch from rim of pie plate. Fold and roll pastry under, even with plate; flute as desired.

8 servings
1 Serving: Calories 150 (Calories from Fat 90); Total Fat 10g (Saturated Fat 2.5g); Cholesterol 0mg; Sodium 150mg; Total Carbohydrate 12g (Dietary Fiber 0g; Sugars 0g); Protein 2g
% Daily Value: Vitamin A 0%; Vitamin C 0%; Calcium 0%; Iron 4%
Exchanges: 1 Other Carbohydrate, 2 Fat
Carbohydrate Choices: 1

KITCHEN TIPS

● For the best results, roll pastry from the center to the outside edge in all directions.

One-Crust Flaky Pastry

Impossibly Easy Pumpkin-Pecan Pie

Prep time: 15 min Start to finish: 1 hr 55 min

1 cup canned pumpkin (not pumpkin pie mix)
1 cup evaporated milk
1/2 cup Original Bisquick mix
1/2 cup sugar
1 tablespoon butter or margarine, softened
1 1/2 teaspoons pumpkin pie spice
1 teaspoon vanilla
2 eggs
1/2 cup chopped pecans
1 1/2 cups frozen (thawed) whipped topping
1/4 teaspoon pumpkin pie spice
8 pecan halves, if desired

1. Heat oven to 350°F. Spray 9-inch glass pie plate with cooking spray.

2. In large bowl, stir pumpkin, milk, Bisquick mix, sugar, butter, 1 1/2 teaspoons pumpkin pie spice, the vanilla and eggs until blended. Stir in chopped pecans. Pour into pie plate.

3. Bake 35 to 40 minutes or until knife inserted in center comes out clean. Cool completely, about 1 hour.

4. In small bowl, stir whipped topping and 1/4 teaspoon pumpkin pie spice. Serve pie with topping; top with pecan halves. Store covered in refrigerator.

8 servings
1 Serving: Calories 260 (Calories from Fat 120); Total Fat 14g (Saturated Fat 5g); Cholesterol 65mg; Sodium 170mg; Total Carbohydrate 28g (Dietary Fiber 2g; Sugars 20g); Protein 5g
% Daily Value: Vitamin A 100%; Vitamin C 0%; Calcium 10%; Iron 6%
Exchanges: 1 Starch, 1 Other Carbohydrate, 2 1/2 Fat
Carbohydrate Choices: 2

KITCHEN TIPS

● Drizzle cooled pie with 1/4 cup melted chocolate chips for a touch of decadence.

Impossibly Easy Pumpkin-Pecan Pie

Double Chocolate–Cherry Torte

Prep time: 30 min Start to finish: 6 hr 35 min

- 2 packages (8 ounces each) semisweet baking chocolate, coarsely chopped
- 1 cup butter or margarine
- 6 eggs
- 1 1/2 cups white chocolate chunks (from 12-ounce bag)
- 1 1/2 cups whipping (heavy) cream
- 4 ounces cream cheese (from 8-ounce package), softened
- 1 can (21 ounces) cherry pie filling
- 1/4 teaspoon almond extract
- 2 tablespoons amaretto liqueur

1. Heat oven to 400°F. Spray 9-inch springform pan with cooking spray. In 3-quart saucepan, melt semi-sweet chocolate and butter over medium-low heat, stirring constantly, until smooth. Cool 30 minutes.

2. In medium bowl, beat eggs with electric mixer on high speed about 5 minutes or until about triple in volume. Fold into chocolate mixture. Pour into springform pan. Bake 15 to 20 minutes or until edge is set but center is still soft and jiggles slightly when moved. Cool completely in pan, about 1 hour 30 minutes. Then cover and refrigerate 1 hour 30 minutes.

3. In medium microwavable bowl, mix white chocolate chunks and 2 tablespoons of the whipping cream. Microwave uncovered on High 20 to 40 seconds, stirring after 20 seconds, until chocolate is melted. Stir until well blended. In medium bowl, beat cream cheese on medium speed until smooth. Gradually add white chocolate mixture, beating on medium speed until smooth. Add 1 cup of the pie filling; beat on medium speed until well blended and cherries are broken up.

4. In another chilled medium bowl, beat remaining whipping cream and almond extract on high speed until stiff peaks form. Fold in cherry-chocolate mixture until well blended. Spread over dark chocolate layer. Refrigerate at least 2 hours but no longer than 48 hours.

5. In medium bowl, stir remaining pie filling and liqueur until well blended. Remove side of springform pan. Serve wedges of torte topped with cherry sauce.

Double Chocolate–Cherry Torte

12 servings
1 Serving: Calories 680 (Calories from Fat 440); Total Fat 49g (Saturated Fat 27g); Cholesterol 190mg; Sodium 190mg; Total Carbohydrate 51g (Dietary Fiber 3g; Sugars 46g); Protein 8g
% Daily Value: Vitamin A 25%; Vitamin C 2%; Calcium 10%; Iron 10%
Exchanges: 2 1/2 Starch, 1 Other Carbohydrate, 9 1/2 Fat
Carbohydrate Choices: 3 1/2

KITCHEN TIPS

- You could use 1 1/2 cups coarsely chopped white chocolate baking bars instead of the chunks.
- Present this pretty dessert on a favorite platter and garnish with fresh mint leaves.

Chocolate Mousse Torte

Chocolate Mousse Torte

Prep time: 35 min Start to finish: 5 hr 10 min

1 pouch (10.25 ounces) Betty Crocker fudge brownie mix

$\frac{1}{4}$ cup vegetable oil

$\frac{1}{4}$ cup water

1 egg

2 bags (11.5 ounces each) semisweet chocolate chunks ($3\frac{1}{2}$ cups)

$\frac{1}{2}$ cup chopped pecans

$\frac{1}{4}$ cup toffee bits

1 package (8 ounces) cream cheese, softened

$\frac{1}{2}$ cup powdered sugar

1 teaspoon vanilla

2 cups whipping (heavy) cream

Powdered sugar, if desired

1. Heat oven to 350°F. Grease bottom only of 9-inch springform pan with shortening or spray bottom with cooking spray. In medium bowl, stir brownie mix, oil, water and egg until smooth. Stir in 1 bag of the chocolate chunks. Pour batter into pan; spread evenly. Sprinkle pecans and toffee bits over batter; press in lightly.

2. Bake 30 to 40 minutes or until center is set. Cool completely on wire rack, about 1 hour 30 minutes. Run sharp knife around side of pan to loosen brownie layer.

3. In small microwavable bowl, microwave 1 cup of the remaining chocolate chunks uncovered on High 1 minute; stir until smooth. In medium bowl, beat cream cheese, $\frac{1}{2}$ cup powdered sugar and vanilla with electric mixer on medium speed until smooth. Beat melted chocolate into cream cheese mixture.

4. Reserve $\frac{1}{4}$ cup of the whipping cream. In chilled large bowl, beat remaining whipping cream with electric mixer on high speed until stiff peaks form. Fold chocolate–cream cheese mixture into whipped cream until no white streaks remain. Spoon mousse over brownie layer, smoothing top. Refrigerate about 2 hours or until mousse is set.

5. In small microwavable bowl, microwave remaining $\frac{1}{2}$ cup chocolate chunks uncovered on High 1 minute; stir until smooth. Stir in reserved $\frac{1}{4}$ cup whipping cream until smooth. Run thin, flexible spatula around side of pan to loosen torte; remove side of pan. Spoon warm chocolate mixture over top of mousse, allowing some to drizzle down sides. Smooth top of torte with thin, flexible spatula. Refrigerate 30 minutes or until serving.

6. Just before serving, gently place 4-inch snowflake stencil on torte. Using fine wire-mesh strainer, sift powdered sugar over stencil. Carefully lift stencil from torte; repeat for additional snowflakes.

16 servings
1 Serving: Calories 520 (Calories from Fat 310); Total Fat 35g (Saturated Fat 18g); Cholesterol 65mg; Sodium 135mg; Total Carbohydrate 49g (Dietary Fiber 3g; Sugars 39g); Protein 5g
% Daily Value: Vitamin A 10%; Vitamin C 0%; Calcium 6%; Iron 10%
Exchanges: $1\frac{1}{2}$ Starch, $1\frac{1}{2}$ Other Carbohydrate, 7 Fat
Carbohydrate Choices: 3

KITCHEN TIPS

- Use a stencil to create a snowflake pattern on top of the torte.

Triple-Chocolate Torte

Prep time: 15 min Start to finish: 6 hr 35 min

1 package (1 pound 3.8 ounces) Betty Crocker fudge brownie mix

¼ cup water

½ cup vegetable oil

2 eggs

1¼ cups milk

1 package (4-serving size) white chocolate instant pudding and pie filling mix

1 container (8 ounces) frozen whipped topping, thawed

⅓ cup miniature semisweet chocolate chips

1 pint (2 cups) raspberries or strawberries, if desired

1. Heat oven to 325°F. Spray bottom only of 9-inch springform pan with cooking spray. Make brownie mix as directed on package, using water, oil and eggs. Spread in pan.

2. Bake 45 to 50 minutes or until toothpick inserted in center comes out clean. Cool completely, about 1 hour 30 minutes. (Do not remove side of pan.)

3. In large bowl, beat milk and pudding mix with wire whisk about 2 minutes or until thickened. Fold in whipped topping and chocolate chips. Pour over torte.

4. Cover and freeze at least 4 hours before serving. Remove side of pan. Serve with raspberries. Store covered in freezer.

16 servings
1 Serving: Calories 300 (Calories from Fat 120); Total Fat 14g (Saturated Fat 5g); Cholesterol 30mg; Sodium 230mg; Total Carbohydrate 42g (Dietary Fiber 2g; Sugars 30g); Protein 3g
% Daily Value: Vitamin A 0%; Vitamin C 0%; Calcium 6%; Iron 8%
Exchanges: 1 Starch, 2 Other Carbohydrate, 2½ Fat
Carbohydrate Choices: 3

KITCHEN TIPS

● Top pudding layer with finely chopped pistachio nuts for a little holiday color.

Triple-Chocolate Torte

Black and White Bundt Cake

Prep time: 35 min Start to finish: 4 hr

½ cup butter or margarine

4 ounces unsweetened baking chocolate

1 cup water

1¼ cups white vanilla baking chips

1 package (3 ounces) cream cheese, softened

3 eggs

2 cups sugar

3 cups Gold Medal all-purpose flour

½ teaspoon salt

1½ teaspoons baking powder

½ cup sour cream

1 teaspoon vanilla

1 bag (12 ounces) miniature semisweet chocolate chips (2 cups)

3 tablespoons half-and-half

Black and White Bundt Cake

1. Heat oven to 350°F. Grease 12-cup Bundt pan with shortening (do not use cooking spray); coat lightly with flour. In small microwavable bowl, place butter, unsweetened chocolate and water. Microwave uncovered on High 1 minute; stir. Continue microwaving at 15-second intervals until butter is melted and chocolate is smooth.

2. In another small microwavable bowl, microwave 1 cup of the vanilla baking chips uncovered on High 1 minute; stir until chips are smooth. In small bowl, beat cream cheese and 1 egg with electric mixer on medium speed until smooth. Beat in melted vanilla chips on medium speed.

3. In large bowl, beat butter-chocolate mixture, remaining 2 eggs, sugar, flour, salt, baking powder, sour cream, vanilla and 1 cup of the semisweet chocolate chips on low speed just until mixed. Spoon 2 cups of the chocolate batter into cake pan. Drop cream cheese filling by teaspoonfuls onto batter in pan, being careful not to let filling touch sides of pan. Spoon remaining chocolate batter on top.

4. Bake 1 hour to 1 hour 10 minutes or until toothpick inserted into chocolate cake comes out clean (white filling may cling). Cool in pan on wire rack 15 minutes. Remove from pan to wire rack. Cool completely, about 2 hours.

5. In small microwavable bowl, microwave remaining 1 cup semisweet chocolate chips uncovered on High 1 minute; stir until smooth. Stir in half-and-half until smooth. Spoon over cake, allowing some to drizzle down sides. In small plastic food-storage bag, microwave remaining ¼ cup vanilla baking chips on High 30 seconds or until melted. Squeeze bag until chips are smooth. Cut small tip from one corner of bag; squeeze bag to drizzle melted chips over cake.

16 servings

1 Serving: Calories 520 (Calories from Fat 230); Total Fat 25g (Saturated Fat 14g); Cholesterol 65mg; Sodium 200mg; Total Carbohydrate 67g (Dietary Fiber 3g; Sugars 45g); Protein 7g % Daily Value: Vitamin A 8%; Vitamin C 0%; Calcium 8%; Iron 15% Exchanges: 2 Starch, 2½ Other Carbohydrate, 5 Fat Carbohydrate Choices: 4½

KITCHEN TIPS

● Keep going with the black and white theme by serving slices of cake with warm hot fudge sauce and vanilla ice cream.

Fudge Bundt Cake with Cashew-Caramel Sauce

Prep time: 40 min Start to finish: 2 hr

1 box Betty Crocker SuperMoist® chocolate fudge cake mix

1⅓ cups water

½ cup vegetable oil

3 eggs

1 bag (14 ounces) caramels, unwrapped

1 cup evaporated milk (from 12-ounce can)

¾ cup cashew halves

1. Heat oven to 350°F. Grease 12-cup fluted tube cake pan with shortening (do not spray with cooking spray); coat with flour.

2. In large bowl, make cake mix as directed on box, using water, oil and eggs. Pour into pan.

3. Bake 33 to 38 minutes or until toothpick inserted in center comes out clean. Cool 10 minutes; remove from pan to wire rack. Cool 15 to 30 minutes.

4. Meanwhile, in 2-quart saucepan, heat caramels and milk over low heat, stirring frequently, until caramels are melted. Stir in cashews. Serve slices of warm cake topped with warm cashew-caramel sauce.

16 servings
1 Serving: Calories 360 (Calories from Fat 140); Total Fat 16g (Saturated Fat 5g); Cholesterol 45mg; Sodium 360mg; Total Carbohydrate 49g (Dietary Fiber 1g; Sugars 29g); Protein 6g
% Daily Value: Vitamin A 0%; Vitamin C 0%; Calcium 10%; Iron 8%
Exchanges: 2 Starch, 1 Other Carbohydrate, 3 Fat
Carbohydrate Choices: 3

KITCHEN TIPS

- Top servings of warm cake and sauce with a scoop of vanilla ice cream.
- Reheat leftover caramel sauce by placing it in a microwavable container and microwaving uncovered on High for 20 to 30 seconds.

Fudge Bundt Cake with Cashew-Caramel Sauce

Triple-Fudge Cake

Prep time: 15 min Start to finish: 3 hr 5 min

⅓ cup sweetened condensed milk
1 bag (6 ounces) semisweet chocolate chips (1 cup)
1 package Betty Crocker SuperMoist® chocolate fudge cake mix
½ cup vegetable oil
1 cup applesauce
2 eggs
½ cup chopped pecans

1. Heat oven to 350°F. Grease bottom only of 13 × 9-inch pan with shortening or spray bottom with cooking spray; coat with flour. In small microwavable bowl, microwave milk and ½ cup of the chocolate chips uncovered on Medium (50%) about 1 minute or until chocolate is softened; stir until smooth and set aside.

2. In large bowl, beat cake mix and oil with electric mixer on low speed 30 seconds (mixture will be crumbly); reserve 1 cup. Beat applesauce and eggs into remaining cake mixture on low speed 30 seconds (batter will be thick and grainy); beat on medium speed 2 minutes. Spread in pan.

3. Drop melted chocolate mixture by teaspoonfuls over batter, dropping more around edge than in center. Stir remaining ½ cup chocolate chips and the pecans into reserved cake mixture; sprinkle over batter. Bake 45 to 50 minutes or until center is set. Run knife around side of pan to loosen cake. Cool completely, about 2 hours.

15 servings
1 Serving: Calories 330 (Calories from Fat 150); Total Fat 17g (Saturated Fat 5g); Cholesterol 30mg; Sodium 290mg; Total Carbohydrate 43g (Dietary Fiber 2g); Protein 4g
% Daily Value: Vitamin A 0%; Vitamin C 0%; Calcium 6%; Iron 8%
Exchanges: 1 Starch, 2 Other Carbohydrate, 3 Fat
Carbohydrate Choices: 3

Triple-Fudge Cake

Fudge Pudding Cake with Ice Cream

Prep time: 15 min Start to finish: 1 hr 10 min

1 cup Gold Medal all-purpose flour
¾ cup granulated sugar
2 tablespoons baking cocoa
2 teaspoons baking powder
¼ teaspoon salt
½ cup milk
2 tablespoons vegetable oil
1 teaspoon vanilla
1 cup chopped nuts
1 cup packed brown sugar
¼ cup baking cocoa
1¾ cups boiling water
4½ cups vanilla ice cream

1. Heat oven to 350°F. In ungreased 9-inch square pan, mix flour, granulated sugar, 2 tablespoons cocoa, the baking powder and salt. Stir in milk, oil and vanilla with fork until smooth. Stir in nuts. Spread evenly in pan.

2. In small bowl, mix brown sugar and ¼ cup cocoa; sprinkle over batter. Pour boiling water over batter.

3. Bake 40 minutes. Let stand 15 minutes. Spoon cake and sauce into individual dishes. Top each serving with ½ cup ice cream.

9 servings
1 Serving: Calories 500 (Calories from Fat 180); Total Fat 20g
(Saturated Fat 7g); Cholesterol 35mg; Sodium 250mg; Total
Carbohydrate 73g (Dietary Fiber 3g; Sugars 54g); Protein 7g
% Daily Value: Vitamin A 6%; Vitamin C 0%; Calcium 20%; Iron 10%
Exchanges: 2 Starch, 3 Other Carbohydrate, 3½ Fat
Carbohydrate Choices: 5

KITCHEN TIPS

- If your family does not enjoy nuts, you can omit them from this recipe.
- Serve this delicious dessert with hot coffee or your favorite tea.

Fudge Pudding Cake with Ice Cream

Brown Sugar Bundt Cake with Rum-Caramel Sauce

Prep time: 25 min Start to finish: 4 hr

1½ cups packed brown sugar

1 cup granulated sugar

1½ cups butter or margarine, softened

½ cup milk

1 teaspoon vanilla

5 eggs

3 cups Gold Medal all-purpose flour

1 teaspoon baking powder

¼ teaspoon salt

1 cup caramel topping

2 tablespoons light rum or 1 teaspoon rum extract

1. Heat oven to 325°F. Grease 12-cup fluted tube cake pan with shortening (do not use cooking spray); coat with flour. In large bowl, beat sugars and butter with electric mixer on low speed until well blended. Add milk, vanilla and eggs. Beat on medium speed 2 minutes.

2. Beat in flour, baking powder and salt until mixture is smooth and well blended. Spread in pan.

3. Bake 1 hour 5 minutes to 1 hour 15 minutes or until toothpick inserted in center comes out clean. Cool 10 minutes. Remove from pan. Cool completely, about 2 hours.

4. In 1-quart saucepan, heat caramel topping and rum over low heat, stirring occasionally, until well blended and warm. Serve warm topping over slices of cake.

16 servings
1 Serving: Calories 450 (Calories from Fat 170); Total Fat 19g (Saturated Fat 9g); Cholesterol 115mg; Sodium 290mg; Total Carbohydrate 65g (Dietary Fiber 0g; Sugars 43g); Protein 5g % Daily Value: Vitamin A 15%; Vitamin C 0%; Calcium 8%; Iron 10% Exchanges: 1½ Starch, 3 Other Carbohydrate, 3½ Fat Carbohydrate Choices: 4

Brown Sugar Bundt Cake with Rum-Caramel Sauce

Browned Butter Pound Cake
with Caramel-Cashew Filling

Prep time: 25 min Start to finish: 4 hr 25 min

Cake

- ¾ cup butter, softened (do not use margarine)
- 1 cup packed brown sugar
- ¼ cup granulated sugar
- 4 eggs
- 1 teaspoon vanilla
- 1½ cups Gold Medal all-purpose flour
- ½ teaspoon baking powder
- Dash of salt
- ¼ cup milk

Filling

- 2 packages (3 ounces each) cream cheese, softened
- ½ cup caramel sundae syrup
- 1 cup whipping (heavy) cream
- 1 cup lightly salted cashew halves and pieces, coarsely chopped

1. Heat oven to 325°F. Grease 9 × 5-inch loaf pan with shortening (do not spray with cooking spray); coat with flour. In 1-quart saucepan, heat ¼ cup of the butter over medium heat 1 to 2 minutes, stirring constantly, until light golden brown (watch carefully because butter can burn easily). Immediately pour browned butter into large bowl. Cool 10 minutes.

2. Add remaining ½ cup butter, the brown sugar and granulated sugar to browned butter. Beat with electric mixer on medium speed about 30 seconds or until well mixed. Add eggs. Beat on high speed 3 to 4 minutes, scraping bowl occasionally, until light and fluffy. Beat in vanilla.

3. In small bowl, mix flour, baking powder and salt. Beat flour mixture alternately with milk into butter mixture on low speed, beating just until smooth after each addition. Pour into pan.

4. Bake 1 hour to 1 hour 10 minutes or until toothpick inserted in center comes out clean. Cool in pan on wire rack 10 minutes. Run thin knife around edge of pan to loosen cake; remove cake from pan to wire rack. Cool completely, about 1 hour 30 minutes.

5. Cut cake into 3 horizontal layers with serrated knife. (Cut top layer first, placing hand on top of cake and cutting from short end to short end, then carefully lift off layer; repeat for middle layer.) Place bottom layer on serving plate.

6. In medium bowl, beat cream cheese and caramel sundae syrup with electric mixer on low speed until well blended. Gradually beat in whipping cream on low speed. Beat on high speed 1 to 2 minutes or until mixture thickens and soft peaks form. Fold in ¾ cup of the cashews.

7. Spread one-third of caramel mixture (about 1 cup) over bottom layer. Top with middle layer; spread with half of remaining caramel mixture (about 1 cup). Top with remaining layer of cake. Spread top of cake with remaining caramel mixture. Sprinkle remaining ¼ cup cashews over top of cake. Cover loosely and refrigerate about 1 hour before serving. Store covered in refrigerator.

12 servings

1 Serving: Calories 490 (Calories from Fat 270); Total Fat 30g (Saturated Fat 14g); Cholesterol 140mg; Sodium 260mg; Total Carbohydrate 48g (Dietary Fiber 0g; Sugars 30g); Protein 8g
% Daily Value: Vitamin A 20%; Vitamin C 0%; Calcium 8%; Iron 10%
Exchanges: 2 Starch, 1 Other Carbohydrate, 6 Fat
Carbohydrate Choices: 3

KITCHEN TIPS

- For a super-fast dazzling dessert, substitute a 16-ounce frozen pound cake for the homemade cake.
- Insert a few toothpicks into the top of the cake before covering with plastic wrap to keep the wrap from sticking.

Browned Butter Pound Cake with Caramel-Cashew Filling

Candy Cane Cake

Prep time: 15 min Start to finish: 2 hr 15 min

Cake

1	package Betty Crocker SuperMoist® white cake mix
1¼	cups water
⅓	cup vegetable oil
3	egg whites
½	teaspoon red food color
½	teaspoon peppermint extract

Glaze

1	cup powdered sugar
1 to 2	tablespoons milk
½	teaspoon regular vanilla or clear vanilla

1. Heat oven to 350°F. Generously grease 10- to 12-cup fluted tube cake pan with shortening (do not spray with cooking spray); lightly coat with flour. Make cake mix as directed on package, using water, oil and egg whites. Pour about 2 cups batter into pan. Pour about ¾ cup batter into small bowl; stir in food color and peppermint extract. Carefully pour pink batter over white batter in pan. Carefully pour remaining white batter over pink batter.

2. Bake 38 to 42 minutes or until toothpick inserted in center comes out clean. Cool 10 minutes. Remove from pan to wire rack or heatproof serving plate. Cool completely, about 1 hour.

3. In small bowl, mix powdered sugar, 1 tablespoon milk and the vanilla. Stir in additional milk, 1 teaspoon at a time, until smooth and the consistency of thick syrup. Spread glaze over cake, allowing some to drizzle down sides. Store loosely covered at room temperature.

16 servings
1 Serving: Calories 210 (Calories from Fat 70); Total Fat 7g (Saturated Fat 2g); Cholesterol 0mg; Sodium 230mg; Total Carbohydrate 33g (Dietary Fiber 0g; Sugars 21g); Protein 2g
% Daily Value: Vitamin A 0%; Vitamin C 0%; Calcium 4%; Iron 4%
Exchanges: ½ Starch, 1½ Other Carbohydrate, 1½ Fat
Carbohydrate Choices: 2

KITCHEN TIPS

- For a pretty centerpiece, fill the center of the cake with wrapped striped mint candies.
- This totable treat is perfect for potlucks. Don't forget to pack a knife and spatula for serving.

Candy Cane Cake

Caramel-Apple Gingerbread

Prep time: 10 min Start to finish: 50 min

1 box (14.5 ounces) Betty Crocker gingerbread cake and cookie mix

¾ cup chunky applesauce

½ cup warm water

2 tablespoons butter or margarine, melted

1 egg

½ cup chopped pitted dates or raisins

½ to ¾ cup caramel topping

⅔ cup whipped cream topping in aerosol can

Caramel-Apple Gingerbread

1. Heat oven to 350°F. In medium bowl, mix gingerbread mix, applesauce, water, butter and egg with spoon until well blended. Stir in dates. Spoon into ungreased 8- or 9-inch square (2-quart) glass baking dish.

2. Bake 30 to 40 minutes or until toothpick inserted in center comes out clean. Cool slightly.

3. Top each warm square of gingerbread with caramel topping and whipped cream.

9 servings
1 Serving: Calories 330 (Calories from Fat 80); Total Fat 9g (Saturated Fat 3.5g); Cholesterol 35mg; Sodium 420mg; Total Carbohydrate 59g (Dietary Fiber 1g; Sugars 37g); Protein 3g
% Daily Value: Vitamin A 4%; Vitamin C 0%; Calcium 8%; Iron 10%
Exchanges: 1 Starch, 3 Other Carbohydrate, 1½ Fat
Carbohydrate Choices: 4

KITCHEN TIPS

- Garnish each serving with 1 or 2 slices of unpeeled apple and a sprinkling of chopped dates.
- To warm a square of cooled gingerbread, microwave on High for 20 to 30 seconds.

Winter Fruit and Nut Cake

Prep time: 20 min Start to finish: 2 hr 30 min

Cake

1	package Betty Crocker SuperMoist® yellow cake mix
1	teaspoon pumpkin pie spice
¼	cup water
⅓	cup vegetable oil
3	eggs
1	cup chunky applesauce
½	cup chopped dates
½	cup sweetened dried cranberries
½	cup chopped pecans

Topping

⅓	cup butter or margarine, melted
¾	cup packed brown sugar
¾	cup chopped pecans
3	tablespoons milk

1. Heat oven to 375°F. Grease bottom only of 13 × 9-inch pan with shortening or spray bottom with cooking spray. In large bowl, beat cake mix, pumpkin pie spice, water, oil, eggs and applesauce with electric mixer on low speed 30 seconds. Beat on medium speed 2 minutes. Stir in dates, cranberries and ½ cup pecans. Spread in pan.

2. Bake 35 to 40 minutes or until toothpick inserted in center comes out clean. Meanwhile, in small bowl, mix butter, brown sugar, ¾ cup pecans and the milk. Spread over top of warm cake.

3. Set oven control to broil. Broil cake with top 4 inches from heat about 1 minute or until bubbly. (Watch carefully to prevent burning.) Cool completely, about 1 hour 30 minutes.

15 servings
1 Serving: Calories 390 (Calories from Fat 170); Total Fat 19g (Saturated Fat 4.5g); Cholesterol 55mg; Sodium 270mg; Total Carbohydrate 51g (Dietary Fiber 2g; Sugars 37g); Protein 4g
% Daily Value: Vitamin A 4%; Vitamin C 0%; Calcium 8%; Iron 8%
Exchanges: 1½ Starch, 2 Other Carbohydrate, 3½ Fat
Carbohydrate Choices: 3½

Winter Fruit and Nut Cake

KITCHEN TIPS

- Instead of the pumpkin pie spice, you can substitute ½ teaspoon ground cinnamon, ¼ teaspoon ground ginger and ¼ teaspoon ground nutmeg.
- For a special treat, top each serving with a dollop of whipped cream.

"Berry Best" Upside-Down Cake

Prep time: 15 min Start to finish: 1 hr 5 min

- 1/3 cup butter or margarine
- 1/2 cup sugar
- 1 bag (12 ounces) frozen mixed berries, thawed, drained
- 1 1/3 cups Gold Medal all-purpose flour
- 1 cup sugar
- 2/3 cup milk
- 1 teaspoon baking powder
- 1 teaspoon vanilla
- 1/2 teaspoon salt
- 1 egg

1. Heat oven to 350°F. In 9-inch square pan or 10-inch ovenproof skillet, heat butter in oven about 2 minutes or until melted. Sprinkle 1/2 cup sugar over melted butter. Spoon berries evenly over sugar mixture.

2. In medium bowl, beat remaining ingredients with electric mixer on low speed 30 seconds. Beat on medium speed 2 minutes, scraping bowl frequently. Pour over berries.

3. Bake about 50 minutes or until toothpick inserted in center of cake comes out clean. Immediately place heatproof serving plate upside down onto cake pan or skillet; turn serving plate and cake pan or skillet over. Leave pan or skillet on cake about 1 minute so sugar mixture can drizzle over cake. Serve warm.

9 servings
1 Serving: Calories 300 (Calories from Fat 70); Total Fat 8g (Saturated Fat 4g); Cholesterol 45mg; Sodium 250mg; Total Carbohydrate 53g (Dietary Fiber 2g; Sugars 37g); Protein 4g
% Daily Value: Vitamin A 8%; Vitamin C 10%; Calcium 6%; Iron 6%
Exchanges: 1 Starch, 2 1/2 Other Carbohydrate, 1 1/2 Fat
Carbohydrate Choices: 3 1/2

KITCHEN TIPS

- Sweetened whipped cream is the perfect topping for this yummy cake.

"Berry Best" Upside-Down Cake

Watermelon Cake

Prep time: 30 min Start to finish: 1 hr 45 min

1 box Betty Crocker SuperMoist® white cake mix

Water, vegetable oil, and egg whites called for in cake mix directions

1 package (0.13 ounce) cherry or other red-colored unsweetened soft drink mix

$^1/_2$ cup plus 2 tablespoons miniature semisweet chocolate chips

1 container (12 ounces) Betty Crocker Whipped® fluffy white frosting

Green and red food colors

$^2/_3$ cup green jellybeans

1. Heat oven to 350°F. Grease bottoms only of two 8- or 9-inch round pans or spray bottoms with cooking spray.

2. In large bowl, beat cake mix, water, oil, egg whites and drink mix on low speed 30 seconds; beat on medium speed 2 minutes, scraping bowl occasionally. Stir in $^1/_2$ cup of the chocolate chips. Pour into pans.

3. Bake 27 to 32 minutes or until toothpick inserted in center comes out clean. Cool 10 minutes; remove from pans. Cool completely, about 1 hour.

4. In small bowl, stir 1 cup frosting with 10 to 12 drops green food color. Stir 10 to 12 drops red food color into remaining frosting. Cut cake rounds in half to make 4 halves. Frost uncut sides with green frosting; press green jelly beans into frosting. Frost top of cake with red frosting; press remaining 2 tablespoons chocolate chips into frosting for seeds. To serve, cut into wedges.

Watermelon Cake

KITCHEN TIPS

- Use mini chips to make sure there are lots of chips and that they stay distributed in the cake.
- Serve cake on green paper plates with watermelon-print napkins.

16 servings
1 Serving: Calories 350 (Calories from Fat 130); Total Fat 14g (Saturated Fat 4g; Trans Fat 0.5g); Cholesterol 0mg; Sodium 260mg; Total Carbohydrate 52g (Dietary Fiber 0g; Sugars 34g); Protein 2g
% Daily Value: Vitamin A 0%; Vitamin C 0%; Calcium 4%; Iron 6%
Exchanges: 1 Starch, 2$^1/_2$ Other Carbohydrate, 2$^1/_2$ Fat
Carbohydrate Choices: 3$^1/_2$

helpful **nutrition** and **cooking** information

nutrition guidelines

We provide nutrition information for each recipe, which includes calories, fat, cholesterol, sodium, carbohydrate, fiber and protein. Individual food choices can be based on this information.

Recommended intake for a daily diet of 2,000 calories as set by the Food and Drug Administration

Total Fat	Less than 65g
Saturated Fat	Less than 20g
Cholesterol	Less than 300mg
Sodium	Less than 2,400mg
Total Carbohydrate	300g
Dietary Fiber	25g

criteria used for calculating nutrition information

- The first ingredient was used wherever a choice is given (such as ⅓ cup sour cream or plain yogurt).
- The first ingredient amount was used wherever a range is given (such as 3- to 3½-pound cut-up broiler-fryer chicken).
- The first serving number was used wherever a range is given (such as 4 to 6 servings).
- "If desired" ingredients and recipe variations were not included (such as, sprinkle with brown sugar, if desired).
- Only the amount of a marinade or frying oil that is estimated to be absorbed by the food during preparation or cooking was calculated.

ingredients used in recipe testing and nutrition calculations

- Ingredients used for testing represent those that the majority of consumers use in their homes: large eggs, 2% milk, 80%-lean ground beef, canned ready-to-use chicken broth and vegetable oil spread containing not less than 65 percent fat.

- Fat-free, low-fat or low-sodium products were not used, unless otherwise indicated.

- Solid vegetable shortening (not butter, margarine, nonstick cooking sprays or vegetable oil spread because they can cause sticking problems) was used to grease pans, unless otherwise indicated.

equipment used in recipe testing

We use equipment for testing that the majority of consumers use in their homes. If a specific piece of equipment (such as a wire whisk) is necessary for recipe success, it is listed in the recipe.

- Cookware and bakeware without nonstick coatings were used, unless otherwise indicated.

- No dark-colored, black or insulated bakeware was used.

- When a pan is specified in a recipe, a metal pan was used; a baking dish or pie plate means ovenproof glass was used.

- An electric hand mixer was used for mixing only when mixer speeds are specified in the recipe directions. When a mixer speed is not given, a spoon or fork was used.

cooking terms glossary

Beat: Mix ingredients vigorously with spoon, fork, wire whisk, hand beater or electric mixer until smooth and uniform.

Boil: Heat liquid until bubbles rise continuously and break on the surface and steam is given off. For a rolling boil, the bubbles form rapidly.

Chop: Cut into coarse or fine irregular pieces with a knife, food chopper, blender or food processor.

Cube: Cut into squares ½ inch or larger.

Dice: Cut into squares smaller than ½ inch.

Grate: Cut into tiny particles using small rough holes of grater (citrus peel or chocolate).

Grease: Rub the inside surface of a pan with shortening, using pastry brush, piece of waxed paper or paper towel, to prevent food from sticking during baking (as for some casseroles).

Julienne: Cut into thin, matchlike strips, using knife or food processor (vegetables, fruits, meats).

Mix: Combine ingredients in any way that distributes them evenly.

Sauté: Cook foods in hot oil or margarine over medium-high heat with frequent tossing and turning motion.

Shred: Cut into long thin pieces by rubbing food across the holes of a shredder, as for cheese, or by using a knife to slice very thinly, as for cabbage.

Simmer: Cook in liquid just below the boiling point on top of the stove; usually after reducing heat from a boil. Bubbles will rise slowly and break just below the surface.

Stir: Mix ingredients until consistency is uniform. Stir once in a while for stirring occasionally, often for stirring frequently and continuously for stirring constantly.

Toss: Tumble ingredients (such as green salad) lightly with a lifting motion, usually to coat evenly or mix with another food.

metric conversion chart

Volume

U.S. Units	Canadian Metric	Australian Metric
¼ teaspoon	1 mL	1 ml
½ teaspoon	2 mL	2 ml
1 teaspoon	5 mL	5 ml
1 tablespoon	15 mL	20 ml
¼ cup	50 mL	60 ml
⅓ cup	75 mL	80 ml
½ cup	125 mL	125 ml
⅔ cup	150 mL	170 ml
¾ cup	175 mL	190 ml
1 cup	250 mL	250 ml
1 quart	1 liter	1 liter
1½ quarts	1.5 liters	1.5 liters
2 quarts	2 liters	2 liters
2½ quarts	2.5 liters	2.5 liters
3 quarts	3 liters	3 liters
4 quarts	4 liters	4 liters

Weight

U.S. Units	Canadian Metric	Australian Metric
1 ounce	30 grams	30 grams
2 ounces	55 grams	60 grams
3 ounces	85 grams	90 grams
4 ounces (¼ pound)	115 grams	125 grams
8 ounces (½ pound)	225 grams	225 grams
16 ounces (1 pound)	455 grams	500 grams
1 pound	455 grams	½ kilogram

Measurements

Inches	Centimeters
1	2.5
2	5.0
3	7.5
4	10.0
5	12.5
6	15.0
7	17.5
8	20.5
9	23.0
10	25.5
11	28.0
12	30.5
13	33.0

Temperatures

Fahrenheit	Celsius
32°	0°
212°	100°
250°	120°
275°	140°
300°	150°
325°	160°
350°	180°
375°	190°
400°	200°
425°	220°
450°	230°
475°	240°
500°	260°

Note: The recipes in this cookbook have not been developed or tested using metric measures. When converting recipes to metric, some variations in quality may be noted.

Index

Underscored page references indicate boxed text or sidebars. **Boldfaced** page references indicate photographs.

M